A Precarious Enterprise

A Precarious Enterprise

Making a Life in Canadian Publishing

Scott McIntyre

Copyright © Scott McIntyre, 2025

Published by ECW Press
665 Gerrard Street East
Toronto, Ontario, Canada M4M 1Y2
416-694-3348 / info@ecwpress.com

All rights reserved. No part of this publication may be reproduced, stored in a retrieval system, or transmitted in any form by any process — electronic, mechanical, photocopying, recording, or otherwise — without the prior written permission of the copyright owners and ECW Press. The scanning, uploading, and distribution of this book via the internet or via any other means without the permission of the publisher is illegal and punishable by law. This book may not be used for text and data mining, AI training, and similar technologies. Please purchase only authorized electronic editions, and do not participate in or encourage electronic piracy of copyrighted materials. Your support of the author's rights is appreciated.

Cover design: Jessica Albert

LIBRARY AND ARCHIVES CANADA CATALOGUING IN PUBLICATION

Title: A precarious enterprise : making a life in Canadian publishing / Scott McIntyre.

Names: McIntyre, Scott (Founding partner of Douglas & McIntyre), author.

Identifiers: Canadiana (print) 20250216337 | Canadiana (ebook) 20250216396

ISBN 978-1-77041-819-6 (hardcover)
ISBN 978-1-77852-494-3 (ePub)
ISBN 978-1-77852-495-0 (PDF)

Subjects: LCSH: McIntyre, Scott (Founding partner of Douglas & McIntyre) | LCSH: Douglas & McIntyre (Firm) | LCSH: Publishers and publishing—Canada—Biography. | LCSH: Publishers and publishing—Canada—History. | LCGFT: Autobiographies.

Classification: LCC Z483.M38 A3 2025 | DDC 070.5092—dc23

This book is funded in part by the Government of Canada. *Ce livre est financé en partie par le gouvernement du Canada.* We acknowledge the support of the Canada Council for the Arts. *Nous remercions le Conseil des arts du Canada de son soutien.* We would like to acknowledge the funding support of the Ontario Arts Council (OAC) and the Government of Ontario for their support. We also acknowledge the support of the Government of Ontario through the Ontario Book Publishing Tax Credit, and through Ontario Creates.

PRINTED AND BOUND IN CANADA

PRINTING: FRIESENS   5 4 3 2 1

Purchase the print edition and receive the ebook free.
For details, go to ecwpress.com/ebook.

For C, with all my love.
She walked with me every step of the way.

CONTENTS

Prologue · · · IX

1. The Lure of Print · · · 1
2. The Eye of the Hurricane · · · 13
3. Working in the Trenches · · · 36
4. One Book at a Time · · · 53
5. Building the House · · · 73
6. Frankfurt Tales · · · 95
7. A Precarious Enterprise · · · 107
8. Trailblazing · · · 122
9. Milestones · · · 138
10. Sharp Words · · · 156
11. A Visual World · · · 172
12. Peace and War · · · 190
13. Good Taste · · · 199
14. The Power of Stories · · · 208
15. Strong Voices · · · 223
16. Warning Signals · · · 239
17. The End of the Dream · · · 261

L'Envoi · · · 276

Acknowledgements · · · 279
Index · · · 283

PROLOGUE

Jack McClelland opened his door at the Bayshore Inn in Vancouver. Floppy blond hair, ruddy complexion, skimpily clad in only underwear — the full McClelland was on display.

"Christ, I'm hungover" were the first words out of his mouth.

It was the fall of 1966, and I and Bob Flick — a photographer whom I'd befriended while editor of the University of British Columbia yearbook — had wangled a meeting with Jack to pitch our book idea.

Jack's charm, immediately apparent, disguised the coiled spring that lurked beneath. Bob and I knew he'd transformed his family company, McClelland & Stewart, into the most aggressive, editorially driven Canadian publishing company of the day. Defying conventional wisdom, he published *Canadian* authors and backed them with assertive sales and imaginative promotion. He'd doubled his company's publishing program and had become a master at persuading the best writers of the day to join it.

Nervous, naïve, idealistic, and optimistic, we wanted to join their ranks.

Jack invited us in, and we began our pitch. We had planned a book of text and photographs to chronicle the audacious dare of Simon Fraser University. The two lead architects on the SFU campus project, Geoffrey Massey and Arthur Erickson, were young and relatively unknown, but the commission had catapulted them into the national and international limelight. Inspired by the acropolis in Athens and the hill towns of Italy, they envisaged a university set on a mountaintop amid a lush West Coast landscape. Reflecting the spirit of the era, the university had a mandate to meld architectural, social, and academic idealism to break down traditional hierarchies.

Jack listened with surprising focus as we explained our approach and why we felt it was the right book for the moment.

Jack cut us short. He'd been up to see the university and didn't think much of the architecture. Still, he said he'd propose the idea to the university's board. If the board was supportive, he'd consider a contract. He neglected to mention his quid pro quo: the university would have to buy 10,000 copies.

We felt empowered. SFU felt otherwise and declined the purchase requirement.

The idea died, but Jack's manic energy ensnared me. I was hooked on the *idea* of publishing.

I blame Jack.

I

THE LURE OF PRINT

Growing up, book publishing never entered my imagination. But books did. Those in our house made a spartan collection: a Bible, some Shakespeare, a collection of first editions from my great-uncle Ernest Thompson Seton. I wasn't an avid reader, not in the way so many people who eventually stumble into publishing seem to have been in their younger years. But images were compelling, be they in children's books or in larger illustrated tomes, which were beginning to become possible with the explosion of offset printing.

Discovering books at an early age, mostly borrowed from the neighbourhood library, I was smitten as much by their material presence as by the words. I was often sick, and books were windows into the world beyond my bedroom. That suggested promise, and their images of distant places fired my imagination.

I grew up in Dunbar, a comfortable westside suburb of Vancouver in Point Grey, which had been carved out of the University of British Columbia Endowment Lands in the early years of the 20th century. It was a quiet place, well endowed with parks and gardens, Anglo-Saxon in its prevailing ethnicity. My father spent his entire career working as a clerk for the Canadian Pacific Railway in an office on Pier BC, home to the company's coastal steamers and now the site of Canada Place. His salary was never high, but he was guaranteed a steady job, and a medical plan that was genuinely progressive for the time. He had been too young for World War I, and too old for World War II. We never had to endure the disruptions that destroyed so many lives during the chaotic years of the 20th century.

My family had deep Canadian roots, all Scots from the Highlands and the Orkney Islands, descendants of the Jacobites who had fought on the wrong side during the rebellions of the 18th century. They were treated nastily by the English and were forcibly dispersed, stripped of their lands and even their surnames, many ending up in Canada.

Ernest Thompson Seton was the most extraordinary of the lot. He was just six years old when he and his family arrived in 1866 to live in a crude backwoods shanty north of what was then old Toronto. His early writings include accounts of venturing north into the wilds of Rosedale in search of animals to sketch. Born a Thompson, he turned to Scottish law to win back rights to his family's inherited surname, Seton. From an early age he was a scrapper, emerging as one of the most influential natural history writers and artists of his time. Words and images seem to have combined in the family genetic code for over a century. Two generations later, my mother's maiden name still included Thompson and Seton.

My mother's Scottish roots stretched back 11 generations to Robert, the 8th Lord Seton, who was created the first Earl of Winton in 1600. She attended Bishop Strachan School in Toronto, while her sister finished a degree at McGill University in the 1920s. The family had been in Canada so long that my mother's Anglo-Irish great-grandfather Hughes had worked on the original Bishop Strachan building as a stonemason.

My father's family had been in Canada since fleeing Scotland in 1831, settling in Elgin County, Ontario. My paternal grandfather, Harry Beecher McIntyre, landed his first job with the Great Northwestern Telegraph Company. After joining the Canadian Pacific Railway in Winnipeg and moving west through a series of small towns, he arrived in Vancouver as inspector of telegraphs in 1912.

The CPR ran through my family's Canadian experience as determinedly as its tracks broke ground through Canada's west. (I'd go on to live my own railway moments, spending four summers as a college student waiting tables in aging dining cars, where white tablecloths, silver table settings, and French service still prevailed.) The frontier anchored my family's experience. Cousins arrived, pursuing a dream of searching for gold during the Cariboo gold rush. The human adventure of colonial British Columbia fascinated my father. He, and our family, lived much of it.

There were artists on both sides of the family. Edwin Holgate was a cousin of my maternal grandmother. He had grown up in Montreal during the early years of the 20th century, studying art there and in Paris. His stories, seldom offered, left a lingering fascination with Montreal during its golden age, and of his friends and colleagues, some of whom were members of the Group of Seven.

My maternal grandmother was of good heart, although in my memory a stoic, religious Victorian widow, wary of sex and worried about my presumably frail health. She had grown up in Prince Edward Island. After settling on the West Coast, she took lessons from Emily Carr, becoming a talented amateur painter skilled at capturing the coast's elusive light both in watercolour and oil.

My strongest memory of when she was living with us, as she did for a few years, is the pungent odour of turpentine, very slow-drying paint, and to my eyes a strange juxtaposition of purple and green characteristic of Carr's forest palette.

—

Books might have been rare in the house I grew up in, but illustrated magazines were ubiquitous. As far back as I can remember, they arrived on a regular basis. Magazines were revelling in their golden age, lionizing postwar dreams — *Holiday, Sunset, Saturday Evening Post, Life, National Geographic*. I was becoming seduced by print. I just didn't know it yet.

There were other omens. At age 10, bored during a summer vacation, I set out to write an outline of world history. That precocious effort didn't last long, but the 30–40 typewritten pages, mostly cribbed from an encyclopedia, ended up stapled together in a flimsy cardboard binding, and abandoned. My mother found it years later. The hand-lettered mock colophon reads "The McIntyre Publishing Company."

Other instincts declared themselves early: an innate fascination with business, and a nagging urge, however ill-defined, to build something. Amongst all the Disney comics that triggered dreams of adventure, *Uncle Scrooge* strode centre stage. Fanciful plots followed Scrooge, a thinly disguised caricature of Andrew Carnegie in spats, threadbare serge coat, and stylish top hat, abandoning his vault of cash to pursue distant adventures, usually in search of riches in exotic worlds steeped in myth and danger. The fictions took hold.

There was one great storyteller in the family — my maternal grandfather, Ernest Cameron Thompson. We called him Gramps. He was in his late 60s by the time I first remember him, a regular guest for Sunday night dinners. He was small, balding, impishly garrulous, and elegantly dressed in the English mode. To my innocent teenage ears, he was an accomplished teller of stories, undoubtedly embellished with subtle exaggeration, that were frequently set in Paris. Photographs show he had been rakishly handsome as a young man, with a full head of hair.

His stories were compelling. Slightly risqué, always discreet in honour of young ears and my parents' nervous concerns, they hinted at all that Belle Époque Paris had to offer. His stories introduced me to a new phrase, "French letters," although explicit detail was lacking. He must have been a scoundrel.

I did learn something of his time in Paris during the Spanish flu epidemic of 1918, when masks soaked in Listerine were the recommended medicine. Years later, when I wrote from Bordeaux, he casually mentioned that he didn't like that city much, as he had spent a brief time in jail there after being arrested as a spy during WW I. He also liked to mention that he had missed sailing on the doomed *Lusitania* because he had been waylaid at a party in New York. Details were always missing in his stories.

Travel animated him, and he had clearly enjoyed life. Whatever money he earned was spent living well. He had been in the fashion and dry goods business in Toronto during the early years of the 20th century. That required annual buying trips to Paris and Brussels, crossing the Atlantic in the sybaritic first-class confines of the great sailing palaces of the day, to acquire lace and other luxury goods for the good burghers of Ontario.

The business must have flourished, as he and my grandmother, a Holgate from Montreal, and their four children lived in a large family home at Yonge and St. Clair in Toronto, with the added perk of a summer house on Toronto Island. Walter Gordon, Canada's interventionist minister of finance, and his family were next-door neighbours on the island. The children all played together. (Much later, I spent nine years on the board of the Walter and Duncan Gordon Foundation, the family's philanthropic legacy, helping disperse millions of dollars to support projects empowering the Indigenous peoples of Canada's North, and projects protecting Canada's freshwater resources. It seemed a resonant reconnection.)

In retirement, Gramps was always on the move, favouring warm places — Saint Lucia, Saint Barthélemy, and Saint Kitts in the Caribbean, and Oaxaca in southern Mexico. After he became a widower, he sailed to Australia and New Zealand every winter on the P&O ships that were then state of the art, and regularly visited Vancouver. He was such a frequent passenger that when he died, at 90, several newspapers in both countries headlined their obituaries "P&O Tommy."

My legacy was his captivating stories. They had to compensate for the absence of any financial inheritance.

—

At Lord Byng, my neighbourhood's junior and senior high school, I was persuaded to run for president of student council in Grade 8 and was elected. The next year, I was invited to become part of a new educational experiment, "acceleration," one of the guinea pigs in the first class. This meant squeezing Grades 9 through 12 into three years.

Ironically, the most useful skill I acquired was touch typing, a course I signed up for impulsively to fill a blank space. By the end of the year,

I had reached a speed of 100 words a minute, which is vastly more practical now than it was then.

In high school, my attraction to the world of print grew even if I didn't quite understand what that meant. My appetite was whetted by a subscription to *Esquire*, then under the inspired guidance of Arnold Gingrich. It was enjoying its editorial zenith with sophisticated graphics epitomizing new possibilities. It was the extraordinary writing that fully ensnared me: Norman Mailer, Tom Wolfe, Terry Southern, Malcolm Muggeridge, Truman Capote, and many of the trailblazers of the "New Journalism." Magazines, rather than books, were at the top of my pantheon.

At the same time, unannounced, a group of teachers entered my second-year class to ask if I might consider becoming editor of the school yearbook the following year. I hadn't thought about it, but the temptation was too great to resist. Suitably flattered, I accepted.

The editor's job turned out to be painless, with a bewildered group of like-minded colleagues learning the ropes of physical print production together. It was, in a way, similar to a magazine, except for page after page of head shots, trimmed with an Exacto blade guided by a Plexiglas template. The yearbook needed a title, and an overarching theme. We selected *The Odyssey*, perhaps foreshadowing what was to follow over the next 50 years.

Byng was a good school, easy for me to navigate. I got top marks, and while many of my friends remained a year behind, regularly playing pick-up sports (mostly touch football) shielded me from some of the disdain many "brains" endured. It helped that I had a decent passing arm and played quarterback.

Our school principal, Col. E.L. Yeo, had become involved with a CBC quiz show then in gestation, *Reach for the Top*. A team selected from four westside high schools appeared in the Vancouver-shot pilot, which must have been well received. When the program was greenlit and launched regionally on CBC, our composite team won four times in succession, the maximum then allowed. The very modest prize money went to the schools involved. In turn, I was awarded one of the scholarships it funded.

Winning it on my graduation night was remarkable, and unexpected. It was one of the first times I caught my father in tears.

—

University lay ahead. Given my family's financial constraints, the University of British Columbia was an obvious choice, and it was close to home. The possibility of travelling to a prestigious university in a distant city was never considered. *Any* university was a great privilege.

My four years at UBC were transformative. As an arts student, becoming increasingly intrigued by the creative world, I felt anything was possible. Entering what was then an Honours Fine Arts program, I soon met such mentors as Bert Binning and Alvin Balkind (with his partner, in life and business, Abe Rogatnick). They both introduced me to what was then Vancouver's nascent contemporary art and architecture community. It was a small, tightly knit world, and ferment was in the air. Alvin, early in his 11-year career as director of the university's Fine Arts Gallery, fired my growing passion for the visual arts. Bert's avuncular style introduced me to art history, and he persuaded me to join the Brock Art Committee, a modestly funded student initiative charged with purchasing contemporary Canadian art for student lounges.

Architecture, which had been my notional professional goal, faded into the background. For many years, I had assumed that would be my path, because I thought it combined my presumed skills of mathematics and art, along with decent financial prospects as a profession. But it was never a passion. The day-to-day discovery of another world — the visual arts, including the skills of making books — pushed it aside.

In high school, I had become fully engaged with the power of film and persuaded my parents to buy a Japanese 8mm movie camera that had three lenses and was exceedingly sturdy, seemingly indestructible. For most of the next decade, it became virtually attached to my body, and in university I became smitten with the subtle bravado of cinema vérité, mostly European, inevitably French. What became christened la Nouvelle Vague, the French New Wave, found its strongest voices in Paris. Amongst the influential new gods were Francois Truffaut and Jean-Luc Godard. Devoted to breaking the established rules of "classical" narrative-based filmmaking, it was extemporaneous, unpolished, disdainful of established practices, under-financed, and young. It was a defiant joust at comfortable society, perfect fodder for a skeptical teenager.

It got worse. I joined the UBC film society, Cinema 16, which led me to discovering the obscure film theory of the Russian filmmaker Sergei Eisenstein. His theory of the power of montage, quickly intercut short scenes, lurched between laboured and unintelligible: indomitably Russian, yet somehow fascinating. I tracked down a copy of his seminal book, *Film Form and the Film Sense*, in a dusty corner of the old Duthie Books paperback cellar, which caused its legendary doyen Binky Marks to smile. His cheerful admonition was, "It's probably too difficult for you."

My incessant wanderings with a camera, and a new discovery of 19th century European music, led to spending the better part of a year rising at 5 a.m. to drive to the beaches surrounding UBC to film sunrises, pastel skies, and endless lapping waves. With a self-taught ability to edit flimsy 8mm film, and driven to create something, I cobbled together 20 minutes of those early morning shots into a single reel, edited to the rhythms of Debussy's *La Mer*.

—

My three-year tenure with the campus yearbook, *Totem*, introduced me to the world of the graphic arts, my future wife, and Robert Flick. Its offices were buried in leftover space in the basement of the Brock Hall annex. I spent far too much time there over the next three years, becoming editor during the final two, when we turned the yearbook into something resembling a magazine. The shift did nothing for sales or my marks, which became mediocre, costing me the cum laude degree Binning and his colleagues had lobbied to get me.

When a very beautiful and very smart young woman who had also been a high school yearbook editor joined the *Totem* staff, I was smitten.

She, not so much. Corky (her nickname then and ever since) was an anthropology student studying under Audrey Hawthorn. She was in the first class Wilson Duff taught at UBC, in 1965, described as "Indians of North America." His introductory words were revolutionary for the time: "The Indians are not dead; they are just sleeping." That memory stuck and would be instrumental in Corky helping shape what became the Douglas & McIntyre commitment to the Indigenous cultures of the Northwest Coast.

Bob Flick was one photographer using his camera in aid of *Totem*. He grew up in Port McNeill, a distant town on Vancouver Island, where his Dutch parents had immigrated following World War II. His father had accepted an offer to become postmaster in the town.

Bob was new to UBC, as idealistic as I was, and as willing to engage in follies. He was blessed with an intuitive, penetrating eye. Lanky and intense with long, blond hair and the remnants of a soft Dutch accent, he had a photographic mantra that was inspired by Cartier-Bresson's search for the "decisive moment." He was consumed by a passion to just "take pictures."

We fell into an episodic rhythm of squeezing in time to photograph sites around Vancouver, which led to thoughts of a large, illustrated book portraying the gritty charms of the city as it then was, in black-and-white images. Bob would photograph, and I would organize, write the text, and design the book. The two of us spent countless hours wandering the city, squandering what time and money we could spare in the naïve hope that we could persuade a gullible publisher to take on the book. Pursuing the impossible impelled me into directions exceeding practical reality.

But trying to get the book published opened some doors. The two of us met with and were offered a contract by Howard Mitchell of Mitchell Press, one of BC's leading regional publishers. The advance offered was $50. We were grateful, but by then we'd set our sights higher.

I graduated in 1965, and that's when Bob and I together conjured up the idea to produce a book about the bold architecture experiment of Simon Fraser University. My father, hoping I would demonstrate more adventurous behaviour, offered me enough money to travel to Montreal with friends and take my chances there. But I felt an obligation to stay in

Vancouver and finish the project with Bob. I joined the Vancouver office of F.H. Hayhurst, a Toronto-based advertising agency. The magazine style of *Totem* had caught the eye of a senior executive. I signed on for the munificent salary of $300 month.

That first, stillborn Vancouver project opened another door that led us, in time, to Jack McClelland. Bob's then wife, Jane, worked in the trenches at Duthie Books and had come to know Jim Douglas, a senior marketing executive at McClelland & Stewart and newly arrived in British Columbia from Toronto. Jim was the BC sales rep for McClelland & Stewart, Macmillan, the University of Toronto Press, Thomas Allen & Son, Hurtig, and McGill-Queen's University Press. Ever enterprising, he had set up his own company to receive commissions, an initiative new to the hidebound Canadian book scene of the time.

Executives of several Toronto houses also encouraged him to set up a separate company, J.J. Douglas Ltd., as a library wholesaler to stop librarians in western Canada from buying their British and American books from international wholesalers. This ingrained habit deprived Canadian distributors of important sales, a significant irritant in our small market.

Jim was the pre-eminent bookman of his time in Vancouver, experienced, energetic, and charming. With Jane's introduction, we met with him, and he seemed sympathetic and expressed support for our Vancouver project. He offered to publish the book himself if we couldn't find another option. As I seemed to be fascinated by the strange world of book publishing, he also offered to introduce me to senior people in M&S and John Gray of Macmillan.

I already had plans to stop in Toronto in early January 1967 on the way home from a brief Christmas escape to the Bahamas. Jim's introductions offered me a capsule overview of two quite different publishing styles. M&S, the more flamboyant operation, focussed on serving authors. Macmillan was more restrained, better organized, and prioritized the book rather than the author. I was immediately attracted to the apparent cachet of M&S to the point that I didn't think it was even necessary to meet the Macmillan people.

I met with Hugh Kane, then second-in-command at M&S. Hugh was in his mid-50s and had thinning hair, a decisive style, and a voice with the resonance of the actor he had once wanted to become. The courtesy with which I was greeted seemed extraordinary. In response to a provocation from Hugh, I blurted out that I didn't know if publishing was for me but was very keen on finding out. Instead of ending any such possibility, my response seemed to open the door wider.

My final meeting in Toronto included breakfast with Geoff Feilding, then executive editor at M&S, who added the caution that publishing was a very poor place to make any money. I wasn't listening very intently.

———

On January 12, 1967, a letter from Hugh arrived with an offer that exceeded my most optimistic expectations:

> I am prepared to make a definite proposal to you. I should like you to consider moving to Toronto and getting into the publishing business for I think that your educational background and your enthusiasm for it would ensure your success. We would probably start you in the Trade Advertising Department looking after special promotions for us, but it would be our plan to give you as wide an experience in the business as possible so that you would quickly find out whether or not book publishing was for you. There is no reason, for instance, why you should not end up in the "Illustrated Book Division" of the Company if that seemed to be where you were likely to make a maximum contribution. We would offer you $7,000 [$65,000 today] per year to start.

Memories of my recent experience in the Bahamas were pivotal. A good friend from university was staying with his father in Lyford Cay, a luxurious private development on the waterfront at Old Fort Bay outside Nassau, where very wealthy families, many from Toronto, owned real estate. We were invited to join him for lunch one day: hot dogs washed down with a bottle of Puligny-Montrachet. Sean Connery was playing bridge at the next table. The moment reinforced my exceedingly naïve notion that if you were bright and diligent, the world was before you.

After lunch, I went for a walk on the beach with my friend's father. He was a Norwegian Canadian who had built a shipping empire in Japan and savoured the good life. Swarthy from the sun and solidly built, he was well aware of his position in life, having been the Norwegian ambassador to Japan and patriarch of one of the richest families in that country.

During our walk, he asked what I was going to do with my life. I responded with my usual ramble that if you were bright and worked hard, you could do anything. He simply countered: "Bright people are a dime a dozen. Only one thing matters in business, and in life. You make decisions, and never look back."

I accepted Hugh's offer.

2

THE EYE OF THE HURRICANE

The offer from McClelland & Stewart was unexpected, as was its timing. Corky and I had already made plans for an extended European honeymoon, including buying a new MGB GT in London (on borrowed money, with a loan secured by my father). Our goal was to head south toward Dubrovnik, in what was then Yugoslavia. A small wedding gift from my parents, intended to pay for furniture, was diverted to pay for the trip. Astonishingly, when I asked Hugh to hold the offer until we returned from Europe, he agreed.

In late June 1967 we arrived in Toronto. I had arranged with friends to take over their two-bedroom apartment on Don Mills Road. We had no car and no furniture, a circumstance that was to last for some months, but we had space, a kitchen, a card table, and a bed. We were close to Hollinger House, a squat, unimpressive brick-faced industrial building that took its name from its address, 25 Hollinger Road, then home to the combined offices and warehouse of McClelland & Stewart.

The publishing scene in Toronto at that time was somnolent. Most of the existing companies were glorified book distributors, importing the books of their British or American principals. Of the handful of Canadian companies publishing books, the largest was Ryerson Press, owned by the United Church of Canada. Editorial risk was not its strong suit.

The most important publishers of Canadian authors were McClelland & Stewart, Macmillan, Clarke-Irwin, the University of Toronto Press, and Oxford University Press. Their bread and butter was textbook publishing, primarily for Ontario. The Maritimes and the West were considered peripheral.

Publishing any book by a Canadian author for the bookstore and library market was viewed as a recipe to lose money because of our small market with two languages. Such risks, however editorially idealistic, were treated cautiously as "add-ons" to the more profitable core business of educational publishing.

Jack McClelland rejoined his father's company after returning from the war, and his style was soon on full display. In 1952, he was named executive vice-president, which meant that at age 30 he became effectively the head of the company, earning the epithet "boy publisher." Marketing and promotion quickly went from tepid to intense. His role models were Bennett Cerf and Alfred Knopf, two great New York publishers, both of whom he had come to know as a young man. He became a master at living on the knife edge in an impossible business. He was not naïve, just determined to put his authors first.

By the late 1960s, M&S was publishing some 70 new titles per year and had a stable of writers that was becoming a who's who of what is now the Canadian literary firmament — Margaret Atwood, Pierre Berton, Sheila Burnford, Leonard Cohen, Matt Cohen, Margaret Laurence, Irving Layton, Farley Mowat, Peter C. Newman, and Gabrielle Roy, to name but a few. It was understood by every person in the company that each of us was somehow part of an extraordinary moment in our country's history — the forging of a national literary culture.

—

When I entered the threadbare halls of M&S as an employee, I had met many of the senior people the January before, so there were some familiar faces.

Names reverberate in my mind as though they were first voiced yesterday: Jack himself, clearly in command, and his indomitable assistant, Marge Hodgeman; Hugh Kane and his polished amanuensis Diane Linton; Dave McGill, head of the trade sales operation, who was blessed with a healthy sense of the ridiculous and usually able to offer a smile when things went wrong, which they inevitably did; Geoff Feilding, executive editor, already contemplating a more lucrative position in the financial world; Pamela Fry, a senior editor who had once worked for Hamlyn in the UK; Bob Wilkie, newly lured from Scotland to become head of production and still retaining his soft Scottish accent; and Paula and Sherman Sackheim from New York, hired to expand a newly established direct-mail program.

Theoretically, I had been hired to join a new initiative designated the Illustrated Book Division, one of many publishing ventures Jack and his colleagues were dreaming up. That division's mandate was to grow the direct-mail initiative while developing high-end illustrated projects in the style of *Horizon* magazine and Time-Life Books. That seemed to fit my skill set, but by the time I arrived the embryonic division was in chaos.

Nobody knew quite what to do with me. I was granted a desk without any real mandate in what was then called the "editorial compound." The cubicles that surrounded me were occupied by editors who seemed as mystified by my presence as I was to be there.

Initial impressions endure. While the editorial compound was enclosed and airless, the openness of my new colleagues softened the uncertainty. Hugh Kane became my mentor, beginning with a liquid lunch on my first day; he added the slight apology that I shouldn't expect this on a regular basis.

Lunch with other colleagues in the spartan Hollinger House cafeteria offered surprises. Blissfully preoccupied while travelling on our Dubrovnik honeymoon in early June 1967 without access to English-language newspapers, Corky and I had entirely missed coverage of the Six-Day War. Frank Newfeld, the enormously talented, sometimes prickly head of design and production for the company, was compulsive about filling in the details. Newfeld was a relative newcomer to M&S, a Czech-born, multi-award-winning book designer who had trained in London and been lured to Toronto to elevate the visual cachet of the program.

His past included time in the Israeli army, where he had been wounded in action in 1949. Moshe Dayan was his hero, as Dayan's daring tank tactics had been to everyone in Israel. This was personal for Frank. His commentary was detailed, and vivid. Skirmishes were re-enacted with salt and pepper shakers, table knives, and forks. We didn't eat much lunch that day.

I hoped to win my spurs with Frank, as we were theoretically going to work closely together if I did indeed end up in the Illustrated Book Division. The moment happened unexpectedly a month later, in the fall of 1967, when Frank showed me an advance copy of Frank Rasky's *The Taming of the Canadian West*. It had newly arrived from Mondadori in Italy, one of the first illustrated books from the new division, which was not yet formally constituted. He was clearly very proud of it. He turned its pages, commenting on the mix of papers and inks that made it special. I pulled the dust jacket off to look at the case design and commented on the choice of cloth and the spine stamping. Frank was visibly impressed at both my knowledge and my willingness to look beneath the dust jacket to assess the book qua book. It seemed to soften his view of the new boy from the West.

—

My introduction to "house style" came at the August 1967 sales conference. It unfolded off-site at the Guild Inn, a once elegant hotel situated on a bluff above Lake Ontario, east of the downtown core. Sales conferences, cornerstone semi-annual events then standard in the industry, were held each August and January, timed to introduce sales reps from across the country to forthcoming seasonal publishing programs.

The M&S event dragged on for several days, introducing the programs of all of the company's distributed US houses: Atheneum; Dodd,

Mead & Co.; Lippincott (including New Directions, Evans, and the trade programs of Lippincott itself); and Little, Brown, Canada, a separately incorporated Canadian entity of the 19th-century publishing house Little, Brown and Company, Boston, and still privately owned and run by family scion Arthur Thornhill Jr. On the final day, the M&S program would be presented with great panache.

Book-by-book introductions from the distributed companies were long-winded, excruciatingly boring, and subject to silent mocking by jaded sales reps, some enduring hangovers. The Atheneum list was superb, introduced with eloquent conviction by its publisher, Alfred "Pat" Knopf Jr., Alfred's son, who had broken with his parents' constrictive demands. Then things lagged, leading to irreverent intrusions. Anna Porter tells a story of Allan MacDougall (then at M&S, later to co-found what became Raincoast Books in Vancouver) and me throwing paper darts. During one interminable session, when the Dodd, Mead & Co. program was being presented by an editor pathetically in love with his own words, a note circulated around the table with a simple message: "Dodd is dead."

Sales conferences were occasions to trumpet authors, as well as their latest projects. Accompanying meals and parties were de rigueur. Food and drink were generous. Plates of lobster and seafood paraded by, backed by an open bar ensuring an endless supply of full glasses.

Stylish demeanour was always on display. My favourite amongst the old guard sales reps was larger than life. Keith Andrews, from Montreal, had served as regimental sergeant-major in the Royal Montreal Regiment during WW II and exuded a sense of command that must have been hard-won. If central casting needed a quintessential non-commissioned officer, they had their man: handlebar moustache, shorn hair, erect bearing, and booming voice, all well wrapped in English tailoring.

Keith favoured Dubonnet cocktails, more gin than Dubonnet — much in fashion, quickly lethal. They accompanied stories, usually ribald, punctuated with deep guffaws erupting from somewhere in his belly. Once, when meeting him with friends outside Toronto's Royal Alexandra hotel on a foggy evening, we were attempting to hail a taxi. Keith let out a sharp, penetrating whistle, another of his signature skills. Suddenly, out of the murk, a taxi emerged. The driver opened the door with the words: "Regimental Sergeant-Major, I'd recognize that whistle anywhere!" This was 23 years after the end of the war.

One evening, Corky and I were amongst his dinner guests in his haunt of choice, the old Windsor Hotel on Dominion Square, when Corky asked for, of all things, a glass of milk. The waiter demurred. Keith erupted, rising effortlessly out of his chair to demand, in an unmistakably authoritative voice, that the lady had ordered *milk*! A glass instantly arrived on a silver platter and carefully nestled in chipped ice. At the end of the evening, Keith whipped off his regimental sash and presented it to Corky in memory of the evening. Corky still wears it.

—

Jack was a brilliant promoter, but there was no one to apply the brakes to his hyperactive drive for more, or his persuasive optimism that the next bestseller would steer the company into safer financial waters.

In early fall, 1968, financial disaster hit. Just in advance of mid-month payday, Hugh Kane telephoned us at home one evening, in tears, to convey news that the bank had pulled the company's operating line. He didn't think payroll was going to be met.

Corky and I had no savings, and no alternatives. In mid-October 1967, my father had died, unexpectedly, of a massive heart attack in the middle of the night. He had been devastated when we moved to Toronto, never quite understanding my passion for publishing. But my parents had made time that August to visit and introduce us to members of the family I had never met. Two weeks after they returned home, the phone rang. Before I even picked it up, I said to Corky, "That's my mother telling us my father just died." The words involuntarily poured out. Two weeks earlier, I had been deeply unsettled by one of the most viscerally intense dreams of my life, which foretold the death of my father.

Following Hugh's call, we took a long walk in Toronto's the Beaches neighbourhood along what in memory is the boardwalk. What the hell were we going to do? The brilliantly crisp fall afternoon, emphasizing the vibrant colours of leaves just past their seasonal peak, slightly softened the mood — somehow, things would work out. And they did. Jack pulled off a miracle. The bank was back onside, although skeptical. But a deep working capital hole had not been filled. The episode marked the beginning of what became an ongoing roller-coaster ride of financial uncertainty.

—

One of the consequences was some corporate restructuring. Because of my advertising background, by Christmas I was granted a new title, advertising and promotion manager of the trade division, inheriting a staff of four and given a mandate vastly exceeding my experience. Soon, Catherine Wilson was hired to take over handling author publicity and became a star over the years. She was loved by the authors she handled and eventually replaced me when I left for Europe in August 1969. We got on wonderfully well, and much laughter accompanied the department's manic activity.

With the bank back onside, Jack turned to the Bronfmans and their investment vehicle, Cemp, for the desperately needed infusion of working capital. He'd come close to securing such support a year earlier but walked away at the last minute when draconian conditions were added.

Rumours flew. M&S was for sale. No, it was not. It had been sold to an American company. No, it had not. Jack wanted out. No, he did not. On a single day, I fielded phone calls from three journalists demanding comment on the latest rumour. It was not even my file. That was just the way things were for a high-profile company in a chaotic environment, when all things Canadian were beginning to matter deeply.

One day, Hugh Kane came down the hall and asked if I had ever done cash flows before. What are they? I asked. He needed my view of the department's planned spending. The ongoing negotiations with Cemp had stalled, and a revised financial plan was urgently required.

Hugh had an unwelcome message. I had to let one person from my department go by the end of that day. Hugh offered to do it for me, but I felt it was my obligation. I had recently hired a new personal assistant, one to be shared with another department, a lovely young woman newly arrived from Scotland. I had a difficult choice to make. That afternoon, I took one of the other longer-serving people in my department, Jo McNeil, out into the bleak parking lot behind the M&S building and asked if she could type from a Dictaphone. She answered, "Yes." It was as simple a decision as that. Letting the newly hired young woman go was excruciating, and of course there were tears. I never got better at letting people go, for any reason.

There was a happy ending. Jack was persistent, and in the spring of 1969, M&S got its required lifeline, an ambitious $850,000 loan. And Jo worked out extremely well, so well that when she retired some 40 years later, she had enjoyed a career as executive assistant to Bob Wilkie of Macmillan, the former M&S production manager who became one of the top executives in Canadian publishing.

—

At M&S, authors were *always* the important story. Sandra Kolber's 1967 book of poetry, *Bitter Sweet Lemons and Love*, is a telling example.

Sandra's husband, Leo, was president of Cemp, and Jack's desperate, ongoing pursuit of fresh working capital necessitated some quid pro quo. It was hardly a coincidence that publishing his wife's book happened to coincide with a full-court press to secure a large loan. I happened to be driving to Montreal at a propitious time and was asked to deliver galley proofs of the project to Leo Kolber.

The book had been typeset by Stan Bevington's Coach House Press, with its cheeky habit of inserting a defiant beaver somewhere in the margins of all sets of galley proofs. Mortised out of the animal's stomach (these were the days of letterpress) was a space for the words "Printed in Canada by mindless acid freaks." Funny for the times, but not for all eyes.

I arrived in Kolber's capacious office on the top floor of Place Ville Marie, a bit cowed by the circumstance but hoping to escape with minimal damage. When Kolber flipped through the galleys, the first thing his eye caught was a page with the irreverent logo prominently displayed. He was not amused. I beat as hasty a retreat as I could manage.

When the book was printed, Coach House Press remained up to the task. Riffing on the book's title, we had decided that all the promotional materials should be printed using lemon-scented ink. How Stan Bevington had found such a pungent substance is beyond me, but never underestimate the guile of a printer. A sharply odorous lemon ink was found, various promotional materials were printed, and I was delegated to drive them to Montreal for the high-powered launch event, which was to be held in the very elegant Classics flagship bookstore on Saint Catherine Street. Everything reeked of lemon: my car, the books, the promotional material, and most of the M&S warehouse, where everything had been packaged up in a great panic so that books could reach the launch event in time.

In great haste, I raced up to the door of the Classics store with a carton of books in my hands, only to be greeted by Louis Melzack, the legendary bookseller whom I had not yet then met, with a swoosh of the arm and the words "Sorry, we're closed." He genuinely had no idea who I was, or why I was there. The mystery was soon cleared up, and I delivered both myself and the books.

The launch event was elegant, with a mix of Montreal's business and cultural leaders in attendance. M&S parties were considered important, attracting all of those "influencers" book publishers can only dream about now. Book launches were essential and important events, and treated that way by the powerful media of the day. Print still reigned supreme, and Canadian books, particularly those from politicians and skilled political observers tackling the charged issues of the day, were breaking out of their historical cocoons, becoming bestsellers.

—

Given M&S's ongoing financial trauma, Jack was always in search of the next bestseller, and he placed his bet on Peter C. Newman's fall 1968 project, an examination of Canadian politics during the episodically quixotic Lester Pearson era titled *The Distemper of Our Times*. The stakes were very high. The advertising and promotion plan to catapult it forward fell to my department.

It was a stretch to come up with what for the book business of the time was an innovative plan. It began with an elegant brochure for booksellers listing all the things that would be done, from pre-publication serialization to posters, bookmarks, and templates for co-op print ads. Our remit was to encourage stores to order heavily in advance and stack the book up prior to publication.

I had reconnected with a former colleague from Hayhurst Vancouver, Glenn Arscott, an experienced, accomplished art director who had also moved to Toronto, joining one of the top advertising agencies of its day, Vickers & Benson. We moonlighted together a great deal, with the result that M&S benefited from professional-looking materials created for a fraction of the normal cost. Glenn and I had great fun conjuring together; the Newman materials were the apogee of our partnership. All that was sacrificed was some sleep.

While printed support materials were useful, author publicity was crucial. That was Catherine Wilson's file. Given the chutzpah of the M&S program, and the established authors we could offer the media, she regularly produced miracles.

Any Newman book demanded major attention during the sales conference that would introduce it to front-line sales reps. Jack presented the book himself, and I was to follow. He moved down to my end of the table, and sat right behind me, too close for comfort. There was no alternative but to press on, putting the potentially fraught circumstance out of my mind. Apparently my presentation passed muster, as during the break that followed, Jim Douglas said, "Remind me never to play poker with you."

With the book in production, I travelled to Ottawa to spend a morning with Peter Newman in his office. His habit was to rise at about 3 a.m., then write to the accompaniment of Stan Kenton's jazz in his headphones for several hours before moving on to his day job as the Ottawa editor of the

Star. We met to review all that we were planning. It was unnerving to sense that Peter was visibly shocked by my young age. The book became a huge success, and our personal relationship grew. We had dreams in common, and Peter had always fantasized about moving to Vancouver. He once told the CBC he wanted to be remembered as a "shit disturber." He succumbed to his western fantasy and moved to Victoria in 1986, living for several years in an idyllically situated house in Cordova Bay. A passionate sailor, he was determined to spend more time sailing the Pacific: "The Pacific Ocean . . . is an empty space filled with wonders."

―

That same spring included Richard Gwyn's biography of Joseph "Joey" Smallwood, *Smallwood: The Unlikely Revolutionary*. A small, intense man with thin hair and large glasses, Smallwood strode tall on the national stage, earning the moniker "the last father of Confederation."

The Smallwood launch event required some theatre, so the details of planning it reached my desk. I was to coordinate with the premier's staff in St. John's to ensure that appropriate Newfoundland snacks and libations would enliven the proceedings. My first telephone call to the Rock did not go well. I was viewed warily as a "mainlander." The subtext was clear: I was just another arrogant big city player with little comprehension of anything beyond the great metropolis. Disconcerted, I mumbled that I was just a kid from Vancouver. It didn't help. I was discovering that English Canada had more than one defiant regional culture.

Eventually, all was sorted out. Edward "Ed" Roberts, Smallwood's then executive assistant, later to become leader of the Liberal Party in Newfoundland and later still lieutenant-governor, was assigned to ensure Newfoundland culture survived the journey west. Screech, that throat-destroying Newfoundland firewater made from the dregs of rum, was provided in abundance. It was accompanied by platters of cod's tongues, scrunchions, some brewis, and to top it off, CPR strawberries. Memories blur, but the event, held in the Newfoundland Room of the Royal York hotel, was a great success.

Richard Gwyn was amongst the last great generation of Canadian journalists, able to practise his craft when Canada still supported quality print journalism and afforded the luxury of time and supportive editors. His astute portrayal of Pierre Trudeau, *The Northern Magus: Pierre Trudeau and Canadians*, would capture the elusive sorcery of the man's character better than anything in print, before or since.

—

M&S authors such as Gwyn were core to the intellectual disarray of the times, including the first stirrings of Quebec's Quiet Revolution. After too many centuries under the thumb of the Catholic Church, a new generation of nationalists was demanding change. Throwing off the crushing mantle of the old Anglo establishment was high on the list of perceived slights to be banished. My first experience of this was Jacques Godbout's *Knife on the Table*. M&S's English edition was on the spring 1968 program, and Godbout had been persuaded to venture to Toronto for publicity. The novel was, in Godbout's words, "above all, the story of a rupture. A rupture between two human beings who love each other but who at the same time have become victims of a situation, in the Sartrian sense of the word." It was a timely metaphor for Canada.

One afternoon, I met with a small group that included Godbout and a couple of recent arrivals from what remained of Yugoslavia for drinks in the bar of the old Inn on the Park. Pierre Trudeau was rumoured to be running for leadership of the Liberal Party, an almost automatic path to becoming prime minister. Some of the theatre of the conversation that followed was undoubtedly for my benefit, as shocking young folk from the West who were perceived as naïve was always good sport. I was indeed taken aback when Godbout suggested, seemingly offhand, that if Trudeau was elected, he would be assassinated.

Quebec nationalism was a wake-up call to English Canada. As Trudeau once suggested, his role was to save Canada, which meant keeping Quebec in the country as an equal partner. Someone else would have to deal with the naysayers in the West who felt that it was their turn. It was a sentiment I endorsed.

—

That same year, M&S published Mordecai Richler's essay collection *Hunting Tigers Under Glass*. Mordecai had moved back to Canada with his young family in late 1968 to become writer-in-residence at what was then Sir George Williams University in Montreal. It brought him home to his beloved city, and his writing about "home" was always trenchant, yet tinged with nostalgia. He was a master essayist with a very sharp pen that matched his unpredictably acerbic demeanour. Once, at a party in Montreal, when I was recovering from a cold and had a very scratchy throat, he greeted me with the words: "You have throat cancer."

With *Hunting Tigers Under Glass*, we were desperate to find a way to somehow differentiate it from the stacks of review copies that regularly arrived on the desks of influential book review editors. The cover art for the book showed a tailless tiger in a bell jar, discovering with alarm that the edge of the jar had sliced off his tail, which was sitting just beyond the glass. At that time, Esso Canada was running the successful "put a tiger in your tank" campaign, and one of its gimmicks featured giving away fake tiger tails.

We acquired a few hundred faux tails and sent them out in mailing tubes, with a graphic showing a distraught tiger glancing ruefully over his shoulder in search of his tail, which of course was in the tube. Whether such silliness had much effect was questionable. I do recall Kildare Dobbs, the influential book review editor at the *Toronto Star*, citing this as an example of how to capture a jaded book reviewer's attention. Silliness, yes. All part of the game at M&S. The book won that year's Governor General's Award for English-language non-fiction.

(When Mordecai learned in mid-1969 that I would be leaving M&S for a five-month wander in Europe with Corky, he phoned to invite us to visit him in London, offering to introduce us to "literary" London.

When the moment arrived, we had no money, and the prospect so terrified us that we never took advantage of the offer. One of many missed opportunities I now regret.)

—

In spring 1969, M&S published *Memoirs of a Bird in a Gilded Cage* by Judy LaMarsh. Outspoken, provocative, usually at odds with her staid male colleagues, she was the only woman in the first Lester Pearson cabinet. As she liked to point out, the odds were 25 to 1. She was never shy about attacking them head-on.

The launch of her book was to be the event of that publishing season in Canada. The book was eagerly awaited by male journalists within the Canadian media, who all had their knives out and sharpened.

I accompanied Judy to have her photo taken by Ashley & Crippen, the Toronto studio then doing all such work for M&S. It seemed a simple task, but what I knew, and she did not, was that the front of the dust jacket featured a wicked caricature of her by Duncan Macpherson of the *Toronto Star*, then Canada's leading political cartoonist. It was brilliant, but nobody at M&S had mustered the courage to show it to her in advance. So there I was with a cabinet minister and instructions to "persuade" her to pose for a back-cover photo in a mirror image of what I knew the front cover was going to become. Naturally, she demanded to know what was up, and as I had a sketch of Macpherson's cartoon with me, I felt compelled to show it to her. I feared a volcano. She remained gracious, and later when signing a copy of her book for me, added the message: "He made me smile *at* the front cover, and *for* the back cover!"

When our conversation turned to her involvement in Expo 67, I rhapsodized about how the site had been developed, and how strategically brilliant I thought it had been to build an island in the St. Lawrence River, just off Montreal, as the sanctioned site of the fair: English and French together, almost the centre of the country, a stylish, sophisticated city light-years ahead of any other in Canada. She hooted with laughter, suggesting that cabinet behaviour was so chaotic that its members couldn't even reach a consensus as to where the washrooms were located. Perhaps an overstatement, but she had made her point.

Driving her back to the Park Plaza Hotel, where she was staying — as did *all* M&S authors then, and as did I over many years — by rote I began driving down the ramp into its basement parking lot. Judy not so coyly asked, "Don't you usually drop cabinet ministers off at the *front* door?" I jammed into reverse and backed up. Arriving at the front door, my MGB GT was so small that it took considerable effort on the part of two doormen to extract her. Again, her humour prevailed. But it had not been my day.

We had arranged a jammed, multi-city national publicity tour for Judy. No one in the media was going to say "no" to a chance to interview a feisty, controversial woman talking about Ottawa politics in what was sure to become a national bestseller. There was, however, a problem. Judy had not fully anticipated the outpouring of blatant sexism that would erupt. Her vulnerabilities were on full display.

She began trying to back out of commitments, beginning with a launch autographing party in the Eaton's flagship store on Queen Street at Yonge in downtown Toronto. It was going to be covered live by CBC national news, with anchor Norman DePoe in charge. The prospect terrified her. Desperate, I actually phoned DePoe to tell him that CBC couldn't cover the event. It took some time for my eardrums to recover.

The event unfolded, and no incidents marred the occasion. But there were 10 days of travel ahead, with an overcrowded media schedule in every city. Each afternoon, Judy would phone me to say that I had to cancel the next day. I would dutifully drive from Hollinger House down to the Park Plaza to sweet-talk her into carrying on. In those days she drank rum, and between the two of us we consumed quite a lot. Duty won out, and she completed a hugely successful national tour through eight cities. Real sales figures were always hazy at M&S, almost as though they were state secrets, but Judy's memoir quickly surpassed 25,000 copies.

Judy's book became a bestseller, but unexpected incidents sometimes derailed our best plans. Eric Koch's "tongue-in-cheek political fantasy" *The French Kiss* suffered such a fate in 1969. A well-known author, broadcaster, and academic, Koch had been amongst other things a producer for *Take 30*, for which he'd hired Adrienne Clarkson, and supervising producer for *This Hour Has Seven Days*, where he'd hired both Barbara Amiel and David Suzuki.

The French Kiss was a wicked satire based on Charles de Gaulle's problematic visit to Quebec during Expo 67. De Gaulle, sensing revolution in the air, shouted the words "Vive le Québec libre!" from the balcony of Montreal's city hall. All hell broke loose, leading to Lester Pearson abandoning his normal diplomatic behaviour. De Gaulle petulantly stalked home.

The French Kiss was a racy read, but it had a problem. There were drugs, some implied sex, and the wayward daughter of a Quebec premier. It was fiction, of course, but the disclaimer on the copyright page suggested that "any relation to people living or dead is entirely intentional." Nobody had caught the potential libel problem. Given the edgy mood of the times, provoking lawyers was not a wise strategy.

In due course, we sent out review copies with a provocative press release hinting at the book's roman à clef backstory. The launch party was imminent, and as the event was underway in the editor's apartment, Jack and M&S libel lawyers discovered the issue. They were not happy.

My first priority the next day became phoning every reviewer to withdraw the book, without offering any reason. To my very great relief, most normally cynical journalists cooperated, with grace. When the book was finally published, our press release carried the headline "The French Kiss Is Coming."

In the spring of 1969, Jack McClelland hired Anna Porter, then Anna Szigethy, as an editor. Over the next half century, after I left M&S and started my own company in Vancouver and Anna launched Key Porter in Toronto, our paths would continue to overlap. We became aggressive competitors for books at the Frankfurt Fair, and from literary agents.

Anna arrived at M&S with great panache: knee-high vinyl boots, long blond hair, multilingual, seemingly unaware of her charms, a wicked sense of humour aided by sardonic delivery, and a compelling backstory. She insists that she was nervous about the new world she had entered. It didn't show.

Anna and her mother had fled Hungary following the 1956 revolution, which Anna had lived through at age 12. They washed up in New Zealand, where Anna found her way into publishing. We seemed to connect immediately, although we were arguably competitors within the halls of M&S.

I was in charge of overseeing the seasonal catalogues, sometimes writing them as well, always to impossible deadlines. Prying necessary information out of the editorial department was a constant challenge. When Anna took charge of the 1969 list, we needed an initial meeting to review the entire program so that the catalogue work could get underway. Anna asked that I go to *her* office, which seemed reasonable, as it was more congenial than mine. But when I returned to my department's small enclave, I was stiffly upbraided for having "caved" to the newcomer. I was oblivious to such politics, and never learned to play that game properly. I should have read more Machiavelli.

—

Anna Porter's arrival coincided with another of unexpected drama — a fresh cash flow crisis, again the result of aggressive publishing without the necessary working capital to support it. It was decided the remedy was to organize a massive sale of overstock inventory, direct to the public. For independent bookstores at the time, this was profoundly heretical behaviour. Jack and his colleagues, undoubtedly dismayed by their real numbers, decided that the need was sufficiently desperate.

The event was to unfold over three days in St. Lawrence Market, a downtown venue of some character, with adequate parking. Truckloads of books were to be transported there, laid out on trestle tables, and flogged mercilessly for the duration of the sale.

I was oblivious to the backstory, as Elsa Franklin originally had been engaged to handle the publicity. She was often recruited for high-profile promotion campaigns, being extraordinary at such things, a force of nature in her own right. She was also a member of the M&S board and Pierre Berton's television producer.

Elsa withdrew, for whatever reason, perhaps because of the absurdity of it all. My department was suddenly conscripted, with a generous budget and an impossible deadline. The plan required establishing an overarching graphic identity, printing ancillary materials, writing and producing a full-page ad in the *Toronto Star*, and organizing a media event that would include authors, as did *all* M&S activities.

Glenn Arscott, bringing his Vickers & Benson connections, was willing to jump into the fray. The frenzy of having to do too much, too fast was par for the course for an advertising executive. Everything needed to unfold at warp speed, within about 48 hours.

Having acquired the modest descriptor "The World's Greatest Book Sale," the event opened on a Sunday, not usually a day of commercial celebration in Toronto in 1969. The trestle tables were loaded, some with theoretically damaged books. Collective breaths were held in anticipation of a sale that would generate both buzz and cash.

When the doors opened, a crowd rushed in. It appeared that this might be a success. But the tables were stripped of the best bargains quickly. That was going to be a problem. We had focussed our advertising on the opportunity to acquire such high-profile gifts as "a world famous scientific encyclopedia" and one of James Fenwick Lansdowne's magnificent books of bird paintings. The few copies of each we had added to the mix as "fabulous" bargains vanished within minutes.

Leonard Cohen arrived for the Sunday brunch, looking as if he had stumbled onto the wrong planet by mistake. Loyal to Jack, and to the cause, he had obviously turned up in response to a personal plea. His first record had just been released, and he was carrying advance copies. Cohen's reputation then was not what it is now, and when he gave Corky a copy, inscribed with the words "Corky, with love, Leonard," she was so unimpressed she left it behind in the building.

(Forty years later, we ran into him unexpectedly in the Warwick Hotel in New York, where we were both staying. Leonard was there for a critical relaunch of his career in the Beacon Theatre. It offered the potential for an amusing story. He was surrounded by an animated group of young women, so we just nodded, left the group alone, and returned to our corner of the bar. He did nod back.)

The Sunday opening was so wildly successful that Jack, undoubtedly out of relief that the sale had not proven a disaster, spent part of the morning inviting me out to his Mustang for amber liquid. On Monday, the Advertising Standards Council of Ontario telephoned to accuse us of false advertising. To replenish the books we had featured, we had to find some new "damaged" copies. I'll never forget Jack wandering the tables with a hammer, bashing the spines of additional stock of those treasured books so that they could be found "damaged" again.

The sale netted M&S some $150,000, unimpressive now but critically helpful at the time. I felt I had made some final contribution to a company that had left such an indelible impression. The sales success assuaged some of the guilt I felt at planning to abandon M&S.

—

By spring 1969, Corky and I had become increasingly unhappy in Toronto. I missed the mountains and the light of Vancouver. The intensity of the literary scene in Toronto, with its incestuous gossip and established pecking order, was weighing heavily on us. I was too young, and too inexperienced in the ways of the world I had encountered, to be genuinely comfortable, although my career was soaring.

On March 24, 1969, I wrote to Jim Douglas, who the previous fall had dangled the notion of my returning west to join his two book enterprises: "After a great deal of careful thought, I have decided that the time has come to leave McClelland & Stewart, although I very much hope to remain in publishing . . . My commitment to publishing remains very strong, and I'll look forward to hearing whether my joining you remains a possibility. Needless to say I very much hope that it does."

We had been saving money, and I remained in thrall of my fantasy for extended travel. That meant Europe. When Jim Douglas confirmed that returning to Vancouver to work for him remained a possibility, adding the carrot that we could follow my dream of building a publishing house, it tipped the balance.

Jim did add a note of caution, writing in December of that year:

> My view of it all is that you should stay in Toronto until we see what can be organized for the future. Either we have a strong financial *income* base or a strong *capital* base but if not, then we are shaky and must have good cash flow right away, which means another source of sure income . . . If you have capital resources then again the problem is simplified . . . But you have no capital . . . then the Macmillan offer must weigh large in your thinking . . . After all, Vancouver is not going to run away.

But plans had been made. I was young enough, and cocky enough about my future chances, to throw caution to the wind.

Corky and I planned to leave M&S in August of that year, wander in Europe for five months, then return to the West Coast in January of 1970. By any conventional wisdom, this was an irresponsible plan. I was just 25 years old, in a dream job in the country's highest-profile publishing house, and risked throwing that away in pursuit of a murky opportunity.

Before giving notice at M&S, and casting the die, a complexity arose. One day in mid-spring, unannounced, Jack called me into his office and asked if I would like to be promoted to the position of executive editor, a critical cog in the shaping of the publishing program.

I had to come clean. He took the unexpected news calmly, at least on the surface. I learned later that he considered the decision immature. It certainly was. What I never discovered was how serious Jack had been about his offer. To have had such an opportunity, at an age when most young people are just trying to figure out what they want to do in life, was a gift that I never fully appreciated until much later.

On August 4, 1969, we boarded a plane for Amsterdam. Our furniture, such as it was, had been shipped back to Vancouver. We had return airfare booked for early January 1970, $2,000 in traveller's cheques, a lease-to-buyback Renault waiting for us, and a credit card. There were five months of travel before us, with no planned itinerary, no preferred route, and little instinct about what might be next. We had even less idea of how the future was going to unfold, other than my still intact dream of building a publishing house, and a job of some sort awaiting us in Vancouver.

After wandering Europe for two months, our plan was to head to the Spanish coast in search of cheap accommodation and warm weather so that I could reflect on publishing, what it might mean, and how a company might be built. Jim had challenged me and was awaiting my thoughts.

Without the discipline of being fully engaged in the fray, I was never good at contemplation. I did write a long epistle to Jim, which he kept, but it disappeared long ago. Ideas conceived in a vacuum are rarely useful in the real world. In retrospect, mine certainly were not. The exercise did force me to put the very intense M&S experience into some perspective.

Three months into our wander, the novelty had worn off. A nagging anxiety was festering. The full impact of having given up everything in the world I had embraced hit home. I felt so guilty that I wrote Jack suggesting I would be prepared to return to Toronto early, if only to help the company through the always critical fall season. Jack never responded.

We drove on to Spain, where we found a very congenial two-bedroom cottage in the small town of Almuñécar, and the days melted away. All too quickly it was time to drive back to Paris, drop the car, and return home.

While we were travelling, Hugh Kane had written offering a very good job with Macmillan Canada, the country's other great publishing house. He and I had resigned from M&S the same day. Hugh had accepted an offer to become president of Macmillan, following in John Gray's footsteps. We were to have lunch, which Hugh assumed would confirm the new arrangement. Hugh had tracked us down in Europe through my mother and wrote one of his warm-hearted letters:

> I remember our conversation in the Buttery at the Inn on the Park when you told me of your decision to resign . . . What was never really clear to me was how much of your longing (and Corky's) to return to Vancouver had influenced your decision . . . I can well believe that the call of the mountains is a strong one and that either or both of you may find it irresistible . . . On the assumption that living in Vancouver is not the single most important factor in your plans for the future, I want you to know that there is an opportunity for you here at Macmillan's which would provide the involvement which I fancy you are seeking; the opportunity for growth and increasing responsibilities; the rewards and satisfactions which I think you would wish. I really cannot think, Scotty, in my thirty odd years in the publishing business of any comparable instance of a situation fitting an individual so beautifully . . . I have no intention of flying over to talk to you at Yalta, but I could perhaps send you some more precise information to think about.

The opportunity was extraordinary, but I wasn't ready to accept it.

We arrived back in Toronto just before New Year's, 1970. We planned to spend a week there making final arrangements for the trip west, staying with one of the M&S editors, Pamela Fry. With considerable trepidation, I joined Hugh for lunch in Toronto's old Arts and Letters Club. Eventually I had to deliver my answer, which was "no," and while it was most decidedly not what he was expecting, he maintained his composure. The spartan bench on which we were sitting suddenly became very uncomfortable.

—

It was only on our return from Europe that I learned I had left one final scar at M&S. The cover of the fall 1969 catalogue featured a very large and elegant, but very declarative, multicoloured "69." It had been designed by one of the new M&S designers, a recent emigré from Czechoslovakia. I had been neutral about the image, so intent on other things that I hadn't focussed on its provocative symbolism. When Frank Newfeld blessed it, I just let it go. It graced the cover of the finished catalogue.

Jack was not quite so impressed. When he saw the cover for the first time, he erupted in fury. Jim Douglas, who had seen Jack shortly after the episode, said he had never seen anyone angrier at someone else as Jack was with me at that moment. Apparently, he thought I had given him my middle finger. There was even a thought that the entire run of the catalogue would be pulped and something more appropriate chosen. A few years later, assessing the episode, Catherine Wilson commented with a wry smirk: "Scott, you didn't burn your bridges, but you sure as hell charred them." But not forever.

3

WORKING IN THE TRENCHES

During the interregnum between leaving McClelland & Stewart and returning to Vancouver to join Jim Douglas, I decided a detour to Frankfurt was an essential pilgrimage. It was not far out of the way, and time was no constraint. Frankfurt had emerged as something between a growing fascination and an obsession, something always just over the horizon but somehow the apotheosis of the world I hoped to enter. Attending Frankfurt only fuelled that obsession, making the return to Vancouver more difficult as my desire to be a publisher warred with the realities of what was possible for me in British Columbia.

The Frankfurt Book Fair, or Frankfurter Buchmesse, remains the great international gathering place for the world's publishing community. It was first established by local booksellers in the wake of Gutenberg's development of moveable type, but its roots extended back much further. Beginning as a marketplace for selling manuscripts as early as the 12th century, the fair evolved into a central hub for the distribution of printed texts and new scholarship. Until the end of the 17th century, it was the most important book fair in Europe. Hardly a sybaritic town, redolent of too many bankers and too much bad food, Frankfurt remains the world's largest book event and the most important one for consummating international deals and negotiating trades of all book-related kinds.

In early October, we drove north from Switzerland without quite knowing what we were doing or how things might unfold. We had little money (Arthur Frommer's *Europe on $5 a Day* remained our bible), so we found an inexpensive hotel, now impossible, near the Hauptbahnhof. In those years, the American military remained a major presence in Germany. The neighbourhood around the train station was an undisciplined, untamed red-light district. Our hotel was distinguished by the presence of a pet monkey in a cage in its main hallway. While the monkey fell asleep when a protective covering was placed over its cage each evening, it was not happy when waking up. Its screeches at an ungodly hour were more effective than any alarm clock.

From the window of our room, we could watch the evening unfold. By midnight, the groupings on the street corners were ready for action: red leather on one corner; white on another; black on a third. The rather relaxed German attitude to sex and its accoutrements was something of a shock to our North American sensibilities, but added to the ambience of the neighbourhood. It didn't seem dangerous in any way, although undoubtedly we missed the undercurrents. The bed in the hotel room was both comfortable and affordable, sufficient for our needs.

We managed to acquire tickets to the fair as "publishing visitors." We began to wander the massive grounds of the messe, heading to what was then Hall 8, where the English-language publishers were clustered.

As we had no particular business reason to be there, we wandered the long rows of publishers' booths with a mix of timidity and awe. We finally searched out and found the Canadian stand, which seemed almost hidden, separated from the stands of the UK publishers for the first time in our country's publishing history. It was home to five lonely Canadian representatives, including Henk Hoppener, newly hired as the first executive director of the Canadian Book Publishers Council. Such a council had been a dream of Hugh Kane's and was considered a coup for the tiny Canadian industry, then made up exclusively of the old-line companies, almost all wholly owned subsidiaries of British or American houses and primarily educational in publishing focus.

What was then External Affairs had begun expressing interest in broadening Canada's literary footprint and had therefore provided some funding. When there is government funding, there are usually bureaucrats in attendance and, inevitably, silly rules. One of them insisted that there could be no alcohol on the stand, which made Canada unique. It took many years to finally persuade government officials to abandon their insistence that there be a Mountie, in full dress uniform, decorating the stand. The perception in Ottawa remained that wherever there was a Mountie, awed crowds would assemble to take photographs and ask for autographs. This didn't seem a good recipe for strengthening international trade. Canadian naïveté took far too long to adjust to the real world.

—

After Frankfurt and our return home from Europe, we took the train to Vancouver in mid-January 1970, and our first few weeks were chaotic. Everything had to be reinvented, connections re-established, family and friends reunited. Most critically, we needed to find an affordable place to live. For the first few weeks, we squatted in the Burnaby basement suite of Corky's parents' home. It didn't take long for me to become impatient.

We launched a hunt for something closer to downtown, and our luck held. We found space in a 1920s apartment building on 15th, just east of Granville. It had sufficient character, a once usable fireplace, a separate dining room, more than enough space for what little furniture we owned, and a garage for the MG. The monthly rent was $125, plus $5 for parking. Vancouver was still that small a town.

My arrangement with Jim Douglas was of course honoured, and the promised $300 a month began flowing immediately.

Jim was in his mid-50s, with thick, dark hair just beginning to show tinges of white, a buoyant energy matched with personal magnetism, a sharp eye for business, and a genuine love of books. He had earned the reputation throughout Canadian publishing as what was then considered a "good book man." As one of the most experienced book men of his time, Jim provided a bridge between the "old school" publishers in Toronto, most of which remained primarily distributors of other people's books, and the new upstarts. His generous offers of free advice gave many a helping hand.

Jim had never lost his unpolished Scottish burr, which befuddled both microphones and dictating machines, to the distraction of his secretaries and many of his colleagues. He was a good fit for the Canada of the time.

A rough and ready working-class district of Edinburgh had been his home growing up. He first entered the business as a teenager, delivering books by bicycle for the local bookseller James Thin. World War II had turned him into a radio operator in the Royal Air Force serving in the Burma theatre. Following the war, he made his way to Canada, eventually ending up in Toronto at M&S, where he quickly made an impact. He had moved west for personal reasons and was rebuilding his life.

His new anchor was a Victoria bookseller, Heather Christie, to whom he had been introduced by Farley Mowat. She became his centre, and treasured life partner. Heather had the innate gift of genuinely engaging and befriending almost everyone she ever met, soon including Corky and me.

Jim's dilemma was deciding quite what to do with me. He proposed that I spend two afternoons a week in his bookstore in New Westminster and the remainder of my time selling the books of his smaller represented publishers on commission. He wasn't ready to part with M&S and Macmillan as, to be kind, I was wet behind the ears, with no sales experience. To fill a perceived hole in revenue, Jim had instead arranged for us to take on selling to BC and Alberta universities for Macmillan's college division on a fee-for-service basis.

It was a harsher transition than I had bargained for. I'd given up an executive position at M&S with a secretary and staff in the centre of what was then a dramatically re-energized Canada for a job I would have to learn on the run, all in the interest of a naïve dream. I hated being behind the desk in a bookstore, and equally hated flogging books to college professors. In both cases, the people I was dealing with knew more about books than I did. It was a sobering comeuppance.

To add to my misery, it rained that spring, mercilessly, day after day, pissing down throughout the first several months of the year, much of which I spent sloshing around university campuses. As much as I hated selling to people who knew more than I did, I hated the rain more. Although I had grown up in Vancouver, I had always been demoralized by the incessant wet.

It was also becoming clear that my sense of Canada had been significantly altered by two years in Toronto. BC culture seemed alien and isolationist, out of touch with what was unfolding in the centre of the country. It was tough not to feel that I had made a mistake. Jack McClelland had expressed his opinion that I would soon be back in Toronto, where all the action was. I very nearly proved him right on several occasions.

I was working 10- to 12-hour days because our income significantly depended upon my generating good sales commissions. British Columbia at the time was blessed with the country's best independent bookstores, one in almost every town or village of significant size. Canadian authors and books were the catalyst. Enthusiasm was contagious.

—

Bill Duthie was the dean but only one of many dedicated booksellers in the vanguard. Dapper in dress, personally generous, elegantly sardonic, in looks a cross between Ernest Hemingway and Alistair MacLean, he retained the demeanour of his time as a tank commander during WW II. He had been Jim Douglas's predecessor as the sales rep covering British Columbia for M&S and Macmillan. Well educated, well connected, and of the old school, Bill's knowledge of books was broad and deep, and he was generous in sharing it.

As an inexperienced sales rep pitching a forthcoming list, I always made Bill my first call. His stories and anecdotes were in equal measure wise and invaluable, fodder on which to base all future sales calls. The icing on the cake was very large purchases, particularly for Canadian books. He led the tribe of believers.

Bill was only one of the characters who enlivened the BC bookselling scene. His alter ego in his store's paperback cellar was Binky Marks, who was equally hospitable. Binky was sui generis: Jewish, graduate of Upper Canada College, collector of erotic first editions, card-carrying nudist, and once a member of the Communist Party who worked with Dr. Norman Bethune during the Spanish Civil War. And he *knew* books.

Vancouver and Victoria had more than their share of passionate, albeit sometimes eclectic, booksellers. Department stores were still important in the book business: Andy Wright of Eaton's, a former military man in the Keith Andrews mould, was determined to bludgeon Eaton's into building a significant book department in its flagship downtown Vancouver store; Woodward's stores, owned locally and run by a scion of the founding Woodward family, mandated genuine bookstores within all of its British Columbia and Alberta locations.

Independent bookstores more than held their own. Jim Munro of Munro's Books, then married to Alice, was the essential stop in Victoria, doubly so when he bought an elegant former bank building and turned his store into one of Canada's best. Helen Hogg's Seymour Books in North Vancouver epitomized what a skillfully curated and superbly organized bookstore could become, and what a bookseller with a degree in bookselling from a German university, and a disciplined iron hand in monitoring inventory, could achieve.

The story was the same throughout the province. For sales reps with the strongest and most saleable lists, aided and abetted by a constant stream of media-friendly wandering authors, explosive commission growth was the promise. When M&S had an important Canadian bestseller, British Columbia could reach 20 percent of the national market. The national chains were slow to penetrate the Rocky Mountains, so independent booksellers and department stores ruled the territory. It was a heady time.

—

Bookselling was full of promise, and I developed what some considered a persuasive tongue. In those days, all book orders still had to be "written up" line by line, by hand. No shortcuts. Corky and I turned a clothes closet in our apartment into my office. An old desk just fit, and many an evening I laboriously hand-lettered page after page of book titles.

The pattern was to sit with a bookseller and leaf through publishers' printed catalogues, page by page, making an individual sales pitch for each book, noting the quantity ordered in pencil on the catalogue page. It was not uncommon to find that, when I was finished pitching and had written up the resulting orders, senior colleagues would vet the orders I had talked the buyer into confirming and cut them. My issue was simple desperation. Hard work blunted the angst of the circumstance.

That basic process still prevails throughout much of the book business, although with vastly more sophisticated tools. This archaic process was always compensated for by the warm personal relationships amongst people who shared a passion for the world of books. Frequently, sherry softened the end of an intense afternoon.

An evolving pattern soon blissfully freed me from both time in the bookstore and the baleful task of trudging through puddles to corner professors in their offices. Commission income was building. In my first year, I generated double what I had earned as an executive with M&S. And because of my Toronto experience, many of the new Canadian publishing houses that were sprouting turned to Jim and me for sales representation in the West. Growth prospects looked promising.

There were still challenges. My first summer back in Vancouver, Van Nostrand Reinhold, an American publisher of specialist art and craft books that was newly established in Canada, asked if I would make a sales trip across the four western provinces to introduce its list to booksellers. The company's new sales manager was Mark Stanton, to whom I would report. Meantime I was at liberty to sell the books of New Press, one of the upstart Canadian publishing houses I was representing, in theory to bolster its meagre revenue potential.

The trip was a monumental slog. The large cities were tolerable, but I was trying to sell the politically charged, nationalist books of New Press and the high-end Van Nostrand books of sophisticated visual culture to customers who didn't have a clue who I was. This tested the tempers, and the limits, of the few bookstores in smaller towns. And I was following a bad wheat harvest.

On the home front, things were settling down. Booksellers were becoming accustomed to my presence, and growing goodwill was producing nicely escalating sales. I never intended to be a salesman for what became almost seven years, but there were compensations. Jim allowed me to buy into both Douglas Agencies and J.J. Douglas, the nascent publishing company. By 1971 I had acquired 40 percent of both, for what in memory was a modest $15,000, although even that seemed a stretch at the time.

I was chafing for us to begin publishing, which must have tried Jim's patience. There was no overarching plan beyond doing the best possible publishing, with no literary reputation and skimpy resources, in a place far from the centre. Privately, Jim would concede that he shared the idea. But for him, fiscal caution weighed heavily. He had never escaped memories of growing up with constrained resources in a very different world, in a very difficult time.

—

In the fall of 1971, Mark Stanton was lured west to join our growing sales agency. The "experiment" of my selling Van Nostrand books across the Prairies had worked well, and suggested to us both that we could work well together. One of the commitments was that the sales agency would soon be renamed McIntyre & Stanton. As a partner and co-conspirator, he was loyal, hard-working, and steadfast. For both of us, earning a commission living remained paramount. That required aggressively selling the books of those publishing houses we represented.

McIntyre & Stanton expanded steadily, signing sales contracts with many of the new, Toronto-based publishing fledglings. A breakthrough of scale occurred when Hugh Kane, whose loyalty I apparently hadn't squandered, offered us sales representation for Macmillan across the four western provinces. One of Hugh's publishing coups had been to secure the memoirs of John Diefenbaker. This required on-the-ground sales support throughout "Diefenbaker territory." We persuaded Hugh that we were the answer to his dilemma. A contract followed.

We benefited from the optimistic spirit of the time. At our peak, we represented 18 publishing houses, including the recently established houses New Press, House of Anansi, Peter Martin Associates, and James Lorimer & Company, while maintaining the core group of M&S, Macmillan, the University of Toronto Press, McGill-Queen's University Press, and Hurtig. J.J. Douglas was a cornerstone, practically and emotionally.

A growing problem was how to handle such a large, diverse range of publishers. Jim was the pioneer. He suggested organizing an event to gather booksellers in one place to sell all the new Canadian titles from all our lists at the same time. We turned the occasion into a social event, dubbed "Canadian Day," launched in the living room of Jim and Heather's West Vancouver house.

The event worked wonders. It saved us an enormous amount of time, generated much goodwill, and grew into a semi-annual series of events in Vancouver, Victoria, and briefly Penticton, anchored by increasingly elaborate lunches with good food and wine. Wherever possible, authors and publishers were in attendance. For several years, Cecil Green Park House at UBC was the Vancouver venue, as was the Empress Hotel in Victoria. They both perfectly accommodated the growing crowd of booksellers, elevating the social cachet of the event.

A personal touch remained central to the occasion. As M&S was the essential list — and the largest, generating the most commissions — its program led the way. I presented it personally. The prevailing tactic to increase orders for new books was to build an "advance" (orders that could be shipped automatically as soon as books arrived in the publisher's warehouse). The trick was to encourage booksellers to stack up copies of any new title to entice buyers, separating it from the competition. Our glib tongues had to ensure success.

Every bookseller received a package of printed catalogues from all our represented publishers. Within each catalogue was the "suggested" quantity, book by book, we proposed that each store should purchase. More often than not, humour greeted our recommendations. "Absurd" was a common response. We pretended not to notice. I have no doubt that, despite all the Sturm und Drang, more books were ordered than would have otherwise been the case. Considerable industry evidence suggested that the more books initially shipped, the greater the eventual sale, marketing and serendipity aside.

—

We had a virtual monopoly on Canadian authors trekking to Vancouver. Jack McClelland believed tours were essential to an author's success. Each fall season unleashed an increasing rat race as more publishers embraced media sprints to ignite sales. That meant managing publicity for 30–40 authors each fall season, sometimes several at a time. We tried to accommodate the crowd without alienating the key media contacts upon whom we relied. As McIntyre & Stanton represented most of the major authors, we could negotiate "favours" and were almost always able to cobble together adequate media schedules, sometimes on very short notice.

But if book tours for both Farley Mowat and Pierre Berton were on the horizon in the same season, competitive spirits erupted. If either of these two were to make an appearance, several hundred copies of their new and backlist titles would be sold. The stakes were high, at least by the bookselling standards of the day. I remember a bookseller, furious at being denied either author for an autographing event, pointing a disturbed finger in my direction, adding: "Do you enjoy playing God?" Books and authors mattered: Intensity came with the territory, and we cared deeply. More than once, a terrible day led me to throw my phone through the wall in my office. The ragged holes that phones left going through plasterboard survived to the end of our lease.

Deemed "M&S Specials" by those enduring them, these sometimes two-week trips were exhausting dramas for authors. When Leo Cahill, the curmudgeonly coach of the Toronto Argonauts (known in the sports world as "Leo the Lip"), was promoting his memoir, *Goodbye Argos*, he summed up this dash across the country: "Christ! I haven't been through anything like this since Korea. And I was a marine!"

I learned what he meant when Roloff Beny came to town to promote his extraordinary homage to Iran's Persian legacy, *Persia: Bridge of Turquoise*, in 1974. We thought we were ready for anything. Not quite. When Roloff exited the plane, he was accompanied by a travelling companion, Lady Joan Ashton Smith. What we weren't expecting was an entire carousel full of luggage. "Didn't Jack tell you to rent a truck?" Beny asked us. All I could do was hail a taxi, bribe the driver with everything in my wallet, jam about 15 suitcases into the cab, and pray that it would all safely arrive at the Bayshore Inn, where Beny was staying. The plan was to visit Eaton's for an autographing party, then proceed to the Queen Elizabeth Theatre, where he was to speak at an event of scale organized by the Women's Canadian Club.

We were already running late when Roloff announced that he wouldn't do the next event without a "talking machine" to record it. Chaos erupted as Eaton's managers raced around the store in desperate search for a tape recorder. One was discovered, just barely in time.

Victoria was next, where we were to fly harbour to harbour on an Otter seaplane. All was orderly until, as the plane descended to an aquatic landing in Victoria's inner harbour, Roloff decided he needed to take pictures. He was wearing a thick sheepskin coat of Iranian provenance, and against all rules wedged himself into the cockpit doorway. Furious remonstrations from the pilot were ignored. After we had landed and safely exited, the pilot approached me with rolling eyes and said, "You will be taking the *ferry* back?"

Roloff had a speaking engagement in the Union Club, one of those lingering bastions of Empire with which Victoria was (and is) still blessed. I think he did well, but I missed the talk. I had been turfed for not wearing a tie. I've been thrown out of better clubs, with less ceremony.

Returning to Vancouver after a long day, we were on a larger commercial jet and landed at YVR close to midnight. The terminal was empty, and the long hallway of Pier B loomed. There were three of us, and one wheelchair. Given Lady Joan's apparent age, I was ready to step up, but Roloff plunked himself into the chair, and before I could intervene, she took over and pushed the wheelchair the length of the empty corridor.

Roloff did concede that Jack had the knack for hiring colleagues who were "very good at dealing with people."

Farley Mowat's trip west to promote *The Snow Walker* in 1975 was the epitome of an M&S Special. Stewart Asgard, a retired naval officer and former mayor of Powell River, owned bookstores in Sechelt, Powell River, and Campbell River. He was also a licensed pilot with his own small plane. He proposed a day of autographing parties in all his stores, racing from one to another over the course of the day. Such events with Farley were always hugely successful, selling several hundred of his books at each outing. When there wasn't time for him to sign every book, I sometimes filled in the gaps, and over time became pretty good at faking his signature.

I had first met Farley wandering the halls of M&S in what memory suggests was during the spring of 1968. He seemed to feel entirely at home, his gift for effusive camaraderie on display. He was in full swagger, his kilt an essential part of the theatre.

Farley had the pedigree. His father, Angus Mowat, was an influential librarian who had fought at Vimy Ridge, and he was the great-grandnephew of Sir Oliver Mowat, the third premier of Ontario and one of the Fathers of Confederation. If he was intimidated by his ancestral heritage, he hid the fact well.

Farley and I were about the same size, shared a certain intensity, and had birthdays one day apart. We bonded. He read me well enough to be masterful at getting under my skin: provocative when he wanted to be, jocular when not, skillful at pushing my buttons. I prefer to recall his crinkly smile, faux bravado, genuine passion for Canada and the creatures that inhabit it, and above all his abiding goodwill. As a bestselling author, and a promoter's dream, he was amongst the few authors who ascended to the apex of Jack's pantheon.

Corky and I met him together for the first time a few weeks later during a typical M&S party. The venue was Ports of Call, an early-1960s assemblage of themed restaurants on the corner of Yonge and Shaftesbury. Each watering hole had its own distinct theme, led by the Bali Hai, where Polynesian drinks (with umbrellas) cost $1.95. This passed for sophistication at the time, before Toronto had fully shed its stodgy Anglo inheritance. Alcohol prevailed and was de rigueur at all M&S events. Corky was intimidated, and in self-defence retreated to a corner. Farley interpreted this as cool distance and judged harshly.

Our trip to Sechelt, Powell River, and Campbell River turned into a very long, intense day. Our last stop was close to a Canadian air force base. Farley had run into an old military colleague, and they cooked up a scheme to commandeer a plane that could fly us back to Vancouver. Using military frequencies, they connected with the crew of a very sleek private jet deadheading back to Vancouver.

"Charter that jet," Farley commanded. I demurred, pointing out that this was Canadian publishing. Sales reps don't normally charter private jets. Farley persisted. I caved. My credit card worked, and we made it safely back to Vancouver.

Farley loved to provoke me, suggesting that Corky and I were never going to last as a couple. When I finally began to push back, tempers flared. At one moment on Vancouver Island, when I had not purchased sufficient rum, in fury I stopped the car. We almost came to physical blows. That would have been monumentally stupid, as well as ineffective.

Reconciliation grew over the next years. It wasn't necessary, given the genuine warmth of our relationship, but there were signals. Once, leaving a visit to our house, he spontaneously gifted Corky his kilt pin. She still has it. His inscriptions in our copies of his books sent a message: in 1970's *Sibir*, "For Corky who is lovely and to be loved — and for Scotty, who is a *good* little S.O.B."; in 1972's *A Whale for the Killing*, "to Corkie, Eric-David [our newborn son], and that bearded brother Scotty. With much love and gratitude"; and in 1979's *And No Birds Sang*, "For Scotty and Corky — with much forgiveness."

—

One of the key drivers for book sales in BC was open-line radio, then ubiquitous. Good ratings allowed such shows to proliferate, fuelled by provocative hosts pushing boundaries, and therefore ratings. The master was Jack Webster, the "Mouth That Roared." He had such clout that he was given his own studio, first in the Hotel Vancouver and later in Gastown, into which willing (sometimes terrified) authors were led to be sacrificed on the altar of hyperbole. While much of his bluster was calculated theatre, Jack was hugely supportive of me and our authors. He once boasted, not unreasonably, that he sold more books than I did.

In the fall of 1971, Mel Hurtig published a book from Duncan Pryde, *Nunaga: My Land, My Country*. He had printed 10,000 copies, a very large quantity for the time. The book had been delayed and was due to arrive late in the season, almost too late for the essential Christmas market. Mel was rattled by the circumstance, not least because of its threat to his cash flow. He was desperate for us to leverage Pryde's forthcoming visit to Vancouver to ignite sales.

Duncan Pryde was a born storyteller. He was also a rascal, well aware of his charms and unconstrained by southern niceties. He had allegedly fathered so many children that he boasted, "Every family should have a bit of Pryde in the Arctic." The woman handling our publicity was exceedingly attractive, and blond. I knew that a watchful eye was required.

Pryde was Scottish, an orphan who had joined the merchant navy at 15, and on a whim had answered a Hudson's Bay Company ad in a Glasgow paper. "Looking for fur traders to go to the far North of Canada" was the come-on. He signed up, came to the country, and embraced the Inuit lifestyle. He learned the language, and much else, eventually becoming an influential figure in the emerging push for self-government in the Northwest Territories.

Jack Webster, also Scottish with a lingering affection for the "old country," was beguiled. These two unleashed a storm during a wild interview that hit all the right notes. At that time Webster had the largest and most loyal following in the Vancouver market, and his audience ate it up. The program was repeated. Book sales exploded. Within two weeks, we had sold almost 6,000 copies, relieving Hurtig of his imagined burden.

No other Canadian regional market could have achieved such success at that time. British Columbia held the podium position amongst Canadian provinces. That golden moment has long since ended with the disappearance of many independent bookstores and the once dominant department stores, replaced by the juggernaut Indigo. BC once offered a perfect blend of supportive media, energetic sales support, effective bookstores, and broad public engagement with a new Canadian spirit.

The flip side of Webster was on display with Maria Campbell, author of a deeply personal and painful memoir, *Halfbreed*, which was published by M&S in 1972. Campbell was Métis, vulnerable, and wary of white culture, for good reason given her adolescent experience. She had taken the unprecedented risk of working with trusted scholars at SFU to tell her visceral story. Friends there had alerted Jim to the manuscript, and while our ongoing contractual editorial restrictions with M&S meant it couldn't be for J.J. Douglas, Jim was able to steer it to M&S.

Maria told a remarkable story, full of searing truths that had been buried for many years. Writing it was an extraordinary dare. *Halfbreed* was the first memoir from an Indigenous writer in almost half a century, and a very painful one to write.

Organizing Maria's Vancouver publicity fell to me. Her account was incendiary. Having been on the street, Maria was deeply skittish around white men, and while I didn't pose any threat, she couldn't know that.

The prospect of encountering Webster terrified Maria. I broke my self-imposed rules for intervening between a media personality and an author and visited Jack, expressing as strongly as I could manage that I would bring Maria to the studio, but trusted him to be sympathetic and tread lightly.

When we arrived in Jack's Gastown operation, Maria's angst was palpable. Once in his studio, a miracle unfolded. Jack visibly drew back, took a deep breath, and honoured Maria with one of the gentlest, most respectful interviews I had ever seen him conduct. With a soft voice, he drew Maria out, and a kind of beatification occurred. Extraordinary.

Many years later, we invited Maria to visit Vancouver as an introducer at the BC Achievement Foundation's literary awards. She had become a deeply respected grandmother, an author of several books, and a politically astute conscience within the Métis community living in Gabriel's Crossing in Saskatchewan. Her Cree great-grandmother, Cheechum, was related to Gabriel Dumont. She once told me a story, without guile, of sensing Cheechum's occasional presence in her kitchen while she was preparing dinner. I didn't doubt it.

The truths of Canadian history haven't vanished. Writers and publishers are filling in some of the gaps. Better late than never. In the astute words of Tom Berger, reconciling with the country's past is essential: "It is our destiny."

—

A fringe benefit of welcoming a steady parade of famous authors, particularly those from McClelland & Stewart and its distribution partners, meant that international figures occasionally appeared. One such was James Clavell.

Following World War II and an agonizing time as a prisoner in the infamous Changi Prison in Singapore, Clavell had built an international reputation as a novelist, screenwriter, and film director. His new book, *Shōgun*, published by Atheneum, was a doorstopper at over 1,100 pages and the first of what was to become his four-book Asian Saga.

When *Shōgun* was published, Clavell and his wife were living in West Vancouver. As he once confessed to me, he valued that splendid isolation with its nurturing landscape and benign distance from the intrusions of world affairs.

He was charming and somehow reflective of the better angels of the Hollywood of the day, at least in public. Tall, with a flushed complexion and gracious manner, he fit the mould. When he realized I would be handling publicity for the book in Vancouver, he got in touch, and we agreed to have lunch. Clavell suggested Aki's, a sushi restaurant on East Cordova in what was then still considered Japantown.

At the appointed hour, we perched on stools as very fresh sushi, and a significant amount of saki, arrived. Stories inevitably followed. I spent the next two hours just listening to anecdotes about Hollywood royalty.

We did arrange an overcrowded media schedule. Every radio program, television show, and newspaper columnist wanted to talk to James

Clavell. Some complained at the book's daunting length. Most seemed to have actually read it. The interviews brought out the best in what was then an exceedingly healthy media scene in Vancouver.

—

With commissions such as these, McIntyre & Stanton expanded to a sales force of 14 reps throughout the western provinces. We were working hard, and our earning power was handsome by any standard. We had grown McIntyre & Stanton into a profitable, sustainable business, but that didn't assuage my impatience to be a publisher. The editorial imperative, idealistic though it was, always overpowered my pursuit for more income. My constant willingness to let publishing imperatives at J.J. Douglas intrude on the agency must have been very frustrating for Mark, although he remained gracious in the face of it.

4

ONE BOOK AT A TIME

My focus on a publishing future preoccupied me throughout my bookselling years. In November of 1970 — less than a year after I'd moved back to Vancouver — temptation, and the attraction of Toronto, intruded in a letter from Jack McClelland offering me a new position. Any potential title was vague, as were the precise details of what he was proposing. He seemed to be offering an extraordinary opportunity to become an influential player helping shape the McClelland & Stewart publishing program:

> There are only a few points that I would make. The first is that unless you are determined to stay in Vancouver, I think you might wait a long time for a better opportunity in publishing. We are prepared to pay well and give you a pretty free hand with the Trade Department. You would have to live with Larry [Ritchie] on the policy, financial and budget side but I think you could manage this. As far as the trade and promotion side, the only interference you would get from me would be on a few books where author obligations existed or where promotion concept related directly to publishing decisions. I'm accused of interfering

in every goddam thing. I hope that Jim can confirm that I have no wish to do this, either now or in the future, but do so only out of sheer desperation when things aren't getting done. I don't really think it is a problem that you would find troublesome once you got settled in. I guess part of the problem stems from the fact that I still believe that every book is important (to the author at least) . . . In any case, Scott, I hope you will weigh this whole thing very carefully. I think you could do a great job for us and I can't think of a better way for you to get unique publishing experience.

I wrestled with my conscience, weighing practicalities against my dreams. This offered a chance to run the publishing program for the most energetic, flamboyant, daring publishing house in the country. It was one of the most important jobs in Canadian publishing at the time, a huge gesture of faith in me. The offer truly scrambled my brain.

An irrevocable decision was required. Corky, as always supportive, had left the decision to me. As the deadline approached, I took a lonely walk along the beach at English Bay, utterly conflicted. It was a bleak day, the sky that colour of washed-out gunmetal grey particular to the West Coast, accentuated by a demoralizing drizzle. I felt very lonely. My self-imposed boxing match went several rounds. In the end, naïve idealism prevailed. The ache of Toronto possibility wrestled with my unfulfilled determination to build something of my own.

When I responded, again with a "no," Jack wrote a very gracious response. It didn't staunch the flow of adrenalin that lingered in my stomach for some days. There was only so much solace Corky could offer.

It was settled. Publishing in Vancouver, albeit initially timid and low-key, lay ahead.

—

Details remained vague. The traditional way of building a publishing house was either to begin with a business base built upon importing and selling

American or British books — the traditional "agency" distribution system — or assembling a pot of working capital and a business plan. Necessary money could come from the founders (often the case in the early years of the last century), benevolent family, or outside investors with an interest in books and a willingness to be patient while awaiting any return on investment.

Book publishing then was still characterized by small-scale, personal passion and, frequently, family money. New Directions Publishing, the distinguished American literary house that introduced many avant-garde European writers to North America, was established by James Laughlin, scion of one of the families that inherited a US Steel fortune. Knopf was funded by parental loans of a few thousand dollars. Some of the English houses that remain household names were established with a few hundred pounds of borrowed or inherited money. Jack McClelland once sardonically mentioned that all you needed to be a publisher was $5,000 and a manuscript. He wasn't far off in that judgement.

None of these circumstances applied to us. Jim and I both had family obligations and mouths to feed. Neither of us had family money. We would have to build cautiously, one book at a time, keeping a canny eye on expenses and the scale of investments in authors. A combination of cash flow from sales, modest bank loans, and sweat equity would have to suffice.

In the 1970s, this was doable, so long as the scale remained small and there were other sources of income. It did editorially constrain the publishing, but we were not playing in the "big leagues," nor did we have any compelling, immediate interest to do so. We were further constrained by our existing sales commission contracts with M&S and Macmillan, which limited what we could publish to things both companies had been offered and turned down.

Jim articulated an initial strategy of building a list one-third regional, one-third national, and one-third international. The editorial shape of the program was under his direction, and reflected his leadership, throughout the 1970s. Guile substituted for working capital.

In the fall of 1971, J.J. Douglas Ltd. launched with two modest regional books. One was a reissue of Captain John T. Walbran's 1909 classic, *British Columbia Coast Names: Their Origin and History*. The reissue was initiated by the Vancouver Public Library to honour the centennial of British Columbia's entry into Canada. Encyclopedic in its reach, almost 600 pages in length, it was a bible to the maritime community along the coast and has remained a treasured rarity since going out of print in 1909.

The University of Washington Press took copies of the Walbran for American distribution, initiating a cross-border connection between our two presses that would continue for 40 years. The press was directed by the alternately charming and bristly Donald "Don" R. Ellegood, a native Oklahoman with horse trading in his blood. He could be dismissive of staff, but gruffly and reliably supportive of those he felt were his equals. He also held his own against his conservative publishing board, which gave him a virtual free hand as director.

The second title, Norah Mannion Wilmot's *Cooking for One*, was a serendipitous surprise. Wilmot's family had lived on the West Coast for many years. She was the first white baby born on Bowen Island. A feisty 86, she had self-published a collection of her recipes that had become a bestseller in Victoria bookstores. The recipes were simple, charming, and practical.

I was responsible for overseeing design and production, and even in those early days, my strong embrace of the physicality of books was evident. Although the production values of *Cooking for One* were primitive, *British Columbia Coast Names* had a Smyth-sewn hardcover with head and tail bands, printed endpapers on a luxurious art paper stock favoured by designers with access to deep pockets, and a dust jacket on an even more sumptuous Strathmore stock. We turned to Hunter-Rose in Toronto for manufacture, a stretch for us at the time. It launched a business partnership that was to last for many years.

Cooking for One became an immediate hit and went through 20 printings over its almost 40 years in print. The *Vancouver Sun* anointed Wilmot "author of the year." William "Billy" Collins, of the eponymous publishing house William Collins Sons & Co., was enchanted, and except for the challenge of differing weights and measures in the UK would have taken an edition.

Shipping was a logistical struggle. Our publishing operation remained tiny: a spare basement space in Jim's house on McKechnie Avenue in West Vancouver and a warehouse in an adjacent closet. Heather packed ordered books by hand, then hauled packages down a difficult-to-navigate hill to the local "post office," a cluttered counter in the rear of a ramshackle wooden grocery store from the 1930s, sitting on rickety foundations. It was called the Black Cat. We never speculated about what that might portend for the future. The bemused proprietors of the store thought our little venture precocious at best, bothersome and of questionable merit at worst.

All true — net sales were $12,000 in 1971 — but we were determined. With a staff of four and more idealism than working capital, we developed an eclectic program of pragmatic non-fiction leavened by an occasional creative risk. While most of the list was catch-as-catch-can, there was always a book that made an impact.

Amongst those that did, David McTaggart's *Outrage! The Ordeal of the Greenpeace III* chronicled a defiant cat-and-mouse chase in which he covered 3,500 nautical miles from New Zealand to Mururoa in a 38-foot sailboat. He dodged the French navy most of the way, determined to give the world evidence of a series of French atmospheric nuclear explosions. It was a tale of brilliant seamanship and political skulduggery, an early symbol of protest against nuclear madness. New Zealand novelist Maurice Shadbolt didn't mince words: "Greenpeace III was *the* protest boat . . . a triumph of seamanship and conviction." McTaggart remained a seminal figure within Greenpeace, which against all odds had been conceived by a ragtag assemblage of idealists who first gathered in a Vancouver church basement in 1971 to hatch a plan.

Herschel Hardin's *A Nation Unaware: The Canadian Economic Culture* had national impact. The author was a public intellectual, and the book provided an astute analysis of how Canada's delicate economic culture balanced public and private enterprise. I thought it was a seminal book. Neither Jack McClelland nor Mel Hurtig agreed. Both had turned it down. Reviews were ecstatic. Douglas Fisher called it "the most exciting

Canadian book since John Porter's *The Vertical Mosaic*." Abraham Rotstein added, "Striking . . . the best overall discussion of Canadian economic history in a decade." Even Allan Fotheringham liked it.

—

1972 was a watershed year for Corky, me, and J.J. Douglas. Our son, David, was born in October and we began the questionable initiative of building an adventuresome house on steep land above a creek.

Helping bring a son into the world was extraordinary. Corky had enjoyed an ideal pregnancy while our son grew inside a perfect beach ball. Her pregnancy had been so trouble-free that we had planned on going sailing with friends the day her waters broke, early in the morning. We drove to the hospital, and I waited, interminably. The birth became difficult, as our son was trying to emerge through her spine. I was banished home from the hospital in the middle of the night to get some sleep.

Farley Mowat was soon to arrive on one of his annual publicity wanders, and of course I couldn't sleep. I spent the early hours of the next morning counting books in the regional warehouse where we stored reserve stock, essential when a bestselling author was imminent. Then to the hospital, where rules were bent and I was allowed to be present, in spite of my bushy beard. After 32 hours, we had a healthy son. Corky's sardonic review of the process: "You lie on your back, put your feet through stirrups, and shit a watermelon."

The birth was very difficult, and Corky was still recovering when I persuaded her to join me for what I felt was an essential M&S event. It was a party, of course. She resisted, and I insisted — not a considerate action. When Corky's fatigue caught up to her, we urgently needed to leave. Farley Mowat and Margaret Atwood helped carry her out.

Our other child that year, *Johann's Gift to Christmas*, tells the story of the writing of the iconic Christmas carol "Silent Night" from the mouse's perspective. Its genesis was a modest bedtime story one of the *Vancouver Sun*'s old guard, Jack Richards, read to his children every Christmas Eve. The story was charming but needed illustrating. Perhaps Len Norris, a long-time colleague of Jack's at the *Sun*, could be persuaded to undertake the work. Norris was the best-known cartoonist in Canada at that time, hugely popular for his gentle mocking of lingering English habits in certain parts of the province, notably the Empress Hotel in Victoria. His brilliant work was all potted palms, deerstalker hats, clipped military moustaches, and amusing remnants of Victorian colonial culture.

I inherited guiding him as "art director," clearly in over my head. Norris was bemused by my behaviour while graciously tolerating me. The book was printed locally, with only four colour images as colour printing was still prohibitively expensive, and saddle-stitched with staples, anathema to librarians and to any experienced children's publisher. We published simultaneous English- and French-language editions, each with a trim size measuring 8.5" x 11" and carrying a suggested retail price of $3.95.

Johann became the mouse that roared, a huge bestseller, burning through many printings by its first Christmas. Local booksellers of the time anointed the season as the Year of the Mouse and the Seagull. The Seagull was Richard Bach's *Jonathan Livingston Seagull*, a fable in novella form that became an international success, selling millions of copies. Good company to be in.

Our little mouse extended its reach. It became something of a cause célèbre in Vancouver after being heavily promoted by the powerful marketing resources of the *Vancouver Sun*, which understood the branding value of two of its own on bestseller lists. Eddy Arnold was talked into coming north to read *Johann* in concert with the Vancouver Symphony Orchestra. A filmstrip for school use was distributed internationally, and the book was sold around the world in nine languages. Scribner's took it on for the US, and publishers in every Scandinavian country licensed it. When we reissued it as a small paperback in 1980, it took on a new life, and it remains in print, having sold hundreds of thousands of copies over the half century since it was first published. It even became a CBC-TV special in 1991, with Sarah Polley as the angel. It remains one of the most successful books in the history of Douglas & McIntyre.

Our house was another risk. We'd gone house hunting when it became clear that Corky was pregnant; the apartment we were renting did not allow children. Because the office was on the North Shore, we hoped to land there. I took a day to drive from Horseshoe Bay to Deep Cove, searching for houses we might be able to afford. The houses on offer were not at all impressive, at least to my eyes.

Serendipity prevailed. A year earlier, we had been visiting North Vancouver and had by accident discovered a new development in the woods, where an architectural practice, Hassell/Griblin, had partnered with a private property developer, Lois Milsom. She was a friend of Arthur Erickson and combined taste and money with an appreciation of good architecture.

They had discovered a patch of second-growth timber on a ravine between two creeks, considered unbuildable land. Taking advantage of recently relaxed zoning restrictions in North Vancouver, they proposed designs that echoed the idealisms of the time and were deeply expressive of what is now known as West Coast modernism.

When neighbours violently objected to the initial designs for a condo, Lois, God bless her, was stubborn. She subdivided the land into seven lots and serviced them underground. But this was 1972, and the lots sat unsold. Years later, Lois told me that we were the first purchasers of one of the speculative lots. We paid $17,000. In 2024, the land alone was assessed at $1.8 million.

We moved in during the fall of 1973. The house remains a West Coast treasure, still our sanctuary, and was recently featured as one of eight included in the UBC's School of Architecture and Landscape Architecture series on notable West Coast houses. Douglas "Doug" Coupland wrote the introduction to it: "That is the magic of the place, that it was built in the first place, and that it has survived, and that it shows us there was once a different, and yes, better way to live life in Vancouver." For us, the house represented a miracle of timing and unexpected opportunity.

—

Small publishing houses were sprouting up everywhere in Canada, fuelled by the improving prospect of government funding, and British Columbia was no exception. A growing collection of new young publishers banded together in 1971 to form the Independent Publishers Association (it became the Association of Canadian Publishers in 1975). Its guiding purpose was to elevate the conversation with government in pursuit of new public policy. The ongoing trials of McClelland & Stewart had left an indelible impression in the corporate community that publishing was badly run, disorganized, and at best a questionable place to park serious money. Media-savvy new publishers, with thin equity bases and unlikely prospects for business investment at scale, were loudly making the case for support.

Government moved with surprising speed and conviction. The Ontario Royal Commission on Book Publishing, chaired by Richard Rohmer, had a far-reaching mandate that extended into all corners of the book community. The final report, 765 pages in two volumes, was released in 1972, outlining a road map for the next decade. One of the first results was a $962,000 loan guarantee to M&S as part of a new program in support of Canadian "controlled" publishers. The Ontario Arts Council began offering block grants to publishers. In Ottawa, the Canada Council and the Department of Industry, Trade and Commerce together offered $1.7 million annually to publishing. The Writers' Union was established. The Association for the Export of Canadian Books was launched, and the folly of the Montreal International Book Fair was expensively willed into being. The publishing community was winning clout, ironic for a business that a 1970 Ernst & Ernst analysis found had total revenues, domestic and foreign, of less than $230 million.

In early 1972, UBC's head librarian, Basil Stuart-Stubbs, and a group of like-minded colleagues sought to gather publishers from the four western provinces together to form a single organization with sufficient clout to stand up against the Association of Canadian Publishers (ACP). There was a strong feeling that the West would lose its independent editorial voice. The meeting attracted a large assemblage of publishing people to Vancouver.

The energy was there; the unity was not. Ultimately the idea died, partially because Jim and I elected to join the national organization rather than an exclusively regional one. We felt good publishing could overcome scale. While it was Jim's decision, sitting beside him when he raised his hand for the vote, I was solidly onside. It made no sense, to either of us, to sit in isolation on the far side of the mountains. A strong national association for English-language publishers would have more clout, particularly in Ottawa. Within two years, British Columbia's publishing community was sufficiently large and energetic to inaugurate the Association of Book Publishers of British Columbia, the first regional group to forge an alliance with the ACP.

At that time, Ottawa had been persuaded to throw some money at "export development." Increased funding led to a series of ambitious programs for everything from bookstores selling only Canadian books in New York, London, and Paris (premature, and hopelessly naïve) to trade missions and a growing presence for the smaller members of the ACP at the Frankfurt Fair.

In October 1974, I made it back to the fair, with a vague mandate and a bag full of manuscripts and books. There were two of us thrown to the wolves as representatives of the ACP, me and Beth Appeldoorn, owner of Longhouse Books in Toronto. As luck would have it, the clout of the Canadian government had given me, presumably through some kind of lottery, a very good hotel room in the Park Hotel, one of those establishments of reputation normally impossible to get into without years of history, or corporate heft and connections.

To a relative newcomer, the fair seemed in equal measure exotic and chaotic, while savvy international publishers were mystified by who we were and what we were trying to achieve. An old guard prevailed, and in its eyes Canada was either still a colony, or irrelevant. I'll never forget the first time I approached a senior editor from a distinguished old-line UK publishing house with the notion that she should think about splitting territorial Canadian rights, particularly for fiction. Her expression was incredulous, and her dismissal utterly patronizing. However noble our mission, we were preaching in the wilderness.

Being relegated to the wilderness allowed us the opportunity to encounter, with little restraint, some of the rituals of the fair. The social side of the fair was in full swing. The Canadian government threw a very ambitious party, with raucous behaviour the order of the evening. Jack McClelland was in his element. He and I spent some time sitting next to each other at a flimsy trestle table, drinks in hand, trading sharp barbs about individuals in the crowd. Jack's were much sharper than mine.

Amongst many memories from that fair, an enduring one was encountering, late one evening or early one morning, the remnants of a party in the Senckenberg Nature Museum, famous for its paleontology department, staggering out of the museum toward a large, concrete dinosaur in the adjacent park. Grown men of a certain age, exquisitely tailored by Savile Row and surprisingly nimble, trying to climb the protruding scales on the back of a stone dinosaur, left an indelible impression. There were few business deals done that night.

I should never make light of the business being done during the fair. It was a time when actual deals were concluded, and contracts signed, particularly by book packagers trying to persuade international publishers to take multiple thousands of copies so that full-colour books with high production and development costs could be undertaken. The large packagers required their representatives to make major sales every day, and working breakfasts each morning debated the possibilities, and the results, while testing the effectiveness (and the patience) of everyone, many with hangovers. In some cases it was a matter of job survival, so the intensity was palpable and the volume of the discussions loud, even when held in supposedly private hotel salons.

This was still a time when many of the great names of 20th century publishing were running their own houses. André Deutsch and Diana Athill held court in the Deutsch booth. Thomas Neurath was to be found in the T&H booth, while his mother, Eva, demanded people visit her in her luxurious suite in the Frankfurter Hof Hotel, the city's best. Paul Gottlieb presided over the frenzy in the Abrams booth. Cass Canfield Jr. was buying books for Harper & Row. Jock Murray was to be found on the John Murray stand. Thomas "Tom" McCormack, Sally Richardson, and Thomas "Tom" Dunne were there for St. Martin's. Anthony "Tony" Schulte was part of the large Random House contingent. Al Cummings and Hugh Brewster were turning Madison Press into one of the most respected and successful small packagers in the world. Jack McClelland was in the midst of negotiating international deals for the Iranian photographic books of Roloff Beny. And Roger Strauss, elegant and regal, sat unobtrusively at his small table in a back corner. For Roger, it was his relationships outside of the fair, with the most accomplished literary publishers of his generation, where his publishing brilliance prevailed.

When major books were to be pitched, authors were often there to help: There was Muhammad Ali, heads of state, Alex Haley, and many of the great and the good wandering the aisles. When Ali patrolled with a coterie of handlers, the contingent was arranged in the form of a perfect triangle, progressing from the front with midgets to the apex, Ali himself to the rear with ever smaller bodies trailing behind. Frankfurt was an *event*. Electricity was in the air, drama was expected, and showmanship didn't hurt. The real action occurred during the drinks, lunches, and dinners spread throughout the week of the fair, usually amongst colleagues of many years' standing.

Upon returning to Vancouver, I enthusiastically wrote long-winded letters to everyone I had met, shamelessly pitching what in truth had been a distinctly mediocre kit bag of possibilities. Aside from establishing relationships with many publishers, some of whom were to remain colleagues for years, I doubt our efforts generated much. I was exposed to the full madness of the fair and the intoxicating opportunities offered by the international book market.

—

J.J. Douglas's nascent program was growing, but only tentatively given remaining editorial commitments to M&S and Macmillan. We were chafing against imposed editorial constraints. Jim, in equal measure pragmatic and prescient, was looking for an alternative arrangement.

He found one in Julian "Buddy" Smith, owner of the book wholesaler Harry Smith & Sons, to whom he had sold the original J.J. Douglas wholesale company some years before. Jim and Buddy quite correctly foresaw that the new Toronto-headquartered bookstore chains — Classics, WH Smith, and Coles — would eventually expand across the Rocky Mountains, threatening the healthy ecology of thriving local independent bookstores. Freight costs were the constraint. It was a reasonable guess that a growing economy, accompanied by a burgeoning interest in books, would sooner or later breach the barriers.

The solution? Build a Western-based collection of quality bookstores to blunt the inevitable. In the expansive spirit of the times, that seemed a promising idea, and Buddy Smith endorsed it. Julian Books was established in 1972, with Jim enlisted to envision and run it.

It began with an audacious idea: buy a number of the best independents — Duthie, Hurtig, and some others — and shape them into a collection of superior, well-run stores with good design, good branding, and centralized purchasing to shave costs. It worked for a few years, until money ran out, and the original intention to go public failed.

The critical gift for us was that this new opportunity freed Jim from his editorial ties to Toronto. Publishing at better scale could begin, although where the resources to do so were to be found remained an unanswered question. Fully embroiled in McIntyre & Stanton, although by then holding equity in J.J. Douglas Ltd. and, as ever, impatient, I enthusiastically embraced the prospect of any ambitious push forward.

—

First Nations cultural and political issues were important to Jim and me, more so to me than to him. Memories of my childhood lingered. Corky's introduction to that world under Audrey Hawthorn and Wilson Duff at UBC had opened my eyes. Most importantly, Indigenous culture, centred on powerful art, offered culturally significant publishing opportunities close to home.

Indigenous peoples were emerging from the shadows in British Columbia, earlier than in most of the country except the North. Powerful historical traditions were gaining respect, although slowly and begrudgingly. Widely diverse and geographically isolated communities, neither covered by treaties nor conquered in war, were rediscovering their roots. Canada was tentatively inching toward a sense of recognition and reconciliation.

An early declaration of our commitment was a little book published in 1973, *The Days of Augusta*, oral reminiscences from Mary Augusta Tappage recorded by Jean Speare. Tappage was born in 1888 in British Columbia's Cariboo country, daughter of a Shuswap Chief and a Métis partner who had been driven west following Riel's defeat. She lived alone in a rustic cabin in Deep Creek, without electricity or running water. It had been her home since 1903. The words were so powerful that we sent Robert Keziere north to photograph Tappage in her cabin and printed the book in duotone, which was expensive for the time.

While ignored in Canada, as was so often the case for us, the book was superbly reviewed in the US in the *Smithsonian Magazine*: "This little book achieves the stature of a contemporary classic of oral literature . . . [It] is so pure, and the language so direct and simple, that it is clumsy, if not embarrassing, to encumber it with words like 'classic,' 'heroic,' 'epic.' . . . It is, in small ways, authentically, each of these." It remains in print and is still used in schools across western Canada. In spring 2024, it was the subject of a cultural event built around Keziere's images and Anne Wheeler's National Film Board documentary about Tappage.

—

By 1975, J.J. Douglas's program was growing, but the list remained small. The following year, Habitat I, the first United Nations Conference on Human Settlements, was to unfold in Vancouver, trailing idealists, policy dares, and high aspirations. That required ambitious responses, including two large book projects. Connections and a growing public profile gave us the edge in winning the right to publish both.

The crown jewel was *The City of Vancouver*, a well-designed and superbly manufactured photographic book intended to elevate the world's view of Vancouver. The city committed to a purchase of 5,000 copies, overcoming normal financial constraints. All the book's contents were to be specially commissioned: text by Barry Broadfoot, photographs from a range of Vancouver photographers (Fred Herzog and Robert Keziere, amongst others), and design by Rudy Kovach, then involved with interior design for Arthur Erickson's extraordinary Museum of Anthropology, which was rising at UBC.

Intended as a gift to the delegates attending Habitat, this was the most ambitious book project originated in British Columbia since Gray Campbell's *Wildflowers of British Columbia*. The city was stepping out onto the world stage, albeit with the usual forelock tugging and internecine wrangling. That was happily overcome with the involvement of the federal government and the advocacy of such important community figures as Peter and Cornelia Oberlander, two Harvard-educated urbanists who were transforming local attitudes. It was a time when audacity was welcomed, and BC had some clout in Ottawa.

Production values needed to be the best then available in Canada, and that was my file. The book was manufactured by Hunter-Rose in Toronto. The images were printed in a mix of process colour and duotone on paper stocks of very high quality, exceeding the normally pinched economics of book publishing. One of the few hiccups occurred when Gordon Campbell, then in a senior capacity working for Mayor Art Phillips, pointed out the preponderance of artificially blue skies. Where the hell is the rain? he asked. A number of photographs with slushy images of rain were added in the appropriate places. Over the years, Gordon liked to remind me of his astute editorial intervention.

The second juggernaut that year was Chuck Davis's hugely ambitious compilation of "everything Vancouver," the telephone directory–sized *The Vancouver Book*. City sponsorship was the brainchild of Ernie Fladell, an intense New Yorker new to Vancouver and to the city's social planning department, who was determined to shake things up. The influx of Americans into Vancouver's cultural fabric was energizing it, pushing the boundaries of the discouragingly staid West Coast establishment, which was skeptical of anything grandiose or cultural.

Chuck Davis benefited from the spirit of the times. He had been given enough money to spend a year creating an encyclopedic homage to the city, covering every aspect of its history, leading characters, and idiosyncratic quirks. The result was extraordinary, a defining gift to a city in transition.

We thought it made a perfect bookend to *The City of Vancouver*. Holding our collective breaths, we printed 11,000 copies at Evergreen Press on newsprint, deemed appropriate for the purpose and the necessity to keep the price down. The retail price, for 480 pages at 8.5" x 11", was $9.95. The risky initial print run sold out quickly, justifying our faith.

—

The sales of those two books boosted J.J. Douglas's net sales to just under $500,000 in 1975. Neither Jim nor I were taking money out of the company, but the authors, and the bills, got paid, and it made me eager to move full time into our small publishing enterprise.

Ulli Steltzer's *Indian Artists at Work*, published in 1976, epitomized my approach. Ulli seemed the perfect embodiment of what Vancouver represented. Born in Frankfurt to Jewish parents, until the Nazi purge, her father was a curator in the Städel, the city's leading art museum. She was forced to spend part of the war in Potsdam, hiding from the Nazis. In 1953, she moved to the United States, settling in Princeton, New Jersey, where she was taught how to use a Rolleiflex camera and fell in love with portrait photography. She ran in accomplished company, commissioned to take portraits of Adlai Stevenson, Robert Oppenheimer, and Martin Buber. Following an architect with whom she was in a relationship, she reached Vancouver in 1972 and just stayed.

Her upbringing dictated that she was always aware of social injustice and willing to take personal risks. Her astute eye soon understood the power of Northwest Coast art. Following her passion, Ulli spent most of the rest of her life photographing the Indigenous cultures that had initially caught her eye. Her work amongst the Haida was so respected that she was adopted by the reigning Haida matriarch, Florence Davidson, and given the name Xuuj Jaad, Grizzly Woman in English.

I met Ulli after she'd started the book project, which had been turned down by several publishers as too regional. Open-hearted, generous, and sensitive to the plight of the disadvantaged, she had a full head of thick hair that was turning grey and a disconcertingly fierce stare. She was wary of male behaviour, suspicious when as publishers we lapsed into character. Any raw moments were always overcome by forgiveness, gracious hospitality, and genuine warmth.

The book combined documentary photography with the words of those she was photographing. She preferred to remain invisible, letting her subjects speak. Robert Davidson, an emerging Haida artist of reputation, noticed it early: "She was just a fine, supportive lady in what we were working to accomplish, finding our way back into the mainstream, when we were muted and shut out of Canadian society for several generations."

There was little interest in honouring Ulli's work or preserving her archive in Vancouver, a black mark on the city's and province's short-sighted cultural imperatives. In frustration, she donated her extensive papers and photographic archives to the Princeton University Library.

—

Undaunted as I was by the risk of publishing books such as Ulli's, the idea of publishing remained firmly embedded in my brain. This dichotomy would plague me throughout my publishing career.

When I told Mark Stanton I wanted to sell my shares in McIntyre & Stanton, he accepted the decision with forbearance. He knew it had always been only a matter of time. Mark followed the agency's established pattern of luring an experienced book person from Toronto to join him as my replacement. He chose brilliantly.

Allan MacDougall was then sales manager at McClelland & Stewart. Allan was a charmer, wonderful with people and blessed with an engaging manner and a wicked sense of humour. He had a brilliant touch with foreign accents, which he used effectively and mockingly, although never maliciously.

Allan had talked his way into the book business in 1972, abandoning his former life as a banker and a cab driver to become a sales rep with M&S. His wife, Angie, matched his skill with people, and happened to be the daughter of Robert "Bob" Andras, a Liberal MP from a Lakehead riding who became an important member of the Trudeau cabinet from 1968 to 1979, including a stint as president of the Treasury Board from 1976 to 1978.

Allan was enormous fun to be around and adapted to the Vancouver community with great élan. Many years later, speaking at his retirement party, I reminded the audience that, as a rebellious young man, he had once crossed Afghanistan by bus and survived to tell the tale. Perfect training for the Canadian book business: all smoke, no money.

Mark and Allan agreed to buy all my shares in McIntyre & Stanton, following a pattern and evaluation process established by Jim. My last day would be December 31, 1976.

Booksellers and many of our colleagues remarked simply that I was nuts. McIntyre & Stanton had expanded to become a profitable, sustainable business, with several hundred thousand dollars of annual commission income. By contrast, book publishing was widely considered to be a sinkhole for money. Certainly, my earning power was going to diminish.

I let my hair down in a letter to Crispin Elsted. He and his wife and co-conspirator, Jan, co-founded and built the Barbarian Press, one of the great private presses in the world. Corky and I were the first patrons. They remain the most treasured of friends. The letter read:

> You can imagine what kind of a year it has been for me between McIntyre & Stanton and the infernal publishing company, but light is in sight at the end of the tunnel, and I am gradually beginning to realize that in about 10 days I will actually be a publisher, more or less. And there is a quiet sort of joy dawning as 10 years of beating my head against a wall can finally be said to have led to that magic plateau. To be able to have time to read; to be able to have time to actually think about things; to be able finally to put all my energy into the making of beautiful books: it's a good feeling after an unduly long apprenticeship... After the chaos of the last few years, this is the first Christmas I

can remember during which I will be honestly relaxed, and it is a lovely feeling.

It eludes me now why I thought the truth of publishing, even in a small company and in the shadow of Jim as publisher, would soften the intensity.

My final gesture was writing letters to the principals of all those companies McIntyre & Stanton represented. I expressed my appreciation and declared my intent for the new adventure. I told Jack, and meant it, that "I wouldn't have missed M&S for the world."

Jack wrote the most gracious letter in reply.

> I feel sad, too, to see the connection severed — or whatever — but that sadness is offset to a very considerable degree by the fact that you are going into publishing directly. I am certain that this will be a good thing for the industry and a good thing for everyone involved in the industry. If that sounds like the comment of an older statesman, please don't be misled. I don't intend to become one. As you well know, I have always considered publishing to be a highly competitive trade. A little industry cooperation goes a long way with me. One of the weaknesses in Canadian book publishing for too many years has been the lack of serious competition. You and a handful of bright young publishers will undoubtedly strengthen the competition and improve the marketplace. This will benefit everyone.
>
> There has been a tremendous improvement in the marketplace in Canada over the last ten years, and you have played an important part in that. I suspect that you may play a more important part in the next ten. I for one would bet on that. So I thank you, Scott, for all you have done for M&S and wish you every possible success in the years ahead. I hope we shall continue to meet frequently and if you ever want to consult, you have only to say the word.

Pretty strong stuff from a publishing icon, as I considered Jack to be, in spite of his company's profound operational and financial flaws. The future was off to a promising start, at least on paper.

5

BUILDING THE HOUSE

It was time to formally change the name of the company from J.J. Douglas Ltd. to Douglas & McIntyre Ltd. We'd planned this for some time but were nervous about cementing the identity while McIntyre & Stanton remained a sales agent for the M&S and Macmillan lists.

The new livery called for a graphic device in addition to our surnames. We both favoured the traditional publishing route of using an animal. Penguin's penguin and Knopf's sleek borzoi were good models, as were their superior publishing programs.

Alfred A. Knopf remained atop my personal pantheon. Established in 1915 by Alfred and his wife, Blanche, the New York publishing house epitomized what an independent publishing house could become when it was driven by passion, taste, and of course the overwhelming strength of the American domestic market.

The Knopfs had set themselves up with a contribution of $5,000 from Alfred's father. Although infamous for eschewing large advances, they quickly made a mark for their adherence to high editorial and design standards, serving superior literary taste. They were in the vanguard of exposing the American market to the literatures of Europe, Asia, and South America. Their secret sauce was imaginative rather than expensive marketing. This unexpected combination helped Knopf leapfrog many of the established old houses, catapulting the program into the front ranks of world publishing.

A Knopf book always had "A Note on the Type" on an unnumbered back page, a quiet homage to the legacy of skillfully designed type and the value it added to the power of the words in which they were set. The artful melding of words with the mechanical means of spreading them has defined the modern world, spawning many revolutions as a side effect. Well-expressed ideas have transformative power.

The defining Knopf visual device remains the iconic borzoi, one of the most recognizable graphic devices in book publishing. Reputedly designed by Blanche herself, it honoured one of her elegant Russian wolfhounds, echoing her refined European taste, which was amplified by her annual trips to Paris in search of high-couture outfits. Visual style mattered. In combination with editorial dare, it always hit the mark with me.

But how to go about finding something appropriate for Douglas & McIntyre? We were both against any strong geographic association with British Columbia or Canada. We wanted something that better reflected the historical values of the international publishing world, with sufficient flair to hint at the importance of both words and superior production values. That eliminated predictable clichés. While my editorial passions in particular were deeply rooted in the Canadian experience, we both embraced the traditional world of book publishing, which was international in its imperatives. Books, all of them, are for the world, and should see the light of day without any impediments from national boundaries.

The new year was approaching. Time was running short if an agreed device was to be ready in time to launch with the spring 1978 program. One day over lunch, at the end of another inconclusive conversation, with uncharacteristic diffidence Jim put a rock from Edinburgh's National Museum of Scotland on the table.

Incised on its surface was the Burghead Bull, a carved image found on the site of a ninth-century Pictish fort overlooking Moray Firth. Jim suspected I would dismiss the idea as too Scottish, but the design had immediate power and appeal. Jim was an Aries; I was a Taurus. We shared Scottish roots: On my mother's side they went back 11 generations, and my father's family had been in Canada for over a century. And a bull was, after all, an animal, a common motif for traditional book publishing houses, so why not? As we were determined to build something far from the centre of the country, a little defiance seemed in order.

The bull was cleaned up in the interest of sleek design, in the process losing some of its parts, but to this day it proudly graces the spines and title pages of all D&M books.

The only complaint came from our dear friend Crispin Elsted, who mockingly suggested that we had selected as a device "a rather gormless-looking cow passant on a field blank." Perhaps I had been rather less than complimentary about his press's bear rampant, which still dignifies all Barbarian Press books.

—

1977 was a transition year. Jim was gradually pulling back, anxious to get on with the next thing, and I was preoccupied by the pressures of my new role.

The list remained modest, reflecting the scale of our working capital, although some of my projects were beginning to make an impact. One of them, *Vancouver's First Century: A City Album 1860–1960*, had grown out of a project under the editorial leadership of the City of Vancouver's social planning department, another initiative from Ernie Fladell. The material out of which we shaped the book had been assembled by his staff into a series of decade-by-decade stories. We took it from there.

Launching the book required something out of the ordinary to establish it in the market. We decided to deliver the books to Vancouver booksellers by hand, out of an antique car, with popular mayor Mike Harcourt and me carrying the books into each store on our shoulders. Duthie Books had ordered heavily, which involved many cartons, more than could be carried easily from one parking space.

Our solution was to make several circuits driving around the block, carrying several cartons on each pass. That meant breaking one of Vancouver's bylaws. It also meant driving past an inconveniently parked motorcycle cop. The first time, he gave us a warning; the second time, he turned his siren on and pulled us over. He was a bit cowed when the mayor stepped out of the car in response. He still felt obligated to issue a ticket. Mike's response was that, as head of the Police Commission, he would have to pay the fine himself, and he did.

The book went on to sell over 11,000 copies during its first season and remained in print, with updates, for almost 20 years. We paid full royalties to the city, which were used to establish the city's "Publishing Reserve." That money still underwrites the City of Vancouver Book Award.

—

By mid-spring 1978, we were displaying the new logo reflecting the change of name, distinguished by that defiant Celtic bull. We hoped it declared intent. Jim remained publisher. I assumed the role of general manager, primarily responsible for marketing, design, and production, with a free hand to pursue editorial projects. Over time, because it fascinated me and we both understood that careful stewardship of skimpy resources was essential in determining publishing priorities, I gradually assumed oversight of financial matters and cash flow. This was an odd witches' brew of responsibilities, but it meant I was closer to my dream of publishing.

To that point, our volume had been so small that renting a small warehouse in North Vancouver was sufficient. But by 1979, with a growing program and a major art book about Emily Carr in the works, we knew we needed a stronger national presence. Clarke, Irwin & Company was one of Canada's prestigious Toronto-based family companies, run by the family scion William "Bill" Clarke, with a full warehouse operation, and we had already established a relationship with that company. It made good sense to expand the alliance. Concurrently, we moved into new quarters on Venables Street in Vancouver, with sufficient warehouse space to be able to accommodate handling western Canadian sales. The offices were still spartan, but luxurious compared to our previous space. It gave us our own building, with some room to expand.

Our 1979 program was an ambitious step up. The spring list was led by *Icequake*, an apocalyptic science fiction novel from Crawford Kilian. The industry bible, *Publishers Weekly*, called it "an absolute knockout." That led Bantam New York and Futura in London to license territorial rights for hefty royalty advances. The book would go on to sell 300,000 copies during its first year, heady stuff for a young house.

The spring list included another important book — Hilary Stewart's *Looking at Indian Art of the Northwest Coast* — which was significant not only because it deepened our commitment to publishing First Nations art books, but also because it brought Robert Bringhurst on board.

We had published Hilary's *Indian Fishing* in 1977, the second of her meticulously detailed explorations of the material cultures of the coast. She was a remarkable woman: compact and clear-eyed, radiating energy. Born in Saint Lucia, she had been shipped off to boarding school in England, followed by six years in the armed forces, during and following WW II. After she landed in Canada in 1951, the power of Northwest Coast Indigenous cultures kindled her imagination. In *Indian Fishing*, original research, the trust earned amongst the Elders who remembered the old ways, careful line drawings revealing traditional methods, and knowledgeable text describing them combined into a book that resonated for the times, and for a growing market. We adventuresomely printed 10,000 copies, unheard of then for so specialized a book, and for which there was no logical expectation of any national market. They sold out.

In 1978, Hilary visited our offices with a colleague, Bill Ellis. They were both deeply affected by the two-dimensional Indigenous art of the Northwest Coast and proposed a "little" inexpensive book to introduce the iconography underlying the art to a popular audience. Their proposed title was *Looking at Indian Art of the Northwest Coast*. We persuaded Robert Bringhurst to design the book.

Robert and I had first crossed paths in the early 1970s, although the circumstance is lost in the mists of time. He was already an accomplished poet and linguist, had taught himself mountaineering, studied with Noam Chomsky and taken Chomsky's advice to learn Arabic, been loaned by the American army to the Israel Defense Forces in the aftermath of the Six-Day War, and survived a harrowing, drug-fuelled odyssey with Neal Cassady. A colleague once called him "the Indiana Jones of Canadian poetry."

I wasn't aware of all this when we first began working together. I did understand his typographic skills, which would result in his writing *The Elements of Typographic Style*, a handbook still serving as a model for many of the world's best presses.

Looking at Indian Art of the Northwest Coast began life as a $6.95 paperback. The University of Washington Press took an edition for the US, and some 40 years later, it has sold over 350,000 copies in North America, remaining in print as an essential introduction to a profoundly sophisticated visual tradition.

While that book was in press, Hilary completed a book celebrating the first decade of Robert Davidson's career. Davidson was a leader in elevating the resurgence of Haida art and was beginning to build a national and international reputation. The book included all the 75 silkscreen prints he had completed up to that time. Again, we turned to Bringhurst for design. The book was printed in Vancouver at Hemlock Printers on expensive art paper, with a palette including Haida traditional colours plus a spot varnish to add snap where appropriate.

Over the years, we struck up a loose understanding that, whenever Robert needed money to pursue his real passion, poetry, we would talk and I would find a way to refill his dwindling exchequer. D&M was always the winner of that bargain. He was one of a handful of those I worked with over the years to whom you could hand a jumbled box of photographs and very raw text knowing with utter confidence that accomplished pages of tight editing and design would be returned, on time. The fee was modest for the work, lower than it should have been for the skill, time spent, and emotional price paid.

Of all Robert Bringhurst's many accomplishments — poet, linguist, cultural historian, typographer, significant contributor to Canada's cultural landscape — it is his ongoing role as mentor and friend that I most treasure. Robert is one of the most considerate, and genuinely brilliant, human beings I have been privileged to befriend. That was proven when Corky became very sick one year with a serious inner ear infection and required regular assistance. We had run out of friends to call upon and were resisting hiring full-time help. Robert came to the rescue, and over the course of a month came to our house daily, in friendship. He cooked omelettes for lunch while spinning remarkable tales. His gift was as restorative as it was selfless.

—

That same year, we helped launch a new Indigenous publishing house, Theytus Books, distributing its nascent program for the next few years, and our fall list touched more deeply on what would become its foundational thematic strands. Hilary Stewart gave us *Robert Davidson: Haida Printmaker*. Audrey Hawthorn's *Kwakiutl Art* was an authoritative introduction to a then relatively undiscovered artistic heritage. I'd suggested to Ulli Steltzer that she spend a summer on the coast photographing remote communities and the people within them. The advance I could offer was only a few thousand dollars, but she accepted it. In partnership with a D&M editor, Catherine Kerr, she travelled by fishing boat up the coast, some 14,000 miles of inlets and bays, recording what she saw in images and words. The result was *Coast of Many Faces*, a gentle hymn of praise to a disappearing way of life. It was a proud moment when the BC Ministry of Education decided to purchase a copy for every school in the province.

The fall 1979 list was also strong, including Roy Peterson and Allan Fotheringham's collaboration, *The World According to Roy Peterson: With the Gospel According to Allan Fotheringham*. And *Cattle Ranch*, the saga of the Douglas Lake Ranch, embraced the romance of British Columbia's frontier history.

The greatest risk was Doris Shadbolt's *The Art of Emily Carr*.

Although art books have always struck fear into the hearts of publishers, they became a cornerstone of D&M's publishing program. Considered risky, very expensive, and tough to sell, publishers viewed art books as ancillary to the essential mission of honouring words. But M&S, the UTP, and Clarke, Irwin & Company had published some superb art books that had sold well. Canadian art books were experiencing a golden moment in the sun. In my view, visual culture mattered, and illustrated books were becoming ever easier to undertake given the evolving possibilities of offset printing and, later, digital scanning.

I'd met Doris Shadbolt in the mid-1970s. She was then at the height of her distinguished 25-year career with the Vancouver Art Gallery. Doris was extraordinary. Always calm, with hair in an elegant French twist and a slightly hesitant manner of speaking, her demeanour camouflaged an astute eye and an iron will. Her groundbreaking 1967 VAG show, *Arts of the Raven*, breached previously rigid boundaries. For the first time, a Canadian curator of reputation had dared the public to consider Indigenous achievement as serious art rather than anthropological artifact.

I was a bit shy when we were first introduced. My diffidence quickly vanished, melting away in the face of her innate grace. She seemed a kindred spirit, and we became close friends. When I asked if she thought it was time for a serious art book honouring the power of Carr's images, she agreed, unhesitatingly. A plan was hatched.

The potential scale of the project weighed heavily on Jim. Doris's concept was to interweave her own critical text with Carr's images and words. The approach was complicated because Clarke, Irwin & Company managed the copyrights of all Emily Carr's writing. Jim had been asked to help the company through a difficult financial period, and given that it was our distributor and in control of our receivables, a cordial solution was required. We set the project up as a joint venture to share the daunting financial risk. Jim led the editorial side, and an editor trusted by Clarke, Irwin & Company would take on detailed work. This was a defining moment for D&M. It was our first art book of such scale, and we'd plunged ahead without institutional financial support.

Conceptualizing the book and working with Doris fell to me. Working on *The Art of Emily Carr* turned into one of the most deeply satisfying experiences of my publishing career. It began when my family and I visited the Shadbolts for a weekend at their blissful summer retreat on Hornby Island. Doris and I sat on the steps of her studio in bright, warm sun, talking about the book, her vision for it, and how the elements might be successfully melded together.

Jack Shadbolt, always robust, energetic, and commanding, was many feet up in a tree with a power saw in one hand and a branch grasped for stability in the other. He was "sculpting" the tree to improve the view from their front deck. Doris was terrified; Jack was fully engaged, indifferent to the apparent risk, entirely focussed on the work at hand.

After dinner that night, Doris was fussing about helping put our five-year-old son to bed. The Shadbolts did not have children of their own, so she had searched the house for a bedtime story. Beatrix Potter was all she could find. When I tiptoed into the room where Doris was reading, reluctant to interrupt, there was a golden glow. It was only from a low-wattage incandescent bulb, but it seemed almost a halo. For a moment I thought: It's true, Doris is an angel.

But then the editorial, design, and production process became complicated. Doris felt strongly that Reinhard Derreth, a leading Vancouver designer with art book experience, should design the book. She had worked with him before and trusted him. We were stepping well outside our normal comfort zone.

We commissioned new photography of all the art, in itself a tricky challenge. Carr's palette was dense and often dark, a visual challenge given the relatively primitive, pre-digital technology of the time. Colour separations had to be done manually, with a camera, rather than scanned, which demanded experience and skill. Paper options were limited if we were to keep even vaguely within our required margins. Reinhard was a perfectionist and resisted compromise. Debates became intense, with Jim and Bill Clarke nervous that I was going to irresponsibly squander precious financial resources. The lack of faith was dismaying to me but felt very real at the time.

As the book's publication date approached, Canada's bookselling community rose to the challenge, pushing us to a first printing of 30,000 copies. For a book carrying an initial retail price of $39.95 in 1979 (equivalent to $158 in 2024), that was a stretch. The printing bill alone was going to reach $250,000. Reflecting a prevailing skepticism about the financial fragility of all Canadian publishers, many printers refused to even quote. Bill Clarke's silver tongue prevailed.

Over time, I learned to become superstitious when projects of this scale were working their way through the system. The greater the financial risk, the more gremlins seemed to disrupt the process. When the books from the Ontario binder, T.H. Best Printing Company Ltd., were working their way across the country to our western warehouse, freight cars containing them were pushed onto a siding with frozen bearings. We lost two weeks in a critical Christmas selling season. That might seem trivial now, but it unleashed panic in the moment.

We had sold a 2,000-copy US edition to the University of Washington Press, and all the books were individually packaged in corrugated cardboard boxes. But the copyright page did not include the legally required "Printed and Bound in Canada" notification. US border guards refused to let the books enter the US. More accommodating than is the case now, and admirers of the book, they actually telephoned us to explain the situation.

Several of our staff trekked to the border and spent a long day gingerly unpacking each book, adding a sticker with the necessary correction to the copyright page, then placing each back into its snug container. The truck containing them made its way to Seattle, and the American edition sold out. Such a simple complexity might seem almost routine now. It was devastating at the time. We never made that mistake again.

Incredibly, all 30,000 copies of the book were shipped to customers. Close to Christmas, Coles reordered another 5,000 copies, and we were sorely tempted to reprint. But we judged that Coles was just trying to protect its stock position for a bestseller. The books would likely be returned immediately following the Christmas season, and we would never be paid for them. We declined the order — a very rare example of caution for any publisher at that time, refusing a large order for an expensive art book in the midst of a Christmas season.

However incomprehensible this may sound to anyone unfamiliar with the strange norms of book publishing, "returns" for full credit have been with the book business since the 1930s. Large customers cynically use the possibility as a very effective way to manage cash flow. For them, not the publishers. This was never helpful when attempting to defuse bankers' skepticism over accepting inventory as collateral against operating loans. The tactic has been perfected by large customers, notably Indigo, ever since.

Our luck held. *The Art of Emily Carr* topped bestseller lists in Canada that fall. Even normally crotchety art critics raved: John Bentley Mays rhapsodized in *Maclean's* that it was an art book "to take to the moon."

When royalties became due, rumours re-emerged that Clarke, Irwin & Company's finances were shaky, which meant that ours were as well. Still, the company sent the almost $60,000 royalty cheque on time. With great satisfaction, and considerable relief, I hand-delivered it, with a bottle of champagne, to the Shadbolts' house. They were not expecting my knock on their door. We drank the champagne on the spot.

Doris later told me, with a defiant sparkle in her eye, that she had spent most of the money remodelling her kitchen. It was, after all, her money, and Jack was notoriously tight-fisted. I spent much time in that kitchen over the years. Jack's contribution was to make the martinis, a task at which he excelled.

I would never make light of the social side of publishing. Deep friendships were made and sustained. While the books always came first, however stressful the process of making them, tension often lingered just beneath the surface. A European colleague once offered the astute observation that the reason publishers and authors are so often locked in a love-hate dance is that they live such similar lives. Books make a mercurial mistress.

My lunches with Doris became unofficial editorial meetings as we discussed what was afoot in the gallery world, what changes were being mooted in Ottawa, and which artists might be ready for a monograph. It was always clear what Doris thought, although she remained unfailingly tactful in her judgements. She conveyed more wisdom with an arch of an eyebrow than emanated from many of the country's leading critics.

With the help of *The Art of Emily Carr*, D&M's sales revenues hit $1.6 million in 1979, a 60 percent increase in 24 months. The book market in Canada was reaching its apogee.

When Jim offered me the opportunity to acquire more shares and become the majority shareholder, I didn't hesitate. It meant another trip to the bank, further increasing our personal exposure. That seemed trivial compared to becoming a full-time publisher in overall command of a program. In 1980, I became majority shareholder, and president and publisher, of Douglas & McIntyre Ltd.

The foundation of D&M was established. Our initial successes had suggested a robust growth pattern. While Jim stayed on the board, at my request, and sometimes offered sharply critical opinions, I had a free hand to put a more personal stamp on the publishing. We felt we could give Toronto publishers a run for their money. Steering a Vancouver-based company onto the national stage was a challenge I relished.

Jim became increasingly peripatetic, heading more often to Scotland, his first love, and to Toronto as the new president of the Association of Canadian Publishers (ACP). As a publisher from BC, Jim was bringing a fresh perspective to the national debate. A proliferation of new, small publishers across the country was aggressively pushing for more supportive cultural policy to offset what the scale of the Canadian market couldn't offer. His authoritative voice was critical.

As I settled into my new role as publisher of D&M, I followed in Jim's footsteps and accepted a term as president of the Association of Book Publishers of British Columbia. The association was lobbying the BC Ministry of Education to open up textbook publishing to local publishers. A rarity amongst provinces, BC still specified grade-wide use of authorized materials and had its own warehouse and distribution mechanism to back it up. BC was, literally, the pot of gold beyond the mountains. I also inherited the cultural file. We continued tilting at that elusive windmill. To our surprise, we won a small victory. Then Minister of Recreation and Conservation Sam Bawlf was persuaded to introduce a small program to support the nascent publishing community. The scale was paltry, but it was a start.

On the national stage, the previous year had been a game-changer for publishers. The industry had spent several years lobbying Ottawa for bolder book publishing support policy. Significant national support for publishing was rumoured to be inching forward in Ottawa. Was it a promise, or just a hope? Georges Laberge, once a Quebec City bookseller, had been seconded to what was then the secretary of state to conceptualize how such an initiative might work. Laberge's proposed solution was an "industrial" program to inject fresh equity into the business. He had devised an ambitious one, in theory. It had made steady progress up the bureaucratic ladder, but had stalled at Treasury Board, bumped from the weekly agenda for several weeks. Time was not our friend.

Patsy Aldana, who had followed Jim as president of the ACP, phoned me with her usual subtlety to announce that Armageddon was imminent. Either the proposal made it through Treasury Board during the coming week, or the possibility might die. The head of the Treasury Board was Robert Andras, Allan MacDougall's father-in-law. After Allan replaced me at McIntyre & Stanton, Corky and I had socialized with the Andrases during their family visits to Vancouver, and I much liked Robert.

Apparently, he was now our last hope. I tracked him down in Vancouver, but he was leaving to return to Ottawa on New Year's Day. We arranged a call for that morning.

The evening before, we had dinner with old friends Crispin and Jan Elsted of Barbarian Press. Andreas "Andy" Schroeder, Sharon Brown, and Robert Bringhurst were seated around a cramped table in the Elsteds' small house near Mission. The evening was a long-standing and much-treasured tradition that we all gather for a meal to linger over, a visit to the Barbarian presses in a separate building across the lawn, good wine, and expansive, undisciplined conversation. Our son was very young and demonstrated the good sense to fall asleep early.

Once the conversation became animated, as it always did, my traditional role was to defend the virtues of Canadian publishing. Dinner was a sympathetic, if skeptical, environment for such a conversation. That night, everyone wanted to know what was going on in Ottawa. I couldn't answer.

Corky and I had another New Year's tradition: a visit to the nearby Order of St. Clare's Monastery to see one of our oldest friends, Claire Blondin. We had first met 10 years earlier in Leysin, Switzerland, hanging our hats in the Club Vagabond, where an unruly assortment of hikers, climbers, and wanderers wasted time. Lasting friendships were easily forged. Some years after returning to Canada, Claire entered a cloistered order, becoming Sister Claire Marie. The order imposed strict discipline, so much so that during our early visits, as a novitiate she was required to remain behind a wire mesh screen.

Times had changed. We could now retell old stories about Switzerland with only a low barrier separating us. This New Year's Day, we had at the last minute been offered a rare privilege: an invitation to join the other sisters for prayer in the convent's small chapel.

I faced a serious dilemma. I had committed to taking Robert's critical call that morning, yet I had accepted Sister Claire Marie's unexpected invitation to join morning prayers.

We joined the sisters in the chapel. Sister Claire Marie was aware of the circumstance, and of its importance. During the service, she asked the small assemblage to pray for a positive outcome. Prayer was soothing, but getting home in time for that phone call was imperative.

We drove home in a fog, my mood darkened by the persistent rain. Then, a miracle unfolded. We had no sooner reached home and opened our front door when the phone rang. "Scott, Bob. How important is this really? Tell me the truth: Is the industry crying wolf?"

I answered with as much conviction as I could muster on the spot.

I have been told various versions of what happened next. The one I prefer is that at the next meeting of Treasury Board, Bob ordered all of the bureaucrats out of the room and simply said to his cabinet colleagues: "The issue is real; it is important; we're doing this."

"This" was a multi-million-dollar fund to inject fresh equity-like funding into Canadian-owned book publishers. Announced in 1979 as the Canadian Book Publishing Development Program, it survived an election and a succession of new ministers — John Roberts, Donald Macdonald, and finally Francis Fox — before ending up in the new Department of

Communications. After months of uncertainty, it officially launched in 1980, part of an announced package totalling $20 million in new publishing support.

Forty years on, it has successfully dodged the slings and arrows of political fate and remains in place as the Canada Book Fund. It now totals about $40 million a year, administered by the Department of Canadian Heritage. Since 1980, over $1 billion has been dispersed to Canadian-owned publishers, English and French alike, providing them and their writers with a lifeline.

The program was the result of years of lobbying, endless background studies, and fierce debate. Bob Andras's directive had broken the logjam.

Perhaps it was the power of prayer.

—

The company missed Jim's presence in Vancouver, but his involvement in the ACP gave us a gift: Patsy Aldana.

Patsy had newly arrived in Canada, a bright, witty Guatemalan American with an undergraduate degree in art history from Stanford, followed by postgraduate work at Bryn Mawr College. She and her then husband had moved north to Toronto in 1971, quickly embracing the animated politics of the day. Patsy soon joined the Canadian Women's Press, a feminist collective, and was instrumental in the founding of the ACP. A quick-minded honesty, although sometimes brutal, defined her.

Patsy was as anxious to establish her own publishing house as I was. She was determined to create a Canadian children's program that would echo the more sophisticated publishing of almost every other English-speaking or European country of any consequence. Her view was succinct: "If you don't have a children's literature, you don't have a national culture." That perfectly echoed my vision for the D&M adult program.

In spite of innate differences, our sensibilities meshed from almost the beginning. Patsy had a fiery, emotive Latin soul. I was a caricature of an Anglo-Canadian Scot, diplomatic to the core, wary of temperamental outbursts, slow to recover from them when they were directed at me.

Our relationship should never have worked, but it did, brilliantly, for over 30 years. We were often yin to each other's yang; sometimes the other way around.

We soon struck an innovative business arrangement. Patsy became a senior executive and shareholder in D&M while retaining ownership of her own nascent company, Groundwood Books Ltd. Groundwood would operate out of Toronto under the D&M umbrella, backed by D&M financing, marketing, and distribution. D&M would pay the bills and benefit from all revenues, including grants, while Groundwood operated as a separate legal entity, retaining ownership of its contracts and copyrights. Patsy would manage the D&M/Groundwood Toronto office, shaping the merged children's publishing programs. Children's and young adult fiction and high-end illustrated children's books would be identified as Groundwood books, while non-fiction would continue to be under the rubric of D&M. Patsy was also given the responsibility of managing the Clarke, Irwin & Company relationship, and was offered space in the Clarke, Irwin building on St. Clair Avenue West.

The alliance was announced in fall 1980 with a full-colour insert bound within that season's D&M catalogues, a rare indulgence for Canadian publishers at the time. The first combined list was modest, just six books, three each from Groundwood and D&M. It was editorially strong, with Groundwood including books from Brian Doyle and Blair Dawson, and D&M publishing Maria Campbell's *Riel's People: How the Métis Lived* and Betty Waterton and Ann Blades's *A Salmon for Simon*.

A Salmon for Simon became a very pleasant surprise. It was awarded the Canada Council Children's Literature Prize by the Canadian Library Association, reinvigorating Ann Blades's career as an illustrator. Betty Waterton had submitted the book to us as text accompanied by her own art, but her illustration missed the mark. I suggested we approach Ann to produce new art.

When Ann was struggling to accurately portray the faces of Indigenous children, we had a long editorial discussion in my living room. As inspiration, I brought out a selection of Ulli Steltzer's photographs of Indigenous children along the BC coast and spread them out on our carpet. Ann took it from there, catching exactly the right facial nuances in perfectly modulated watercolour. The book remains in print almost 50 years later, having sold several hundred thousand copies in six languages and nine countries.

—

Shaping a publishing program requires a mix of market intuition, fiscal discipline, and a necessary occasional dare. The critical task of any publisher is to set standards and determine the overall contours of the program, which is not as straightforward as it appears. An appetite for risk is essential. Nothing in the creative world is predictable. Luck helps. Magic, while rare, can become transcendent.

This is the essential role of the publisher. Not the marketing department. Not the accounting department. Not individual editors. I was adamant about creating a culture that would support that inviolate principle: editorial independence from arbitrary financial or market constraints, which had been a staple of independent publishers worldwide before deep pockets, requiring sufficient sales to support vastly increased investment, became dominant. Editorial imperatives inevitably suffer in such circumstances. Call me naïve, but the freedom to allow instinct to trump market necessity has led to most of the great publishing, including most of the books from the last two centuries that are now considered seminal.

As far as economic possibility allowed, we took an organic, intuitive approach to building D&M's program. We were never naïve about numbers and the urgency of making them work, nor about market possibility. Our steadily growing bank operating line precluded wearing rose-coloured glasses. In the trenchant words of Alfred Döblin, a distinguished 20th-century German literary figure: "The publisher casts one eye at the writer, the other at the public. But the third eye, the eye of wisdom, gazes unflinchingly at the cash register."

Given my introduction to the business at McClelland & Stewart in the late 1960s, and my innate tendency to romanticize the process, I embraced prevailing traditions. Jack McClelland once suggested that the essence of publishing, particularly in Canada, was to find and publish the best of what was on offer, in all genres, embracing all points of view. Inspired eclecticism was the mantra. That resonated with me.

My personal approach to publishing was becoming more sharply defined. I deeply valued everything about the métier. Words always came first, which meant that editors were treasured. The classic definition of an editor is to discern what a book is trying to become and guide it there. That can prove tricky. Words are slippery things, always under the glare of subjective judgement, and the author's ego. And the best editing is undermined if the book's physical production values fail to honour the words. Even before entering publishing, I had become entranced by elegant typography and good-quality paper. The craft of publishing infused our approach to making books. It was central to D&M's philosophy. Knopf, with its unmatched editorial, design, and production standards, remained a lodestar.

I knew none of this would be possible without good people. From early in our history, we were blessed by the calibre of management and staff we were able to attract. Loyalty was valued; longevity was normal. The pattern was evident by the early 1980s.

On the editorial side, I single out Saeko Usukawa, who eventually became our editorial director. I first met Saeko in 1970, when she was an editor working at Macmillan in Toronto. She was a second-generation Japanese Canadian who had endured her early years living in an internment camp, where her parents had been banished during WW II. A residual diffidence reflected that experience.

She began freelancing as an editor for D&M in the late 1970s, joining us full time a few years later. As is the case with the best editors, her authors grew to love her. She edited some 10 books a year for us, a number which she and I would debate as insufficient. I often lost, as her gentle presence was impenetrable. That quiet confidence also defused many an author's ego.

Saeko's deep respect for the written word became a critical asset for D&M. Wade Davis likes to say that she was the best editor he has ever worked with, a view shared by Wayson Choy, Bill Richardson, Douglas

Coupland, and Robert Bringhurst. She worked quietly, discreetly, putting in sufficient hours day and evening to fix raw prose or steer fiction characters closer to the author's intent. Her authors anointed her the "Great One."

Her visual acumen was an added gift. That gave her superior skill at melding text and image, a rarity in the constrained editorial universe of Canadian publishing. She could even charm chefs. John Bishop and Rob Feenie adored her. Her careful work on complicated projects won her the 2007 Tom Fairley Award for Editorial Excellence, the Oscar for her discipline, which she won for her work on Roald Nasgaard's massive, 432-page *Abstract Painting in Canada*.

Saeko could discipline me with a well-turned phrase, never delivered with intensity or temper. When cancer caught up to her, she retired early, at the age of 63. She spoke briefly but emotionally at her retirement party, with all our staff in attendance wanting to honour the moment, then burst into tears. Not knowing quite what to say in response, I hesitated. Nancy Flight, editorial director of Greystone, a D&M imprint, and another long-time D&M employee, stepped in to save the moment.

In some deeply felt yet never fully articulated way, the bond between the two of us had grown over the years. When she was dying in the hospital, her partner, Peggy Thompson, let some of us know that the end was imminent. Corky and I went to the hospital. Saeko was not awake. I just held her hand for some minutes, reflecting on our almost 40-year relationship.

I have singled out Saeko because she embodied the corporate culture I tried to nurture across the company. My door was always open. Anyone could come into my office at any time, even when I growled in response to the intrusion, and say anything to my face, without fear of retribution. Approachability softened many a raw edge in a small business all too often disrupted by temper.

—

My focus was always on the creative side: acquiring books and overseeing editing, design, and production. I never gave the same attention to marketing, surprising given my background.

Sales and marketing were in the hands of Susan McIntosh, who joined us in 1981. A former university bookseller who was based in our Toronto office, she often single-handedly ensured national accounts bought large quantities of the lead books on any D&M list. Tall, knowledgeable, and persuasive, she commanded the centre of the country, differentiating us from our "regional" colleagues. She managed a national sales force of commissioned sales reps, which at its peak reached 15 people, with presence on the ground in every major city. Susan was a valued part of management for 24 years before eventually departing to become VP of marketing at McGill-Queen's University Press, which offered a softer financial landing than we could have provided.

Rick Antonson, with whom I had crossed paths for years as co-conspirators in running small publishing companies, had become a friend over that time. Rick was devoted to his own company, Antonson Publishing, but his love of books, personal magnetism, and energetic good nature suggested an alliance could work. After a brief courting, Rick joined us as VP, general manager, in 1982. His mandate included overall operational responsibility for most of the company. The following year we bought the assets of his company.

Margaret Reynolds joined us as promotion and marketing manager in 1982. She was with us until 1986, when she escaped for a sabbatical year in France. Upon returning, she was hired as executive director of the Association of Book Publishers of British Columbia, a position she held for 34 years, transforming the stature of the association with the federal and provincial governments.

Both Rick and Margaret were enormous fun to be around. Good-natured repartee was constant, and laughter the prescribed medicine. A singular ritual with Rick was debating the size of initial print runs, often in an open forum with staff as amused witnesses. The exercise became characterized as watching a tennis match, never knowing who would ace the winning forehand. This led to an annual Christmas ritual with just the two of us, christened the "I told you so" lunch. Much good-natured point-scoring unfolded, lubricated with a certain amount of wine. Over

35 years later, we still have that lunch, a prized seasonal tradition. But with less wine.

With a growing team and more aggressive publishing, the 1980s were kind. Sales grew from $1 million in 1978 to double that by 1982. By the end of the decade, they had passed $5 million.

—

Financing this type of sales growth was stressful enough; achieving it without decent operating profits or fresh equity defied the odds. A steadily expanding operating line of credit at the Bank of Montreal and generous supplier credit solved the issue, but we were playing with fire. Good publishing and growing sales allowed my innate optimism to prevail.

This all made corporate and logistical sense, but it was Canadian publishing. Financial fragility was a constant threat. As a result of the Ontario Royal Commission, Clarke, Irwin & Company had secured a hefty loan guarantee with the Ontario Development Corporation (ODC), in the mid-1970s one of many new government initiatives resulting from industry lobbying. Nationalist rhetoric had replaced profitability. With the disintegration of the Ontario education market, the bedrock supporting the old guard, and the inevitably mercurial opportunities of the bookstore market, by 1980 the Clarke, Irwin government guarantee had reached $1.6 million. The writing was on the wall. The ODC was not happy.

The ODC and book publishers together made an unholy alliance. Following some years of difficult financial results for Clarke, Irwin, the ODC unilaterally pulled its loan guarantee in early 1983. Clarke, Irwin was in receivership, with all our receivables caught in limbo. On paper we were bankrupt. The ODC executive with whom I had to deal emphasized his concern when, confirming that the plug had been pulled, he added, "I'm just a fucking plumber."

Fortunately, the industry still retained a gracious side. Harald Bohne, director of the University of Toronto Press, and a gentleman schooled in the old ways, ensured that the UTP's distribution operation would take us in, virtually overnight. Patsy spent a stressful weekend overseeing the movement of all our books from Clarke, Irwin & Company into the UTP warehouse before the receivers locked the doors. We avoided the usual curse of a distribution move devastating next season's sales.

Jim, Patsy, and I worked our government connections intensely to recover our receivables. After some very nervous moments, we were eventually made whole by three governments — Ottawa, Ontario, and British Columbia — acting in concert.

It took a miracle for British Columbia to step up. The early 1980s were a time of official government austerity in the province. Richard Vogel, deputy attorney general, was sympathetic to our dilemma, and knew how to pull the right levers. He and I had established a bond over a lunch some months earlier, and for a reason I never fully understood, he pulled through. Several existing government programs were tweaked in our favour. We came off life support.

The Clarke, Irwin & Company debacle was just a trial run. Peter Mayer, at the time head of Penguin International, once leaned over to me, in his inimitably intense manner, to emphasize that the only thing that matters in any third-party distribution agreement is that you get paid on time. I felt he was just being in character, scoring points.

He was right. We learned that lesson the hard way. Financial concerns would force us to move our distribution five times even as we invested heavily in building the program, expanding into areas such as educational publishing.

6

FRANKFURT TALES

From 1975 on, the Frankfurt Book Fair became a cornerstone engagement on my calendar.

In an era before computers, fax machines, or even affordable long-distance telephone calls (a fact often discovered by Americans who learned too late, and to their horror, what transatlantic telephone calls actually cost, by the minute), the fair allowed face-to-face meetings, with colleagues who had long since become friends, and freewheeling conversations, usually over a meal or in a bar, which allowed camaraderie and passion to tilt the persuasive balance.

The ritual for me began in Paris. In the early 1980s, a small group of like-minded publishers who were also friends began to gather there prior to the fair, ostensibly to discuss publishing issues and share wisdom. David Godine and George Gibson were there, both at that time working in David's eponymous Boston-based publishing house David R. Godine, as were Jon Beckmann, publisher of our new distribution partner, Sierra Club Books, and Tom Woll, an old friend, then running his family publishing house, Vanguard Books. I confess I never got the hang of late dinners or much animated conversation in very good bars being the antidote to jet lag. Practice improved the outcome somewhat, but never quite overcame it.

Future gatherings became increasingly social, and as word spread in New York and London about our conclave, other publishers and agents of our acquaintance began to invite themselves in. The gathering eventually turned into something of a circus. We were hardly alone in gathering in Paris before the fair, as many publishers took advantage of the opportunities, particularly those who had travelled more than halfway around the world.

Until overcrowding took the edge off what for us had begun as an intimate gathering of colleagues, it was a lively grouping of characters representing an elevated level within their respective companies. Andrew Nurnberg, literary agent par excellence, joined us from London. Frederick "Fred" Hill, from his eponymous literary agency in San Francisco, turned up. William "Bill" Shinker, then of HarperCollins New York, and his wife, Susan Moldow, publisher of Scribners, joined for two years, Bill once having stepped off a Concorde from New York. Susan Weinberg and Robert Riger arrived, both then working with the Book of the Month Club or its siblings; Martha Levin joined, later moving on to run Doubleday Anchor. Joe Spieler of the Spieler Agency was new to the business when he joined us, and as once a race-car driver was responsible for us making record time that year on the drive to Frankfurt.

An essential component of the ritual was the drive from Paris to Frankfurt the Monday before the fair. The intent was to find the best restaurant we could, anywhere in an arc extending from Brussels to Strasbourg, where the finest meal could be found. This was something of a challenge, as most establishments were closed Monday nights. Our track record was pretty good: We found great restaurants in Paris, Brussels, Bernkastel; Strasbourg, Riquewihr; and, twice, sustenance in a daunting old kurhotel in the Black Forest, Schloss Bühlerhöhe.

The night we stumbled across the Schloss Bühlerhöhe, I was designated guide. Driving from south to north along the Black Forest High Road on a dreadfully wet, nasty night, our first stop was a rustic Bavarian chalet, full of exuberant hunters. It seemed a possible oasis. But the assemblage, dressed menacingly in the loden green manner of the country, lounging in a smoky, dark space, lustily singing, with real guns and fierce dogs, suggested that we didn't want to spend the night as extras in a 1930s movie. As my colleague was Jewish, we felt that moving on seemed much the better part of valour.

We carried on and discovered, at the end of a long and uncertain drive, a romantic pile of stone from another era. It seemed a run-down although imposing relic, built in 1912 as an officers' club, at one time host to such distinguished guests as Konrad Adenauer. The restaurant's best days were behind it. We ate well, aware that we were almost alone in the dining room, except for one table occupied by a seemingly lonely single woman. The empty restaurant, and the moment, felt surreal. The next morning, when we departed to head north, we discovered that the castle was on the brow of a hill just above Baden-Baden. We had hardly been isolated in the wilderness.

The Schloss was such a revelation, and the hospitality so memorable, our gang returned the following year. HarperCollins was paying, so the wine flowed. Late in the evening, Susan Moldow had to fish me out of the women's washroom, into which I had inadvertently stumbled. The next day, on the frantic drive up the autobahn to Frankfurt, Susan further distinguished herself by quietly mending my torn sports jacket with needle and thread while sitting in the back seat. It is the only time I ever benefited from a distinguished New York publisher demonstrating domestic skills. Publishing is full of surprises.

Each year, our collection of travellers varied, and we limited ourselves to one car. The camaraderie was always warm, often providing literary discoveries. Andrew Nurnberg once handed me a manuscript and asked what I thought. Reading a few pages, I turned up my nose and asked, as the work was decidedly raw and thin, who the clearly unskilled author might be. Mikhail Gorbachev.

The literary world was never far from our thoughts. Frankfurt required very intense work, and full engagement was required. Real results were expected. The accompanying social activities were a bonus.

The Frankfurt Fair retains its lustre as *the* essential business gathering of the book world, in spite of rapid digital evolution. The 2024 event was the 78th since the end of WW II. It attracted 230,000 visitors and 4,300 exhibitors, with 3,300 events condensed into its frenetic five-day duration.

At every Frankfurt Fair, two things outside of publishing were a determining part of the experience: the weather, and the hotel that might be found.

The weather, always unpredictable, was more often a concern. When it was cold with pelting rain, often the case given Frankfurt's geographic position on the edge of the European plain, it could be truly miserable, accentuated by taxi lines that stretched uncovered for hundreds of metres. Combined with little sleep and an array of bad habits, Frankfurt Fever all too often translated into the real thing. A friendly German once chided me, warning against the foehn, a deceptively lethal wind that blows off the Taunus Mountains situated just a few kilometres west of town: "It will not blow out a candle, but it will kill a man."

More positively, the area offered an array of elegant hotels that were just far enough removed from the chaos of the fair to offer respite, usually including very good food. The jewel in the crown was the Schlosshotel Kronberg, an architecturally overblown late Victorian conceit built for the dowager German Empress Victoria (Queen Victoria's eldest daughter) in the late 1890s.

Many a dinner was organized there by the well-connected. Those dinners were always an event, and a sought-after invitation. The Canadian book manufacturer Jean-Pierre Gagné held an annual dinner there for clients, of which we were one, and it matched the most sumptuous of the events in town. Thames & Hudson often held its annual dinner for its international sales colleagues in the hotel, and that led to much mischief, and not a few hangovers.

The fair featured an endless array of parties, most of them easily crashed with or without an invitation. And there were the required bars where it was good to be seen, especially the Lippinzaner Bar in the Frankfurter Hof, the town's most elegant hotel (matched by the Hessicher Hof, closer to the fair, with a bar and a nightclub, Jimmy's, of equivalent stature). One of the noted badges of honour, perhaps apocryphal, was to be able to drink all night in the Lippinzaner and still struggle to the stand early the next morning. Some made it a habit, although as the years passed and people aged while business pressures mounted, more rational behaviour became essential.

During the fraught years of the late 1970s, when the Baader-Meinhof gang was at large, creating havoc across Europe, security became noticeably more intense. In the middle of this marauding, a full regiment of the German army, complete with field kitchen, was stationed on the fairgrounds just behind the hall housing the English-language publishers. It was disconcerting to walk past in the mornings, although in some respects reassuring. Security in all the buildings was strengthened, with the Israeli stand patrolled by military personnel with unsheathed Uzis.

One night, colleagues and I were being taken to dinner by Jack Riede, a Dutch Canadian then acting as a "special emissary" for William Jovanovich, who was in the middle of building what was then Harcourt Brace Jovanovich into a large publishing conglomerate. Quintessentially Dutch — lean, agile, chiseled face, unruly blondish hair, great charm, a roguish gleam in his eye — Jack was instrumental in helping establish a separate Canadian presence at the fair.

During the war, Jack had led a Rotterdam-based Dutch underground group dedicated to helping downed Allied aircrew escape. I'd actually worked with Charlie Hahn, a Canadian who had flown rescue planes into Holland, at M&S. On the ride to the restaurant, I mentioned Hahn's name, and of course Jack had a story. He'd met Hahn, then a jittery pilot, while trying to get a round of escapees out of the country. Years later, when Jack once again met with Charlie in Toronto, Jack asked him for details: "Did you have a gun trained on me?" "You bet I did" was the reply.

Nearing the restaurant, we parked, seemingly at random, on a sidewalk near the centre of town. We detected a low rumble, and a Tiger tank moved slowly out of the alleyway facing us. As a trained linguist and translator, Jack spoke the German language flawlessly but detested anything German and was not shy about expressing his views. A soldier with a lethal-looking weapon hopped off the front of the tank, where he had been riding, and began walking toward us. Fearing what Jack might let loose, I found myself thinking, "Couldn't we just get a parking ticket?" Nothing happened, Jack bit his tongue, and the evening unfolded with élan. He was host, and very good company, with an endless reservoir of very funny stories.

The fair was often pitched into the centre of current geopolitical action. When Erich Honecker, the long-serving ruler of East Germany, resigned on October 18, 1989, setting in motion the events that shortly thereafter brought down the wall between East and West Berlin, the fair had just concluded. The growing tension in the political air had been an unavoidable undercurrent. During the fair, the impending fate of what in the West was known as the "wall of shame," and in the East as the "anti-fascist protection rampart," hung in the air. In retrospect, it seems somehow appropriate that what became known as the Rushdie Affair succeeded in dominating conversation that year. Salman Rushdie's novel *The Satanic Verses* had been published the year prior in the UK, and its publication had triggered a fatwah issued by Ayatollah Ruhollah Khomeini denouncing the author and calling for his murder. This dramatically elevated the necessity for increased security throughout the fair, and in every hotel in the city. My regular hotel had refused the Penguin contingent its long-standing quota of rooms, a decision not at all graciously received. A measure of balance was achieved when the German book trade named Vaclav Havel winner of its annual Peace Prize on the last day of the fair. Books, and their publishers, were front and centre in the unfolding dramas of the time.

One year later, when German reunification was officially passed into law on October 3, 1990, a visceral eruption of joy spread across the city, and throughout the fair. I remember trying to reach one of many celebratory events in the centre of town, only to be caught up in the largest traffic jam imaginable. I never made the event, but the crowds milling about throughout the old town were ample demonstration of the power of what we now know became a tipping point in history.

When it came to the business of Frankfurt, I alone, as majority shareholder in D&M, had overall responsibility for the company's financial survival. I was more comfortable with borrowed money than Jim had been and put a great deal of energy into maintaining a strong relationship with the Bank of Montreal as our rotating operating line grew larger. The ability to talk *books* rather than money was always a relief.

An average fair, certainly by the late 1970s and 1980s, meant some 50 to 60 meetings, one every half hour — some very intense, some more enjoyable, some full of pleasant surprises. In a world before the ubiquity of seamless digital communication, maintaining friendships while pitching the most important forthcoming publishing projects was a necessary activity. Faxes were the new technology. Even long-distance phone calls were both expensive and ineffective. There was no substitute for personal connection. For smaller houses such as D&M, establishing a presence at the fair was critical to being taken seriously by an international audience. If luck held, it was also a golden opportunity to not only sell books but buy important projects for Canada.

There was a downside. Many an editorial director would shudder in horror at what their Frankfurt colleagues, particularly the ruling executives, had acquired during the fair, sometimes on little more than a whim. Exit strategies needed to be triggered, resulting in the "Frankfurt handshake" becoming less than a badge of honour.

This was often caused by what became rather sardonically known as Frankfurt Fever, the all-too-frequent outcome of publishers vastly overbidding for books, seduced by the intensely competitive spirit of the fair. For these books, there was usually no simple exit strategy, other than very large write-offs at the end of the day when the acquired books proved disastrous in the marketplace and were all too quickly relegated to the remainder bin. As Mordecai Richler once sardonically remarked in another circumstance: "More to be remaindered than remembered."

In the early 1980s, to my delight, Harper & Row agreed to take on European distribution for Douglas & McIntyre. At that time, the company's international division was given a long leash and managed by Ulli Bruno, an extroverted Swede who had previously made her living as a jazz singer in Stockholm but was now living with her young daughter in the Netherlands, where the Harper distribution centre was located. She was energetic, irreverent, and iconoclastic, which she once demonstrated by riding her bicycle up and down the overcrowded aisles of the fair.

Whether or not it helped sell books was moot. Her advocacy resulted in our being given the street-facing windows of the leading bookstore in Helsinki for, of all things, Hugh A. Dempsey's *History in Their Blood: The Indian Portraits of Nicholas de Grandmaison*, a collection of overly noble pastel portraits of the First Nations inhabitants of the Canadian Prairies. Our sales were never spectacular, but the possibility was something we tantalizingly dangled before authors, agents, and art gallery directors.

That connection sometimes led to unexpected opportunity. Cass Canfield Jr., son of Harper & Row's iconic publisher, sought out our booth to talk about our forthcoming *The Architecture of Arthur Erickson*. Finally, D&M was going to have a chance at publishing a tribute to Erickson's work. We had planned an ambitious first printing of 10,000 copies, and Canadian manufacture, but that was going to be a stretch. It was the highlight of the fair for us that year to have an experienced international publisher from a distinguished family appear in our booth, and express real interest in acquiring a significant quantity of our edition for the US market. Better still, he followed through, committing to 4,000 copies. Thames & Hudson took another 2,000, allowing us to reach a first printing of 15,000.

A favourite memory is Ben Jacobs, a colleague who happened to be in a booth across the aisle from our own, discovering James "Jim" Delgado's *Across the Top of the World: The Quest for the Northwest Passage*. We had prepared an elegant dummy with sample pages, but to my great disappointment, the book had elicited no real international interest. On the last day of the fair, Ben, intrigued by the material, suggested the book might work for his company, Facts on File. Indeed it did. His company sold an edition to a specialist book club. That sale, combined with a co-edition for the British Museum, led to a first printing of 50,000 copies, an example of Frankfurt serendipity at its finest.

By the early years of the 21st century, working the fair to maintain an international presence had become a matter of faith for Douglas &

McIntyre. For many years I attended alone, but as the company (and the size of our stand) grew, I was joined by Rob Sanders, Rick Antonson, and occasionally other staff. We were granted pride of place within the expanded Canadian section at Frankfurt, which made a perfect focal point for our growing programs. Staff from the Canadian embassy in Berlin began attending, including the Canadian ambassador on several occasions. As the most comfortable chairs happened to be located at our stand, important guests often found refuge there. The annual Canadian cocktail party, held in the aisle opposite the Canadian national stand, by necessity spilled across the aisle into our space.

—

Returning home from the fair through London was often problematic, particularly during the late 1970s when seemingly never-ending strikes and labour slowdowns created havoc in air travel.

One year, I found myself in a cramped, overloaded plane full of publishers and agents heading home. We sat on the ground for a *very* long time waiting for takeoff clearance. Impatience quickly erupted. The pilot was adamant that, while on the ground with the doors closed, we were deemed to be in international airspace. That meant that smoking was prohibited, but the bar could serve. If the doors were opened, the bar would have to be shut down, but smoking was possible.

One of the passengers was George Weidenfeld, amongst London's most distinguished publishers, later anointed a lord. He happened to like cigars and did not suffer rules gladly. Weidenfeld, a large man, at least in girth, stormed up the plane to the front doors, insisted that one of them be opened, and lit a pungent cigar. The entire plane shook as he moved up the aisle. Cigar finished, he strode back to his seat, and the bar reopened.

—

My initial encounter with the spring alternative to Frankfurt, the London Book Fair, was in 1977 when it was still so small that it could be accommodated within the Intercontinental Hotel on Park Lane. The fair had been launched in 1971 by Lionel Leventhal as a specialist fair for booksellers and librarians with all of 22 exhibitors. It grew over the years into another essential date on the publishing calendar. It now attracts over 1,700 exhibitors and 25,000 attendees from 100 countries.

The more important part of that trip was that it gave Corky and me a chance to visit the Victorian headquarters of the distinguished, two-century-old Scottish/British publishing house of John Murray. The sixth John Murray in the lineage, nicknamed Jock, was a friend of Jim Douglas, and I had come to know the publisher's managing director, Nick Perrin, so we had a standing invitation.

Our visit was fascinating. The place reeked of all the quirky idiosyncrasies of multi-generational London publishing: cramped quarters in a heritage-listed, 19th-century building; an address on Albemarle Street in Mayfair, just a block from Brown's Hotel; a library topped with a glass cupola that leaked when it rained and couldn't be touched in a listed building; a seventh-generation scion with no great talent or passion for publishing theoretically running it, one who had named his son Octavius in high hopes.

We were ushered into the "Green Room," the inner sanctum of a great publishing house. Founded in 1768, it had been the literary home of Disraeli, Tennyson, Scott, Melville, Goethe, Darwin, Jane Austen, Byron, Patrick Leigh Fermor, and a host of other writers whose voices had dominated the 19th and early 20th centuries.

John Murray's wife, an archivist, was in the process of trying to make sense of the company's historical records. Some of them sat around the extremities of the room, stored in flimsy cardboard boxes, awaiting attention. Two very fragile chairs sat on either side of a rickety table under large, intimidating portraits of Disraeli and Gladstone. Instinctively, I sat in one of them. The admonishment was immediate: "We don't sit there anymore. That's where Byron met Scott!"

The group assembled around us amusedly recalled their recent experience with a Canadian academic. He had requested photocopies of some letters he judged important to his research for a monograph on Byron.

Jock sent him the originals. When the scholar dutifully returned them, they were received, date-stamped, and sat amongst other papers in Jock's in-basket for months.

We discussed distributing Murray books in Canada, as Nick Perrin and I had become friends, but the dollar volume would not have made it worthwhile. Nick had once suggested he might be prepared to invest in Douglas & McIntyre. "What kind of dividend do you pay?" When I replied that we had never paid a dividend and likely never would, the conversation abruptly ended.

As a cautionary tale about publishing, Murray was sold to Hachette and is now a minor imprint within the mighty monolith Lagardère. John Murray the seventh wanted out, as his son was not interested in inheriting the business. Under UK tax law, if the company moved beyond family ownership, a huge tax liability was on the horizon. Nick Perrin managed the solution. The buildings on Albemarle Street were sold, although a bronze plaque acknowledges their provenance. The Murray archive was sold to the National Library of Scotland for 31 million pounds.

—

Book fairs, but particularly Frankfurt, were the pinnacle of what the world of book publishing meant to me: adrenalin-driven, chaotic, and yes, utterly draining. But they were central to the functioning of the tight-knit "clan" that distinguished the world of book publishing, and they blunted, at least temporarily, the discouraging business realities of a changing world.

Memories of that other world, and the last great days of independent publishing, remain indelible. One memory in particular stands out.

I had worked with Mordecai Richler at McClelland & Stewart, and our paths crossed occasionally over the intervening years. In 1997 I was delightedly taken aback when he spotted me on the D&M stand and suggested we go for a drink. He was in Frankfurt promoting the Italian edition of *Barney's Version*. How could I refuse? The fact that I had a sufficiently large hole in my schedule to be able to accommodate such a thing seems surprising now, but it offered itself up.

Off we went in search of a bar. The amenities within the fair buildings were never salubrious, and I knew that having a drink with Mordecai required tracking down some decent single malt Scotch.

We found a source: a half-timbered, faux-Bavarian tavern in the back of the hall. It was open, and there was space, as it was the middle of the afternoon. There we were, just the two of us, a server of a certain girth and a certain age in a dirndl, and one half-empty bottle of single malt out of reach high up on a shelf.

Out appeared one of those rolling ladders used in libraries, up went our server, down came the Scotch, and lively conversation ensued. Mordecai was furious at Jack over some perceived slight, and I felt compelled to come to Jack's defence, although why eludes me. Naturally, I paid. It was the only time in all my Frankfurt years that a bar bill exceeded the cost of a hotel room during the fair.

7

A PRECARIOUS ENTERPRISE

In 1979, when Douglas & McIntyre had a chance to jump off a cliff, we took it.

BC had launched a thorough review of its social studies curriculum for elementary schools and announced an adventuresome new one covering Grades 1–6. The curriculum document promised to give some preference to books "written and published in Canada." The province's education minister, Brian Smith, went further. The ministry's intention was "to give social studies a Canadian and BC point of view — not an American branch plant view."

The mood in the country had shifted. The new nationalists — led by lobbying from the upstart Association of Canadian Publishers, publishers such as Mel Hurtig, educators, academics, and even politicians — were pushing for Canadian-made textbooks, rather than "materials" adapted by American multinationals. The leading voices on the Committee for an Independent Canada, including Jack McClelland and Peter C. Newman, couldn't be ignored. The media were engaged. Getting materials both written and published in Canada into schools was a mantra hard for politicians to dismiss. Ever since Ryerson and Gage, two of the oldest, most established educational publishers in Canada, were sold to American companies in 1970, rhetoric had escalated. The Ontario government's Royal Commission on Book Publishing promised solutions.

Educational publishing made compelling business. Clyde Rose, the pugnacious publisher of Newfoundland's Breakwater Books, nailed it: "For many publishers who came on the scene in the seventies, the choice was obvious: either get a toehold in the lucrative educational market or face almost certain annihilation in the trade."

In British Columbia, the government still bought textbooks grade-wide, a diminishing practice in other provinces. There were about 45,000 students per grade, and they could all be reached through a single sale to a government body. BC was the treasure trove beyond the Rockies.

An open competition for books was launched in 1980. The game was formally afoot. Eventually 21 companies — every multinational operating in Canada, augmented by a smattering of small Canadian companies — geared up to participate.

One of them was Douglas & McIntyre.

Scale attracts furious competition, and this was amongst the few lucrative possibilities on the horizon for Canadian educational publishers. Legions of motivated sales reps, often backed by senior executives, trooped west, pitches honed and promises in hand, in search of profit.

Rigid attitudes were softening, but slowly. When Jim Douglas had first confronted Dr. Pat McGeer, BC's minister of education in the early 1970s, the dismissal was stiff: "If you can't make books cheaper and better than your competition, we have nothing to discuss."

Presuming a BC-based company with something of a track record might have an inside edge, freelance consultants began knocking on our door. Business possibilities were tempting, but we had no idea what we were getting into. Belief and naïve optimism have always been essential components of book publishing.

The most persistent consultant was BC-based Bill Clare, a salesman of the old school with slicked-back hair, a glib tongue, and a car from a previous decade with fins and the width of an ocean barge. He had 20 years' experience in educational publishing, including a stint as president of the Canadian Textbook Publishers Institute, an amalgam of the multinationals operating in Canada at the time. He had orchestrated the last lucrative BC social studies victory for Fitzhenry & Whiteside in Toronto. He was also a congenital optimist: "Go for it. You can win. You know all the writers and illustrators. We'll just need a few pretty images and some words. Piece of cake. Everything will be easy. Trust me." He was a character straight out of Arthur Miller's *Death of a Salesman*.

Bill kept his ear to the ground within the ministry in Victoria, detecting nuances Toronto visitors missed. Aware of the forthcoming competition, with one eye on the potential scale of a win and the other on his imminent retirement, he had assembled a team of consultants and teachers in anticipation of what might be forthcoming.

His team was led by Carol Langford, an elementary school teacher from Surrey and faculty associate at Simon Fraser University, who was considered a "brilliant educator." She also had been a key member of the provincial review team. Carol was in her late 50s, wiry, energetic, and wedded to the cause, with a furious work ethic and an acute sense of mission. Originally from San Francisco, she was impatient with indecisiveness and driven by a search for pedagogical perfection. She was a perfect leader for the enormous task ahead. She also knew the curriculum, and its needs, inside out. Her energy intensified after hours, when she and her husband were ardent Scottish dancers.

Her chosen colleague, Chuck Heath, was a polar opposite, a teacher-librarian driven by effusive enthusiasms, a cheerleader with diplomatic skill, a peacemaker by instinct. Their joint involvement became the glue that blunted rough edges, holding a disparate group together — teachers, befuddled authors, general editors, and me, most new to the focussed disciplines of the educational world.

—

Jim, preparing to retire, was itchy to move on to the next thing, particularly if it offered the possibility of spending more time in his beloved Scotland. But winning would be transformative for the company. The potential windfall would be several million dollars of very profitable sales that could fuel our publishing program.

Jim and I agreed the challenge was worth it. Our discussion mirrored that of choosing the Burghead Bull as D&M's graphic device: One of us has to do it. My background, visual as much as editorial, seemed a better fit. I was also younger, better able to benefit in the future from a win of scale. We didn't quite flip a coin, but that was the spirit of our discussion. I would take on the educational challenge, while Jim would postpone his retirement for a year to continue leading the existing D&M publishing program.

An initial meeting of the players who had committed by that time was organized to test the waters. Many of the teachers and consultants had not met before. Yet here they were, sitting in a cavernous SFU boardroom. The mood was tentative. Skepticism prevailed. What could a "regional" trade book publisher possibly know about creating textbooks?

I felt as though I were on trial. Reading the room, in desperation I invented some rhetoric, some of it over the top: The power of books to empower change was critical to all healthy societies. Educational excellence enhanced by content generated by talented writers and artists was a revolutionary concept for textbook development in British Columbia. The province had the opportunity to lead Canada. We could beat the multinationals.

The rhetoric hit home. Animated conversation began to dissolve barriers. The room brightened; the energy was palpable. Everyone was on board.

—

To blunt financial risk to the mother ship, we established a sister company, Douglas & McIntyre (Educational) Ltd., incorporated in August 1980. General editors Carol Langford and Chuck Heath, Bill Clare, and all the teachers and authors would work, gratis, for eventual royalties. The shareholders would take on the risk, with equity split four ways, each shareholder holding 25 percent — Jim Douglas, Marilyn Sacks and her husband together, me, and as a deemed fourth shareholder the existing trade company, which was to provide backup services, accounting, space, and some management support, including my time.

Marilyn was a loyalist editor who had been the company's bedrock from almost its beginning, with a sweet disposition, except when she was angry. She and her husband were native New Yorkers who had moved north from L.A. Marilyn's bible was the *New Yorker*, which she had read fervently for years. Her husband, Don, was the opposite: He was from the New York school of hard knocks, with an abrasive side. Both were, in their souls, lovely people.

The three new shareholders agreed to contribute $25,000 each as start-up capital. We felt that might cover the cost of the work required to join the competition. Patsy Aldana was offered an equal opportunity but declined, deeply skeptical of the entire process, the scale of risk, and the energy it would strip away from the company's existing publishing.

This structure was Jim's model. It seemed simple and clean. But it was to provoke some hostility along the way, as books were published and generous dividends escalated. The imminent retirements of both Jim and the Sackses left shadows of expectation, as well as inflated hopes.

Carol's laser-focussed, analytical mind went to work, balanced by upbeat cheerleading from Chuck Heath. They created a template translating the curriculum's "desired outcomes" into books.

This grew into a program of 23 books of varying lengths, called Explorations: six little books for Grade 1, ten for Grade 2, three for Grade 3, two for Grade 4, and one large book each for Grades 5 and 6. Each grade would have a single accompanying teacher's resource manual. In all, 3,000 pages of textbook, plus 1,200 pages of supplementary teacher's material. We planned to take 10–20 percent of every book to finished pages, with type and sophisticated visuals in place. And it all had to be completed in under six months to meet the ministry's announced submission date.

—

The challenge before us was staggering. We needed to quickly engage a disciplined, energetic, and creative team to meet an impossible deadline.

Carol, Chuck, and the teachers would manage pedagogical necessity. Finding key writers and illustrators fell to me, although everything was vetted by Carol's eagle eye.

We needed a Vancouver-based manufacturer to emphasize the entirely made-in-BC undertaking. Evergreen Press, then British Columbia's largest commercial printer, knew what was at stake. Evergreen had the necessary equipment and experience. Better, they had an existing relationship of trust with senior people in the ministry. Evergreen's involvement gave us a competitive advantage. It was a deliberate, important piece of the puzzle.

Evergreen gifted us an early word-processing unit to short-circuit all typesetting. Senior executives experienced at working with the ministry committed time to advise us. In turn, we agreed to award Evergreen all manufacturing, should we win. That company's controlling shareholder and president, Glenn Hyatt, had known Jim for years and retained a soft spot for regional publishing. He made the perfect ally.

—

The available space in our building was cramped, and less than elegant. It was an unfinished, empty room adjacent to our warehouse, with a low ceiling and minimal light penetrating through small, high windows abutting the outside sidewalk. Education staff had to be squeezed into it. We cleaned the room up, added basic partitions, and dubbed it the "war room."

Our innovation was commissioning published trade authors to undertake many of the books, with a few to be written by in-house editorial staff. Within a month, we had contracted all the writers we sought. The scale of potential earning power won over the skeptics. What we hadn't fully absorbed was how tight the straitjacket of educational requirements could be. Curriculum "congruency" was a new concept for writers accustomed to writing for a general audience.

Worse was the requirement for "grade level readability," determined by a rigid measure called the Fry Readability Graph: count syllables, then sentences, then calculate an average for each, per 100 words. This was the accepted standard for establishing reading level. Whatever we thought about the mechanism, developing our proposal was not the moment to test boundaries. For Grades 1–3, this translated into short, direct sentences using basic vocabulary, a profound shock to many newly commissioned writers.

There were additional implicit constraints, although far less than is the case now: ethnic and gender balance, genuine respect for Indigenous cultures, anodyne politics. The response of some authors unleashed an entirely new vocabulary. I bore the brunt. But we didn't lose a writer, testament to our team's growing diplomatic skills.

Our newly hired art director, Rick Staehling, stolen away from *Vancouver Magazine* because magazine work seemed better training for what lay before us, once summed up his view of the process: "I'm nothing more than a fucking traffic cop." Not what he had signed up for. But he did magnificent work. I took him to lunch occasionally to defuse mounting frustration. Several beers re-established a mellow state.

—

Developing sample material opened doors into new worlds. For me, it was the chosen sample chapter for *Exploring Canada*, our notional Grade 5 book. Amongst the topics, the book dealt with immigration, and we had decided upon Manitoba's Icelandic community as a successful example. Crawford Kilian, a published novelist, college professor, and already a D&M author, was to write it. I offered to help with research.

Our Winnipeg sales rep was a direct descendant of the first Icelanders to arrive in Willow Point, Manitoba, in 1874. The community archive was stored in her attic. As I was regularly commuting east, stopping in Winnipeg was easy to arrange.

What I found in our sales rep's attic pointed me to the local library in Gimli. There, I unearthed a cache of early letters, a revealing portrait of hardship tempered with grace, shaping life in a harsh new land. Badly placed stoves melted the frozen ice floors of rough shacks. Indigenous communities welcomed the strangers, saving them from the ravages of smallpox.

I arrived home with packets of original material, rich fodder for Crawford. My parting gift was a dozen frozen Winnipeg goldeye, wrapped in dry ice and newspaper. I hadn't encountered that many dead fish since serving them to bewildered passengers while working summers in a CPR dining car.

—

With ever-shifting deadlines, nerves rattled by gossip filtering out of Toronto about competitors, garrulous coaching from Bill, and unrelenting intensity from Carol, work pressed ahead. Carol did most of the heavy lifting.

The astounding thing about the work was that, once it was underway, disparate pieces of presentation material came together remarkably smoothly. Goodwill overcame inevitable frustration. My most stressful task was maintaining peace amongst the shareholders and the board. Keeping the bank onside was easier.

In May 1981, 50 cartons of polished presentation material were packed into Bill's car. Everyone on the team, which at its peak exceeded 40 people, was exhausted. Pride in the achievement was visceral, although muted. These remained, after all, early days in an open competition.

—

Even though the level of genuine risk remained small, Jim had assumed the role of protector of the Sackses. I felt a constant level of implied doubt about how things were unfolding.

Carol felt undervalued, for good reason. She once privately confessed to me that Jim terrified her. He had slipped into the role of Scottish patriarch, with a priority of protecting minority shareholders. As a defensive measure, Carol and I established a ritual of weekly lunches out of the office to share frustrations and concerns, theoretically calming the waters.

It was essential to push shadows aside and carry on. By a quirk of nature, I was able to stay calm under duress. That was to serve me well throughout my publishing career. The irony is that I was CEO of the company. A fit of temper from me would have triggered serious consequences, not least within the ministry.

—

With materials formally submitted in time to meet the ministry's deadline, we could only wait. And wait. Mechanisms within any government ministry are opaque, even when functional. This competition broke all existing norms. New rules and procedures had to be invented. Reviewing sample material rather than finished books was a revolutionary concept. The ministry had been surprisingly transparent about its hopes. Deputy Minister R.J. Carter set the cat amongst the pigeons when he said, out loud, "All things being equal, or even not quite equal, Canadian and BC materials and curriculum get the nod."

As weeks passed, our concerns grew. I sometimes felt I was playing a game of snakes and ladders — two steps up, one step down, venomous creatures in the shadows.

By mid-fall 1981, still lacking any definitive answer, despair was growing. Under mostly self-imposed duress, I approached an influential friend, Walter D. Young, for help. We had worked together before and knew each other well. Walter was a Rhodes Scholar and a professor of political science at the University of Victoria. Critically, he was a good friend of the minister, Brian Smith. Might he arrange for a private meeting with the minister, for a quiet chat?

The three of us convened in the soothing study of Walter and his wife, Beryl, in their Oak Bay home. Dark wood walls, a lit fire, and congenial warmth offered promise. But the minister had taken a look at our materials, focussing on our final Grade 5 sample pages, which dealt with the anxious road to Confederation. He had a master's degree in Canadian history from Queen's University. One double-page spread included graphic novel–style characters reducing complexity to simplistic snippets, pro and con, encased in bubbles. The minister was not impressed. I resorted to defending pedagogical necessity. To my relief, Walter jumped in with support, emphasizing the groundbreaking importance of the moment, BC's leadership, and the necessity of finally having Canadian materials in British Columbia's schools.

We made it through the door. By early spring 1982, unanimous agreement within the ministry authorized offering contracts. We had won out over competition for all of Grades 1 to 3, with Grades 4–6 to be shared with our lead competitor, Prentice Hall.

Response within the Toronto-based educational publishing establishment was explosive. There were 19 very unhappy competitors. Gladys Neale, feisty doyen of Macmillan's educational unit, was outraged, quoted by journalist Laurie Bildfell in the industry trade publication *Quill & Quire* as saying the decision "was a serious threat to all of us . . . an approach that is especially galling, not to mention costly." She later added privately to me that we had been "unfair" because we had spent "too much money." She neglected to mention that Ontario had controlled the agenda for almost a century. When the draft contracts for the textbooks arrived in April, our bank, the Bank of Montreal, required copies of them as security against the substantial operating loan we needed to fund the program's development. But the contract had been cobbled together from existing highways department boilerplate and included the dreaded words "Subject to Treasury Board approval." That rattled the bank, which decided that the security offered by that language was insufficiently ironclad.

By then, my personal relationships within the ministry were strong. It didn't take long for that wrinkle to be ironed out. I had Deputy Minister Jim Carter on my side. Still, Jim Douglas and I had to put our personal houses up as collateral. Corky, as always, bit her tongue and agreed.

It was now full steam ahead. Two general editors, eleven teachers, eight illustrators, a cartographer, five photographers, multiple photo editors and photo agencies set to work developing 3,000 pages of finished textbooks plus ancillary material, in record time.

Under Glenn Hyatt, Evergreen's support remained steadfast, its advocacy as effective as its manufacturing skill. By early spring 1983, total manufacturing costs for the program were budgeted to reach $2.5 million.

While sharp pencils had already been employed, I felt there was opportunity to push for more. Ever compulsive about numbers, I kept a running grid of manufacturing costs for the entire program, where unit costs were quoted, and regularly re-quoted, to the fraction of a penny per unit. The program totalled over 600,000 units.

Glenn and I arranged a lunch at the Vancouver Lawn and Tennis Club, one of his regular haunts, to discuss the issue. He was a martini man, and his were larger than mine. When he asked what more he could do to help, I calmly replied, "I need 10 percent." Done. That added $250,000 to our bottom line over the next few years. The economics of trade publishing paled in comparison. And Glenn bought lunch.

The principal book for Grade 2 had become a challenge. Its core pedagogical purpose was to expand the Grade 1 introduction of "family" to the next step up, "community." Words were minimal. It called for storyboards rather than text. Two writers of reputation had attempted, and failed. Time was running short. What the hell, I thought. Having absorbed the intense rigours of educational publishing for almost a year, I'll try it myself. This unexpected offer was endorsed by Carol.

The "community" we had chosen was on a planet distant from Earth, where newly arrived explorers were building a settlement from the ground up. Over a weekend, I conjured a narrative and sketched storyboards. Three thousand words for a little book of 112 pages, *Exploring a Space Community*. We invented a new world, with illustrations from Richard Allan, generously supplemented with photographs of real communities on Earth. The book went on to sell 100,000 copies. As author, I chose a pseudonym, Hugh Gordon. It was my father's first two names reversed, a personal homage to a fine, loving man.

The Grades 1–3 materials were delivered in 1983, Grade 4 in 1984, Grade 5 in 1985, and Grade 6 in 1986. We had further complicated the process by committing to publish everything in French as well as English. This was our decision, idealism surpassing practical reality.

Over three years, we shipped 40,000 copies each of all the books, except those for Grades 4 and 5, where we shared the market with Prentice

Hall. Twenty-three textbooks plus six extensive teacher's resource books, all in English, were published and shipped, on time. Five thousand copies of every textbook in French were also shipped, somewhat later given the complexities of translation.

Whenever there were frustrations and issues, personal goodwill prevailed. The higher purpose of defying the odds, creating books that might change Canada, remained the guiding light.

Naturally, the potential scale of financial windfall focussed attention. Authors, teachers, general editors, and Bill Clare together shared royalties that on average reached a combined 10 percent of revenue. Over the company's first six years, we paid $1 million in royalties.

—

Books are demanding taskmasters. Books for schools doubly so. The emotional risks, as well as the rewards, can be high.

Dr. Lorna Williams, whose Indigenous name means Woman Who Walks in Peace Among Her People, wrote one of our little Grade 2 community books, *Exploring Mount Currie*. Now a distinguished scholar, member of the Lil'wat First Nation, and global expert in Indigenous language revitalization, she was new to the idea of a book, and at a low ebb in her life. We again met, many years later, in Government House in Victoria. When she heard my name, she hugged me and whispered: "You changed my life."

Bill Reid was less enthusiastic about our Grade 4 book, *The Haida and the Inuit*. The illustrator for both cultures had done several books for us. His meticulous art was culturally accurate and highly rendered. He did the Inuit half of the book first, then seemed to run out of steam. His Haida figures were squat and clumsily drawn.

Bill was a defiant purist about everything relating to Haida culture. When he came across a copy of the finished book, he was furious. He called me, and in what for him was a disconcertingly sharp tone, objected to the depiction of Haida people as "fucking little troglodytes running around on the beach." "Withdraw the book," he demanded. I neglected to tell him that 25,000 copies sat in a warehouse in Victoria, in the midst of being shipped to schools across the province. We feared that outrage might translate into our offices being picketed. Happily, those dark clouds receded quickly. The issue disappeared, without consequence, so far as we knew.

—

Even with such success, money remained a simmering issue. The waters calmed once books for Grades 1–3 were shipped in early 1983. Revenue for the educational company passed $1.5 million that year, with healthy dividends for shareholders.

Work was proceeding smoothly for the remaining grades. Our financial modelling suggested three good revenue years ahead, from the Explorations program alone. Interest was growing from other provinces as well for parts of the program, with opportunities for ancillary custom materials steadily increasingly. Alberta, the Northwest Territories, Saskatchewan, Manitoba, Ontario, and Newfoundland commissioned new materials, all under the Explorations banner. Several of the books, in French of course, had even penetrated Quebec. Revenues remained steady at between $1 million and $2 million per year, generating healthy operating profits.

Frustrations and complaints had diminished. The ministry, the bank, and even the shareholders were happy. Better, the reviews were good. The leading journal covering educational publishing, the *Canadian Review of Materials*, offered a strong endorsement: "Explorations gives us something new, something that has been carefully conceived, logically planned, painstakingly written, and attractively produced."

An unexpected windfall occurred when our competition, Prentice Hall, backed out of creating the substantial Grade 6 book. The larger-than-expected purchase order for that grade was for 60,000 copies of an expensive hardcover. The number on that single purchase order touched $1.5 million.

By spring 1986, all six grades had been shipped, with total revenues for the previous three years reaching $6 million from BC alone, close to $8 million in total for D&M (Educational), including those stand-alone books being shipped to other provinces. Cash flow was good, our equity base was strong, and annual dividends were continuing to reward the original shareholders.

After much scrutiny of forthcoming curriculum opportunities, we made the decision to next invest our resources to create an elementary-school health program, Young Canada Health. Senior people with expertise were set to work conceptualizing books that would meet the needs of the two provinces in the midst of revising their elementary health programs, Newfoundland and Alberta. We felt confident that a skillful combination of pedagogical diligence and superior editorial, design, and production values would allow us to repeat the miracle of Explorations. We were slow to recognize the inevitability, and speed, of looming pedagogical and technical evolutions.

I could back off day-to-day oversight while Carol, with her extraordinary discipline and energy, was ensuring work was unfolding as it should. I nominated her president of the education company, and the board agreed. It was time for me to turn my attention back to trade publishing.

—

There remained a lingering financial edge between the two companies, which fell on Jim and me. One exchange illustrates the friction.

In 1985, a dispute over costs associated with each company's use of office space within our building, including equipment and fulfillment, verged on rancorous. As the needs of education alone had triggered significant expense, I proposed that education pay 90 percent of the capital improvement costs. Jim dismissed the idea, suggesting it involved "a lot of gall." I replied tersely, "Without education, trade would have incurred no costs whatsoever . . . I firmly believe that education paying for the majority of the alterations therefore is fair." This touched the low point in a relationship that, while strained at times, had seldom descended to that degree of prickliness. In retrospect, I had pushed too hard.

That disagreement was short-lived. A similar dispute the next year over retained earnings was amicably resolved when education softened its stand in recognition that these companies were "children of a common mother." The board of the trade company responded by expressing "its fervent hope that the matter can now be laid to rest." Peace was restored. It grew into a lasting peace. Education's shareholders further demonstrated goodwill when, two years into the intracompany sales agreement, cash flow wasn't sufficient to allow the agreed instalment from D&M to be paid. The requirement was waived, an extraordinary gesture of support.

My personal priority had always been to orchestrate a merger between the two companies, legally still two separate entities. Finishing Explorations had achieved all we had hoped for, and more. It had been an extraordinary success, perhaps unique in the history of Canadian educational publishing.

In my soul, I had always been a trade publisher, fully engaged in the legacy business that was then enjoying its apogee. I wanted to return to my first love, authors and their books.

This seemed a propitious moment to merge both companies into one strong, single unit, strengthening our business base and our combined balance sheet. All shareholders were amenable. Genuine goodwill had been re-established amongst all the shareholders. I asked Jim to stay on as chair of the board, and he agreed.

Carol and her team were skeptical, increasingly inured to what they viewed as inevitable. Carol had always felt that education's achievements were undervalued, and she was right. Patsy remained silent.

The companies formally merged in spring 1987. This required a court blessing, as BC corporate law keeps a wary eye on companies merging to hide financial weakness in one of them. But everything was promising. Money was agreed, with a down payment, the balance to the minority education shareholders spread out over three years.

Market reality would quickly intrude. As distinguished UBC educator Penney Clark would later sum it up, educational publishing was "a precarious enterprise."

8

TRAILBLAZING

Thanks in part to D&M's share of educational revenues, a more secure financial base allowed our trade program to thrive in the 1980s. The program continued to centre on books about people and places in British Columbia, First Nations, and visual art, but because our ambition sometimes exceeded the constraints of small markets and our always stretched working capital, we sought out partnerships with private sponsors, companies, and government.

BC's economic base was shifting as the predominance of the resource economy wound down. Many of the province's large forestry, mining, and industrial companies were merging or being sold internationally, and the founding dynasties were confronting their legacy. Most of these companies were still being run by men of a certain age, which ensured that books remained important.

We required several basic understandings to accept such projects. We had to be comfortable with the editorial approach. We needed to be confident that the CEO was onside, so that second-guessing underlings could not derail the necessary scale of resources. And we needed evidence of clear and timely decision-making, with someone senior within the organization demonstrably in charge.

A mix of age and ego of corporate owners led to the commissioning of many company histories: MacMillan Bloedel; BC Forest Products; Rogers Sugar; Seaboard Lumber and Shipping; the Council of Marine Carriers; Westcoast Transmission; and BC Hydro. While these projects were healthy commerce, they also preserved much of the province's early industrial and business history. They were animated by anecdotes about the larger-than-life characters who had shaped British Columbia's frontier economy.

The best of these projects allowed books of editorial scale and market success to be published and became an adventure in and of themselves. In 1980, a relationship we had been building with the Bank of Montreal and the Glenbow Museum in Calgary bore fruit. The result was *History in Their Blood: The Indian Portraits of Nicholas de Grandmaison*. One of our authors, Don Peacock, was influential within the Bank of Montreal and had alerted us to the opportunity.

De Grandmaison was born into a French family of noble heritage in 1892 czarist Russia. He was sent to military school as a young man, then to East Prussia as an officer in the Russian army. Captured early in WW I, he learned English in a prisoner-of-war camp. Following the war, friends helped him attend St John's Wood Art School in London, then pushed him to immigrate to Winnipeg.

Drawn to the romance of the Canadian Prairies and their Indigenous inhabitants, he ended up in Banff, where he began to make a living painting portraits. By the 1930s, he was focussing on Indigenous peoples, working in pastels. He found "the Indians" willing sitters, and those portraits sold best. He spent time capturing the subjects he found on the Blackfoot, Stoney, Sarcee, and Blood reserves in southern Alberta. In business, he was a pragmatist, with a burnished charm that served him as well as his increasingly accomplished technique did.

One of the business leaders who first discovered his portraits was Fred McNeil, president and CEO of the Bank of Montreal, who happened to have a ranch in southern Alberta. The bank soon had a growing collection of de Grandmaison portraits gracing its head office.

When I first met with its senior executives, the bank was still headquartered in its heritage building on St. James Street in Montreal, now rue Saint-Jacques. Following René Lévesque's stunning electoral victory in late 1976, the bank joined the exodus of the business community, moving its headquarters to First Canadian Place in Toronto the following year. That new, very sleek construction, at that time Canada's tallest office building, guaranteed the bank a place in the sky, with suitably ostentatious offices.

The bank also had a new president, William Mulholland, a former Wall Street investment banker and awarded US army officer with a passion for Western cowboy art. His mandate was to shake up the bank, and he most certainly embraced the opportunity. In the words of one Toronto journalist, "He chewed through underlings with a chainsaw." I was to experience that style.

With the 1982 annual meeting of the International Monetary Fund and the World Bank set for Toronto, the bank required something extraordinary as an appropriate gift for attendees. A book was decided upon, honouring their proprietary collection of de Grandmaison portraits. We won the right to create it. The book was to be amplified by a de Grandmaison show in Calgary's Glenbow Museum, both book and show shaped out of the bank's collection.

The mandate for developing the book was simple: no holds barred. Russell Harper, then Canada's leading art historian, was commissioned to write an introduction, and Hugh Dempsey, director of the Glenbow, agreed to write the main text, accompanying 64 of de Grandmaison's Indigenous portraits. A trusted bank employee, Rae Turley, was to be my liaison, and the bank committed to buying three editions: 2,000 copies of a regular edition; 1,700 copies specially bound in cloth and slipcased for all the delegates to the IMF and World Bank meeting in Toronto; and an over-the-top, elegantly crafted "chairman's" edition of 225 pages, bound in expensive leather, exclusively for Mulholland's personal use. The chairman's edition was to be created by the high-end limited-edition unit of Herzig Somerville, then the best in Canada for such indulgences.

Sorting all this out took several trips to Montreal and Toronto. They sometimes involved dealing with Mulholland personally, which was never predictable. They also required visits to the executive suite on the top floor of First Canadian Place. Pale, lime-green walls lined extended corridors, off which were large, elegant rooms, one of which housed a grand piano, with hovering serving staff in immaculate white livery. Several original Frederic Remington bronzes and a hallway lined with de Grandmaison pastels struck what to my eye were discordant notes. On the way in to meet Mulholland for the first time, I muttered to myself, rather too loudly, that this was "Versailles in the sky."

When I first met Mulholland in a cavernous room, as a reflexive gesture of greeting I offered him my hand. His never left his side. In defiance, I left my empty hand hanging. It took several seconds for his to be raised in response, perhaps the longest few seconds of my career. Several hundred thousand dollars were at risk.

Mulholland was completely focussed, very fussy about every detail of his personal edition. The choice of leather required long discussions and a careful perusal of multiple samples. Given the subjects of de Grandmaison's pastels, there were some rather lame remarks about skins with arrow holes.

As the date of the IMF and World Bank gathering approached, everything was set to go when a disaster, so often typical of such projects, unfolded. Tanning the leather for the chairman's edition had gone awry, and it was not going to be ready in time.

Given the scale of the project, I felt obligated to travel to Toronto to personally give Mulholland the news. When I called Rae to explain the circumstance, ready to meet my doom with the chairman, she responded, only half in jest: "Don't bother coming. Just send your skin."

I never learned how everything was worked out. Somehow, the leather was tanned in time and books were delivered as promised. I still have my skin.

The project was extraordinarily successful. In addition to the bank's almost 5,000 copies, an American publisher, Hudson Hills (distributed in the US by Viking), took 5,000 copies, and we went on to sell out of 5,000 copies in Canada. The project was greeted with good reviews and generated revenue of almost $700,000, a heady and very welcome sum for the times.

Everyone in the bank seemed pleased. With some prodding, we were able to extract a personal letter of praise under the chairman's signature. As the Bank of Montreal was also D&M's business bank, copies of that letter quickly found their way onto various desks within the bank's BC regional headquarters.

—

Our strand of books focussing on British Columbia and Indigenous cultures expanded, driven by a blend of personal interests and circumstance. The best material crossing our editorial desks was often deeply rooted in the cultures of place.

An early signature success was 1980's *Bull of the Woods*, the autobiography of logging legend Gordon Gibson Sr., written with Carol Renison. Gibson was known as "a tough man, a fast friend, and a hellish enemy." He made a fortune in the sawmill business, then turned himself into a politician. Every step of the way, he broke rules, took risks, and defied categorization. He was the perfect man for a frontier province. The book sold 15,000 copies in hardcover and a further 10,000 in our own mass paperback edition.

I first encountered Bruce Hutchison in 1982 when D&M was offered the chance to publish what he considered a children's book, *Uncle Percy's Wonderful Town*. Its nostalgic setting was a small town in BC's interior, modelled on Kamloops, home to a diverse cast of characters typical of the province at that time. It included an uncle who had studied at Oxford and had served in the British cavalry during the Boer War, and petit Trudeau, a 6-foot, 300-pound blacksmith. Appearances from historical figures Sir Wilfred Laurier and BC Premier Sir Richard McBride added a touch of realism. Hutchison had joined our list with the help of former M&S colleagues Hugh Kane and Frank Newfeld. Ever optimistic, our first printing was 10,000 copies, which sold out.

Bruce was an icon of Canadian journalism. Born in Prescott, Ontario, in 1901, he began his career at the age of 16, working for the *Victoria Times*. He spent time with the *Winnipeg Free Press* before returning home to the *Times*, finally becoming editorial director of the *Vancouver Sun* in 1963. His 16 books, beginning with *The Unknown Country* in 1942 (actually commissioned by an American publisher), won two Governor General's Awards and a long list of national newspaper awards.

His beat was politics, and he spent much of every year travelling, meeting with prime ministers and presidents. Trains were then the preferred mode of transport, offering long evenings with colleagues, watered with generous doses of strong liquid and delving into the issues of the day. His travels always included extended stays in Washington, DC, where amongst his close friends and neighbours were George Ball, George F. Kennan, Dean Acheson, Walter Lippmann, and McGeorge Bundy.

Bruce was a true Edwardian gentleman, free of the bile that taints politics today. It is inconceivable now to think that, not so long ago, men and women of conscience were rebuilding the western world with optimism and goodwill, in the wake of a devastating war. We seem to have forgotten how central to these conversations Canada had become.

In the mid-1980s, Corky, our son, David, and I spent the weekend with Bruce at his "country" house, a rustic family retreat on Shawnigan Lake. We were given a tour of Bruce's writing cabin, a small heritage structure hovering over the path down to the lake, by his son, Robert, a former Olympian and BC Supreme Court judge. David, a young teenager at the time, slept on the porch of the main house. On a desk in our small cabin sat an ancient Remington typewriter, very like the one I had grown up with and still used. Several years later, in high school, David came home from school one day to report that in English class they had read a piece from Bruce Hutchison, and he "couldn't get his voice out of my mind." I knew we had done something right.

Dinners in Bruce's Victoria home often included house guests from his eclectic circle of friends and admirers. Amongst them was Percy Rawling, a local character, effusive of tongue and round of girth, who had once blown up Turkish bridges for T.E. Lawrence during WW I. Victoria was a haven for the flotsam and jetsam of the end of Empire and a turbulent century.

I became enormously fond of Bruce, and our relationship grew. I always kept something of a discreet distance, but his insights opened my eyes to a time when politics remained a gentleman's business. Differences could be settled with rational discussion, or perhaps a good Scotch. We would go on to publish him four times, including an anthology of his best writing, edited by Vaughn Palmer, *To Canada with Love and Some Misgivings: The Best of Bruce Hutchison*.

—

Hugh Brody, a British anthropologist and filmmaker, also came to us with a publishable manuscript. The book detailed his experience living amongst the Dunne-za and Cree peoples in the northeast corner of British Columbia. His UK publisher, Faber & Faber, was skeptical. Indigenous people, and an obscure Canadian setting, seemed a stretch. In alternating chapters, the manuscript combined anthropological observation with personal experience, informed by deep scholarship and shaped with fine literary style. The story dared to break new ground, reflecting the trust that Hugh, a London-based, white European, had won from the people he portrayed, a rarity for the time.

Hugh's introduction to Canada had been an encounter with the far North as a research officer with the Northern Science Research Group in the 1970s. He was escaping the confines of the comfortable world in which he had been raised, barely aware of his family's Jewish heritage in the pre-war Mitteleuropa of civilized Vienna.

A young man enthralled by the idea of "the wild," he had been smitten by a Canadian friend's descriptions of the fishing and open land in a faraway country. Arriving in Canada's North, he was transfixed by "a vast, wild, forested free terrain. A set of terrains. A whole universe of space and freedom. Canada became a place to believe in . . . I [struggled] to find the words with which to share the beauty of the land and the joy of being shown what it was and what it means to the people of the North . . . I felt at home, in the depths of my being."

Hugh's embrace of the North and its Indigenous peoples grew deeper over time. He was a listener, quietly and respectfully absorbing stories, spellbound by the sounds and the world they revealed. He was rewarded with an Inuktitut name: Mirqukuluk, "wee hairy one." Unpretentious humour, based upon respect.

When Hugh decided to seek out a Canadian publisher, his friend, the lawyer and passionate Indigenous rights advocate Leslie Hall Pinder, suggested he try this newish Vancouver-based publishing house, Douglas & McIntyre.

I met with Hugh to discuss possibilities. He was delicate of feature and gentle of manner, yet with fierce resolve when defending ideas. In conversation, his instinctive modesty melted away. It was evident that we could build an ongoing author-publisher relationship based on mutual respect. (Over the next 30 years, that turned out to be the case. For each of the five books we did together, while Hugh engaged agents and intermediaries in other territories, his Canadian arrangements were made directly between the two of us, usually sealed with a handshake. Paperwork could follow.)

We published *Maps and Dreams* in 1981, and it was taken in the US by Pantheon Books. The idea of Indigenous hunters dreaming their hunting territories, guided by those same dreams when out on the land, was profound. The book struck a chord and is now considered a classic of Indigenous studies. It remains in print, 40 years and 20 printings later.

Disappointingly, the book was never nominated for any significant award, not even for the Governor General's honour I strongly felt it deserved. When Corinna Eberle, who managed media work for us in Toronto, approached *As It Happens*, then at the apex of the Canadian media pyramid, about a possible interview, the response was brutal: "Land claims. We don't care about that shit anymore here." As was all too often the case, reviews in Canada were tepid. The best came from Paul Theroux in the US: "A wonderful book, full of travel and people . . . it is superb anthropology, challenging many of the accepted notions about the lives of hunters."

What we were publishing was groundbreaking. In 1982, we published *During My Time: Florence Edenshaw Davidson, A Haida Woman*, a trailblazing "ethnobiography" from Margaret B. Blackman. Davidson was a deeply respected Elder, daughter of the greatest Haida carver, Charles Edenshaw. She was close to the centre of Haida culture and represented a prized, although fragile, link with the past. The book remains a cornerstone contribution to Indigenous and women's studies throughout North America.

In 1984, Hilary Stewart returned to D&M with *Cedar*, a work of scholarship and rediscovery. In meticulous, impeccably researched drawings and accompanying text, she revealed the technology of the cedar tree, known to the peoples of the coast as the "Tree of Life." Every part of the cedar tree was used to benefit the material well-being of the people. It too remains in print, approaching sales of 75,000 copies in North America. In total, we'd go on to publish 11 of Hilary's books, keeping all of them in print. Her scholarship, reflected in drawings and words, rescued traditional knowledge that few non-Indigenous people up to that time had been prepared to acknowledge.

Ulli Steltzer accepted another dare from me, this time to travel to the Arctic to record Inuit culture. With another small advance from D&M, augmented by generous supporters, she ventured north. She travelled and photographed on her own, no small feat given the geography and the climate. Once, while photographing on a beach fronting the Arctic Ocean, an icy wind froze the oil in her camera. She persevered, and in 1985 we published *Inuit: The North in Transition*, with a US edition taken by the University of Chicago Press.

—

Throughout the early 1980s, we were haunted by the question of how to follow the enormous success of *The Art of Emily Carr*.

One candidate seemed an obvious choice.

Bill Reid was emerging as an artist of international stature. Moving past the constraints of his early career as a CBC radio announcer, his art was blending rediscovered Haida roots with superior technique. Reid was born in Victoria, and his father was of American-Scottish-German ancestry, his mother Haida of the Raven moiety. Charles Edenshaw was his great-great-uncle. His Haida heritage ran deep, and when he returned to Vancouver from Toronto in 1951, he began to explore the world of his maternal ancestors. Working in a newly absorbed visual language, he melded great natural skill with a passion for, in his words, "deep carving," the well-made object. His exquisitely worked jewelry had been compared to the work of Cellini and Fabergé. He moved beyond that to mastering argillite, cast bronze, cedar, and even wire, ink, and paper.

The director of the University of Washington Press, Don Ellegood, and I visited Bill and Martine Reid in their apartment in Point Grey. We were there for a social visit but also to see Bill's current project, a suite of 10 delicately rendered, wittily sophisticated pencil drawings depicting Haida mythology. Bill, ever puckish, characterized them as a "good selection of bestiality, adultery, violence, thievery, and assault, for those who like that sort of thing."

They were masterful. It struck me that if Bill could conjure stories to accompany these drawings, we might make a little book that could form an introduction to Haida mythology. As always with Bill, that took some negotiating, but he ultimately agreed. Bill would complete the stories, and D&M and UWP would publish them jointly, as our two presses so often would for significant books revealing the cultures of the Northwest Coast.

Months dragged on. Ever anxious for what we thought would make a fine gift book for the Christmas season, I felt my patience begin to wane. Bill's Parkinson's disease was advancing, and his energy flagged. He had completed eight of the ten necessary stories, and they were everything we had hoped for: gently sardonic, clever, full of the spicy humour so characteristic of Haida culture.

Uncertain where to turn, I thought Robert Bringhurst might be the right voice to complete the stories, while gentling Bill along. I talked to Doris Shadbolt, my conscience in such circumstances, asking whether she thought Bill and Robert would get along. She was hesitant. I felt it was worth the risk and made the call. Robert completed the stories and secured Bill's blessing, and *The Raven Steals the Light* managed to make the Christmas market in 1984.

We made a limited, slipcased edition with a tipped-in photo of Bill as a frontispiece and a signed colophon page, plus a regular hardcover edition. A paperback edition followed in 1996, with an introduction by Claude Lévi-Strauss. It remains in print, having passed North American sales of 60,000 copies. The fact that such books were making a difference by bringing complex, sophisticated Haida culture to the world was hugely satisfying to me.

Doris Shadbolt began writing her pivotal book, *Bill Reid*, in 1984. Again, gremlins tested the moment. We had commissioned new photography of all Bill's work, which in itself was tricky as many of the early pieces were gold. It was October 1985, the book was coming out in January, and I was about to leave for Frankfurt when Doris took an initial press sheet to show Bill, proudly confirming our commitment to create a book of international quality.

Not quite. One of the images depicted a delicately carved, glowing gold box. Somehow, a museum curator had placed the lid on backwards, something only a experienced eye could have spotted. Bill insisted that the sheet had to be reprinted with the lid correctly placed, which was virtually impossible given the shortage of both paper and timing. Doris was in tears when she returned to my office to give me the news. My adrenalin was exploding. At that time, such a circumstance would have been financially disastrous.

I vetoed the idea. Bill dug in his heels. Soon we had a legal letter from a lawyer I had never heard of in Haida Gwaii demanding that the book be pulped. As it happened, we were between lawyers, which put us in a tight spot. I left for Frankfurt uncertain of the outcome, fearing that the scale of the project had unleashed a major crisis.

I felt so vulnerable in these early years that loose-cannon lawyers had an effect out of all proportion to the issues involved.

Fortunately the immediate problem was averted by a happy accident. The printer, Hemlock in Vancouver, had over-ordered paper. The sheet with the image on it was reprinted. When I returned from Frankfurt, I discovered that another sheet had also been reprinted because the image of one of Bill's great bronze pieces had been inadvertently flipped. The paper supply had held out, and no one had even felt it necessary to upset me further with the news.

My sense of irrational foreboding whenever Frankfurt was imminent lingered for some years. *Bill Reid* turned into a great success. Our first printing of 8,000 copies sold out over 24 months, a gratifying result for a $50 hardcover. We did a second edition some 15 years later, and the book remains in print as a paperback. Defiance and, more importantly, sheer good luck had defeated potential disaster. Raven was amused, I think, but satisfied with the outcome.

—

Many years earlier, Bill Reid had telephoned with a simple message: A group identifying themselves as the "Islands Protection Society" was fighting a recently granted provincial licence to harvest the legacy trees, and everything else, in the heart of BC's South Moresby Wilderness. Two young men, John Broadhead and Thom Henley, were in the midst of pulling together a group of prestigious scientists and accomplished photographers to create a book of words and images to reveal the enormity of what Canada, and the world, might lose. Seldom had I been given such specific instructions: "Scott, this is a meeting you should take."

After some delays, perhaps reflecting island time, *Islands at the Edge: Preserving the Queen Charlotte Islands Wilderness* appeared in 1984. It created a sensation, most critically in Ottawa, where it became a calling card for activists and lobbyists pushing for the creation of a national park. Seldom do books make that immediate an impact.

Gwaii Haanas National Park and Haida Heritage Site was established in 1988, jointly managed by the Government of Canada and the Council of the Haida Nation. *Islands at the Edge* was the first high-end advocacy book that helped elevate the battle to save some of British Columbia's wilderness areas, and it became a model for more. Clayoquot Sound and the Stein River Valley were the next beneficiaries. This was a decisive reminder to me of the power of individual voices, and the influence books can have on Canadian politicians and culture.

Bill Reid remained central to our relationship with the Haida and their sophisticated mythology. He spent five years, beginning in 1986, imaging and shaping what many consider his masterwork, *The Spirit of Haida Gwaii: The Black Canoe*. It was commissioned as a centrepiece for the courtyard of the new Canadian embassy that was under construction in Washington, DC, designed by Arthur Erickson. The finished canoe is a magisterial six metres long, a Noah's Ark filled to overflowing with the beings of Haida mythology.

Bill had asked Ulli Steltzer to chronicle its evolution in photographs, from first clay model through plaster cast to bronze casting. Ulli's photographs were for a book that we had committed to publishing, with a text from Robert Bringhurst. Writing the text was the moment Robert fully entered the Haida world. His words were brilliant, revealing the stories animating the creatures in the canoe while perfectly echoing Ulli's photographs.

The canoe was unveiled in its position in the embassy's front pond during a ceremony on November 19, 1991. Ulli photographed the event, and I made a point of being there. As the ceremony began, Haida royalty arrived, in full regalia, moving with serene dignity from the steps of the US Senate building to the forecourt of our embassy. Their pride was palpable; the audience was full of faces recognizable from US television news.

The event that followed was worthy of the moment. It was the first time I had seen the finished work, and it didn't disappoint. When I asked Bill how he had achieved the lustrous black surface on the cast bronze, without hesitation he responded, "Kiwi black shoe polish." A perfect riposte, entirely in character for Bill.

We published the book under the title *The Black Canoe: Bill Reid and the Spirit of Haida Gwaii* a year later. It remains in print in a second edition, many thousands of copies later.

—

In 1987 we got lucky when we won the right to publish Rick Hansen's story. Rick had just returned from his 40,000-kilometre wheelchair journey through 34 countries, the Man In Motion World Tour, and was recuperating in a small house in Kerrisdale, on Vancouver's west side. Jim Taylor, Vancouver's most accomplished sports journalist, had agreed to work with him on the book to follow. D&M had already won the right to publish it, but initial encounters are always significant.

Four of us met in the understated living room typical of such houses: Rick; his future wife, Amanda Reid; Jim Taylor; and me. I didn't know quite what to expect. What surprised me, and I will never forget, was the penetrating gaze of Rick's eyes. Many months of high oxygen intake impact a human body. Amanda was calmly observing in the background while Jim, Rick, and I sounded each other out.

I sensed that Rick was someone who quickly judged people. As a small-town boy just emerging into the extraordinary limelight that would shape his future, he exhibited a hint of the wariness his background suggested.

There was no wariness at all in the connection between Rick and Amanda. She had been his physio on the long journey, his "lifeline." They were clearly smitten with each other and left the distinct impression that they were just hoping we would soon exit so that they could get on with other things. It was a wonderfully human moment, a clear measure of them both.

Rick had been a gifted natural athlete until an accident at the age of 15 left him paralyzed from the waist down. Instead of giving up, by sheer force of will he rebuilt his life. He became a star Paralympic track and field athlete, won six medals in the 1980 and 1984 Summer Paralympics, and competed in 19 international wheelchair marathons. Tenacity was his middle name.

Inspired by Terry Fox's audacious run, Rick decided on a similar dare. His modest proposal was to circle the globe in a wheelchair. Without any elaborate organization, sponsors, or even a detailed plan, his small band left Vancouver in a beaten-up van in March of 1985.

Two years, just over 40,000 km, and 34 countries later, having wheeled an average of 50 km a day, the odyssey reached home. It was a singular demonstration of courage, conviction, and sheer physical resilience. Rick, accompanied by his small group of supporters, had pushed his wheelchair twice from coast to coast across the US and Canada, throughout Europe as far as Moscow, across the Arabian desert to Bahrain, down the east coast of Australia, through New Zealand's North and South Islands, and, for emphasis, China, Korea and Japan.

When Rick and his caravan crossed the border into BC heading for the final stretch home, expectation was high. Huge crowds lined the route. As Rick wheeled down Hastings Street, he passed close to our offices on Venables Street. The entire D&M staff walked a few blocks to join the cheering from the curb. We were greeted with a vigorous thumbs-up.

When the procession entered BC Place Stadium on May 23, 1987, 50,000 people rose to their feet as one. An honour guard of Canada's elite wheelchair athletes accompanied Rick on a circuit of the stadium. Up to that moment, he had already raised $26 million for spinal cord research. The journey was over, but the future beckoned.

His book was the next challenge. We were pushing for a finished manuscript in time to publish in fall of that same year. Guided by Jim Taylor's experienced hand, he and Rick buckled down with total focus. As excitement about the book accelerated, and Rick's status as a genuine Canadian hero exploded, our first printing grew to 65,000 copies. Every copy of the press run was shipped in September, before formal publication a month later. Quite a step up from British Columbia Premier Bill Bennett's early admonition: "Don't forget. A book called 'Almost Around the World by Wheelchair' won't sell shit."

The first time Rick visited our warehouse/office, we had made arrangements to ensure the route up our building's narrow staircases in a wheelchair would be manageable. He arrived at the back of our warehouse and *walked* through it, then up the stairs, on his own, relying only on his braces.

Over the intense weeks that followed, the book climbed to number one on national bestseller lists, where it stayed. Rick's humility never wavered. A better word to describe it is grace.

Some years later, while I was working with Olympic organizer John Furlong on his book *Patriot Hearts*, Rick entered the conversation. The opening ceremonies for the 2010 Olympics called for Rick, in his wheelchair, to move up an angled ramp at a critical moment during the opening ceremony. The producers choreographing the event were worried. No one in a wheelchair could master such a steep incline, and the attempt would unfold in front of an international TV audience of hundreds of millions of people. I reminded John that no one should ever tell Rick Hansen that he cannot do something. At the event, Rick moved seamlessly up the ramp.

The awards for Rick's extraordinary achievement flowed. I have no doubt that his greatest satisfaction is that his foundation has raised over $300 million for medical research in aid of people with disabilities.

Few Canadians have made as bold a mark on the world as Rick Hansen. Michael J. Fox put it simply: "Rick is still a hero to me . . . He'd tell you he's just a guy with a strong belief that anything is possible."

9

MILESTONES

The early 1980s set the pattern. The Canadian market had been kind to us, and we were determined to continue on the path of steady growth. Optimism continued to reign. In June 1987, Douglas & McIntyre purchased the shares of the educational company, which was to continue functioning as a separate division. By then, sales in D&M had reached $5 million, on top of continuing educational sales of $2 million. Our combined revenues were close to those of McClelland & Stewart and supported by a strengthened balance sheet. The building blocks of what I optimistically assumed could grow into one of the country's largest independent publishing houses had fallen into place, one by one.

We had survived Clarke, Irwin & Company's bankruptcy and welcomed supportive new distribution through the University of Toronto Press. Our national and international reputation was growing.

Under Patsy Aldana's determined leadership, the Groundwood program was thriving, piling up national and international awards. Co-edition sales to some of the best American publishers of their day — New York–based legends Margaret K. McElderry, Jean E. Karl, and Julia McRae amongst them — elevated possibilities. Patsy was increasingly admired for her uncompromising taste, earning a reputation as one of the best children's publishers of her generation. Groundwood's corporate freedom within D&M was a critical part of that. There were no bean counters pushing back. In 1986, Groundwood launched an international children's fiction competition. As always with Patsy, it had a political edge: Only entries from the Scandinavian countries, Brazil, and Canada could qualify. Patsy's rationale: "We live in the shadow of dominant publishing countries." She was doing something about correcting that.

Overall, D&M/Groundwood revenues were growing 10–20 percent per year. By Groundwood's tenth anniversary in 1988, its revenues, including Canadian distribution of the UK's Walker Books, had reached $2 million.

—

The D&M trade program was flourishing, but by 1988 the education division, which had defied the odds for almost a decade, was in trouble. Our ambitious Young Canada Health series was running two years late, and curricula in the largest potential markets, Newfoundland and Alberta, were constantly shifting. Even for Explorations, the comfortable world of guaranteed quantity purchases was over. Teacher choice and multiple resources were the new mantras. The Ministry of Education's Victoria warehouse was on the verge of shutting down, pushing schools to be on their own, expected to buy directly from publishers.

It was becoming clear that education's numbers were not going to work, not in time. Our existing level of investment to develop speculative textbooks for a fracturing market could not be sustained. We did not have a sufficient capital base, nor the ability to borrow the money needed from our still supportive bank. Our existing shareholders did not have the resources to help, and there were no new pots of speculative equity that we could discern.

As a last attempt in search of promise, I embarked on an extensive national tour visiting ministries of education, beginning in Newfoundland and moving west. It was an exhausting three weeks, intensely focussed on curriculum discussion, mostly with people I had never met before. Three weeks on the road, without either compelling stories to repeat or unexpected good news, was a trial. I found no joy anywhere. Carol had no answers. And the Young Canada Health program could not be pushed ahead faster.

I made a very lonely decision. The assets of the educational division had to be sold. However difficult the decision, it was quickly endorsed by the board. Over dinner in our house, I delivered the news to Carol. Outwardly, she was controlled and stoic, utterly in character. I doubt she was surprised. Inwardly, she must have been seething. She felt betrayed. She had sacrificed a great deal, including her teacher's pension and some of the best years of her professional life, to join us. Her royalties had been substantial, but I doubt they fully assuaged the pain. Her legacy was that, by sheer force of will, she had turned Explorations into the preeminent Canadian social studies program of its time.

We contacted the half-dozen Canadian educational publishing houses we thought might be interested. Nelson Canada, then a division of Thomson International, topped the list. Its CEO, Alan "Al" Cobham, had previously suggested to Carol he might be interested. Nelson Canada ticked all the boxes. It had the resources. It was already at work on a parallel mid-grade health program, which meshed perfectly with our own. It was Canadian-owned, a necessity under Canadian ownership rules. (In 1985, Marcel Masse had introduced his signature Baie Comeau policy. The new policy had one ambition: to repatriate ownership in Canadian publishing companies, at the same time bolstering the financial stability of those companies, specifically by enabling them to benefit from greater scale. It was a defiant and ultimately unsuccessful gesture. The hardball it triggered was played quietly, behind the scenes.)

My discussions with Nelson moved quickly and smoothly, despite my initial reservations, which reflected a lingering ACP bias against "the other guys," all large multinationals. Over meetings held in Toronto, Al and I got on well. He fit the mould perfectly: flawlessly tailored with perfect hair, calmly disciplined.

Negotiations progressed seamlessly, and I was able to increase the originally offered amount to better recognize work in progress. The deal closed in July, accompanied on signing by a single cheque for over $700,000.

All remaining staff were let go. We stretched to ensure generous severances. It was with an aching heart that I joined Linda Turnbull, education's former marketing director, in our warehouse one afternoon to finish packing the skids of our educational archive for shipment to Toronto.

—

In these years I was engaged in another challenge, this one voluntary. Prime Minister Brian Mulroney launched negotiations with the US for a new free-trade agreement of unprecedented scale. Everything, potentially including culture, was to be on the table.

Political debates soon exploded. Everything we held dear was going to be trampled by the American elephant. Doomsayers were out in full force, nowhere more loudly and intensely than in Quebec's cultural community. This had to be listened to in Ottawa.

To defuse the panic, and ensure effective business input, Mulroney formed 15 sectoral advisory groups on international trade (SAGITs) to offer advice. Each was to be made up of business leaders, with regular, detailed, and confidential briefings covering the progress of negotiations.

One of the designated groups was to deal with culture and the arts. I was asked to join it, a rare opportunity for a cultural emissary from western Canada to join an important national debate. From my first meeting in fall 1986 through to the dismantlement of the system almost 20 years later, including one term as chair, this gave me a front-row seat during the country's, and the world's, evolving trade wars. A side benefit was the high-powered access to much of the Ottawa bureaucracy, including ministers and deputy ministers.

My colleagues on the first SAGIT included an impressive group of luminaries from the Canadian art, book, film, and sports worlds. The initial meeting began calmly enough. Soon, conflicting emotions flared. Paranoia was in the air. The group's prevailing mood softened as briefings became more frequent and more transparent. Simon Reisman had been appointed Canada's lead negotiator, and there was little doubt he could successfully keep the Americans at bay. Apparently, and encouragingly, marching orders from cabinet to Canadian negotiators had specifically emphasized that the final agreement had to protect Canadian culture.

For Canadians, the heart of the agreement was not tariffs but market opportunity. Canada sought broader access to the flourishing American economy. The US wanted access to Canada's energy, water, and cultural industries. When the end was in sight, Canadian negotiators dug in their heels and insisted on a "cultural exemption," a world first within a trade agreement. The exemption meant that Canada's fragile cultural industries were off the table. The ability of Canadians to hear, see, and read their own voices — enabled by subsidies, quotas, ownership requirements, or any of the other measures in the cultural toolbox, without reprisal — was protected. In practice, this meant without fear of *American* reprisal. Canadian *ideas* were judged so essential to Canada's national interest that measures to strengthen their reach had to be liberated from the normal commercial imperatives of trade agreements.

It later emerged that cabinet minister Flora MacDonald had been the quiet champion of the fight to retain the cultural exemption. Initially both Simon Reisman and our Canadian ambassador to Washington, Allan Gotlieb, had been firmly opposed. MacDonald's ferocious defence of both the idea and the necessity was genuinely heroic and may have saved the exemption. It has since been included in every recent trade agreement. Such political courage is rare.

—

In the summer of 1987, Douglas & McIntyre's VP, general manager, Rick Antonson, decided to return to one of his first loves, the tourism business, and departed for a new job in Edmonton.

Rob Sanders and I had come to know each other during ACP meetings and had always gotten on well. Searching for Rick's potential replacement, I felt Rob would be a good fit. It was agreed, with goodwill all around. In late summer 1988, Rob parted company with Western Producer Prairie Books in Saskatoon, where he had been publisher, moving further west to join D&M. My hands remained full running the newly combined

D&M with the inevitable residual rough edges of corporate integration. I named Rob to inherit my role as trade publisher but kept a hand in shaping the D&M program, always my first love.

Rob encountered a new world, culturally very different from the one he had left. He was a package of robust energy and great enthusiasm, sandy-haired and blessed with the thick-set body of the hockey player he had once been; as he put it, he was not shy about on-ice scrums in corners against the boards. The hockey temperament lingered. Its downside was the occasional volcanic eruption of temper, sometimes unexpectedly, which was disconcerting for anyone encountering it. The volcano mellowed over time, but led to some exhausting moments along the way. In his core, Rob was good-hearted, and I much liked him.

One of Rob's publishing strengths was illustrated natural history, a nice balance to the highly visual art books that were becoming a staple of the D&M program. He brought with him a book from the last days of Western Producer that had been languishing in final form ready for press, Candace Savage's *Wolves*. We resuscitated it and published the book in fall 1988. It turned out to be the right book for the right time. High-end photographic books were still avidly sought around the world. *Wolves* went on to sell some 300,000 copies in several languages and several countries. It set the tone for what would become a defining strand of a new imprint.

When I named Rob publisher of the program, there were, in effect, two publishers, never a workable arrangement. My diminished involvement was beginning to show, and Rob was still settling into the role. The D&M list seemed to be losing focus. Revenues were static and were beginning to reflect softer publishing. With the shedding of the education division, my itch to be fully in charge of the publishing had returned. Rob didn't respond well to working in the shadows.

As mutual frustrations grew, we knew we had to find a solution. We had grown fond of each other, and Rob had real publishing strengths. We wanted to find a structure that might work. In late 1992, we agreed on a path forward. Rob would have his own imprint, identified with its own name and logo, thematically separated from the established strengths of D&M. His list was initially to be small, with a clear editorial focus acceptable to Rob: natural history, ecology and the environment, sports, guidebooks, and the backlist of Western Producer, the publishing unit of the Saskatchewan Wheat Board, which he had built as a publisher and which we had purchased earlier that year.

His list would be demarcated by subject area, with those that logically fit within Rob's mandate moving to his newly constituted separate operating division. Greystone Books was launched that year, initially anchored by high-end photographic books about wildlife, the offspring of *Wolves*, building upon our existing distribution partnership with Sierra Club Books. That program was the San Francisco–based publishing offshoot of the Sierra Club, launched in 1960, and we had won Canadian distribution rights to its expanding program in the early 1970s. Our publishing tie to the club became a cornerstone of the Greystone program, as Sierra Club began buying healthy co-edition print runs of all Greystone's illustrated natural history, 15,000–25,000 copies of each book. It grew into a very happy, and profitable, relationship.

D&M had also recently won the right to become the publisher for the nascent publishing program of the Suzuki Foundation. As that seemed a better fit with Greystone, I passed it over. I had become friends with David and Tara Cullis Suzuki, so it was a wrench to give up a direct relationship to the foundation, but we were, after all, one family.

To Rob's great credit, he expanded that partnership to include all of David Suzuki's own prolific output, plus award-winning books on environmental issues. The list became the anchor of the now independent Greystone Books Ltd.

—

The 1980s had been an intense, exhausting decade. We had survived massive change, emerging with a strengthened balance sheet and fresh publishing energy. The decade ahead promised smoother sailing.

In 1994, Lawrence "Larry" Stevenson's private equity venture, Pathfinder Capital, merged SmithBooks and Coles into a new entity to create Chapters Inc. Stevenson, an MBA and former paratrooper, set out to conquer Canadian bookselling. Short of hair and crisp of manner, he had grandiose plans, with both the energy and the financing to pursue them. The stodgy publishing business was ripe for disruption. He was the one to do it.

Conscious of having to satisfy Canada's Competition Bureau, which meant seeking allies from within the business, he and his colleagues courted a cross-section of those in the industry who were deemed "influential." Adding a respected western voice was still considered valuable, and politically prudent. Chapters had attracted former premier of Ontario David Peterson to its cause and had divided up the list of those to be pursued.

Returning from lunch one day, I spotted a phone number on top of my inevitable pile of message slips that happened to have a 416 area code. The name that followed was David Peterson. Intrigued, I asked my assistant if that might be the former politician David Peterson. She made a face. Yes, it was, but her family had grown up in his Ontario riding, and she wasn't a fan. I was lucky the message had survived.

I returned the call and listened to the pitch. The Canadian publishing sector was deeply divided about the creation of a new juggernaut. There was much apprehension about what that might portend. Large groups of branded bookstores were proliferating in several countries, seemingly well funded — Waterstones in the UK and both Barnes and Noble and Borders in the US, amongst others. I sided with Avie Bennett, whose view was "Better to be inside the tent looking out than outside looking in." I accepted the invitation to go inside.

Early in the unfolding process, I happened to be meeting with Larry in the Rooftop Bar of the old Park Plaza in Toronto when Jack McClelland walked by. Larry and Jack had not met, so I introduced them. Jack, in his inimitable manner, waxed effusively about how superstores were going to transform the industry.

But Chapters was a business play rather than a book play. Its investor prospectus emphasized the possibility of unsold books being returnable to publishers for full credit. A store could order new books with impunity and without financial risk. Publishers would be left holding an empty bag rather than useful cash from paid invoices. Always seduced by the prospect of windfall sales, publishers fell for the lure of large orders. Wallpaper, the cynics called the stacks of books ordered to fill the explosion of new shelves. False hope, the realists suggested.

In 1996, Heather Reisman arrived on the scene, launching Indigo Books and Music Inc. With the significant resources of her husband, Gerald "Gerry" Schwartz, at her disposal, a lifelong passion for books, and a not indifferent eye on the main chance, she saw an opportunity. Big-box bookstores were proliferating throughout the English-speaking world, and all had walls of empty space to fill, catnip to publishers.

The question remained: What would this mean for Canadian publishing?

—

One of the foundational myths of the Canadian book business is that you must distribute the books of international publishers to reach profitable scale. Only then can you afford to squander sparse resources on publishing original Canadian books. This remained holy writ late into the 20th century, an inevitable colonial legacy. Historically, it did make good business sense.

In the 1990s, with sales growing steadily and publishing flourishing, we fell into the trap of pursuing Canadian distribution for larger US and UK companies. Old connections had given us the great art book publisher Thames & Hudson, and we had added Sierra Club and several small Seattle-based publishers. Groundwood had landed the prestigious UK children's publishing house Walker Books, which soon included its ambitious new US offshoot, Candlewick Books. We felt we could accommodate others.

In 1995, as a result of ongoing market turmoil in Canada, we were approached by a large UK publishing house, Orion Publishing Group, which was being forged into a major by the mercurial Anthony Cheetham. Cheetham was born in Mexico City to a British diplomat and spent his early years in Vienna, Paris, and Budapest, before spending time at Eton and Oxford. He entered publishing when he joined the New English

Library, working at several publishing houses before co-founding Century, later Century Hutchison, and cashing out by selling the company to Random House. His long-standing colleague and founding partner in Century, Peter Roche, was his maestro of financial oversight. Anthony was accomplished at growing sales, discovering bestselling authors of popular fiction, and always keeping a sharp eye on the profitable horizon.

Established in 1991, the next year, Orion bought the assets of the fading, prestigious, high-end publishing house Weidenfeld & Nicolson. That company's co-founder, George Weidenfeld, was kept on in an advisory capacity and given the title of executive chairman. A fixture on the London social scene, Weidenfeld was one of Vienna's postwar gifts to London publishing, famous for his upscale parties and his unmatched networking — he "knew everybody." His habits included profligate spending when it came to entertaining. In the words of Peter Roche, he was "definitely a non–executive chairman. We wouldn't let him near the money."

Orion was a shooting star for several years, growing at an annual rate of 33 percent, with profits to match, until it was sold to Hachette UK in 1998. Its self-described values were "agile, ambitious, and committed." Emphasis on "ambitious."

Winning Canadian distribution seemed transformative. We had "beaten" Penguin and anticipated dramatic sales growth. Contract terms were more generous than anything we had previously experienced, with one small caveat: Books were bought firm sale; none could be returned to Orion for credit. And Orion published popular fiction in mass paperback format, including such authors as Maeve Binchy, Penny Vincenzi, and Michael Connelly.

To cement the new relationship, I travelled to London to meet the principals in their eponymous building on Upper St. Martin's Lane. They soon pressed me to speculate about what dollar volume we might generate in Canada. With not-very-useful Orion sales history badly printed on floppy computer spreadsheets, I retired to a bar on Charing Cross Road to make sense of it all. My invented numbers suggested that we would invoice $2 million during our first full calendar year. To my eventual delight, that vague prognostication proved accurate.

In July 1997, Farrar, Straus and Giroux (FS&G) offered its Canadian distribution to us. Founded in 1946, FS&G was of manageable size and one of the most prestigious of the remaining New York independents, with an editorially distinguished list. Walls in the squished reception area of the company's seedy quarters fronting Union Square were papered with certificates from its 21 Nobel and 26 Pulitzer Prize wins, infinitely more impressive than the surrounding cramped offices. Even the throne room, where Roger Straus himself held court, natty in dress and profane in language, was shabby. It was effectively guarded by his long-time amanuensis, Peggy Miller, who was imperious by nature but whom I grew to much like over time. The publishing made up for the distinctly unglamorous quarters. The list was full of authors of extraordinary reputation, and I liked and trusted the people.

Winning FS&G was the result of the usual combination of persistence, luck, and timing. The company had a subsidiary-rights VP who had, over an extended tenure, won clout within the company. In a previous life, Judy Klein had been a broadcaster for the CBC in the Yukon and was a free spirit. We got on well, sometimes over lunch in Danny Myers's Union Square Cafe, effectively the faculty club for senior FS&G executives. The power corner in its lower level, where Roger Straus had a deeded table, was hallowed publishing territory.

FS&G was looking for a new Canadian distributor, and Judy put our name into the mix. She must have been persuasive. A contract was offered, and we signed it. Still stupidly naïve about the perils of distribution in a Chapters world, we accepted another contract based on firm sale, without return privileges.

The great attraction of distribution is that it provides a steady stream of already finished books whose acquisition and production costs have been absorbed by the originating publisher. Established publishing programs, often with high-quality backlists, bring immediate access to a range of authors, including bestselling authors, that a small Canadian house could never attract on its own. Books from established authors are coveted by major customers and make very effective calling cards. Confessing my bias, distribution is not creative publishing; it is basic business. Not glamorous but, if tightly managed, consistently profitable.

The disadvantages are significant: Scale of supply remains in the hands of others; contracts can be ended or withdrawn, sometimes arbitrarily, often the result of corporate restructuring; and sales expectations are usually unrealistically high. Most disconcerting of all, depending upon the contract, books returned from sellers may or may not be sent back to the principal for full credit. Returns can destroy everything.

The growth of superstores accelerated two trends. Average discounts demanded by the large Canadian customers increased, without any commensurate break from the international publishers providing the books. An inexorably increasing rate of returns for full credit, a minimum of 30 percent and sometimes over 40 of total purchases, became a fact of life. Buying books from principals without equivalent return privileges is a kiss of death. We would learn this the hard way.

—

In Canada's new superstore environment, getting books into stores was the easy part. Total D&M net sales escalated from about $8 million in 1994 to $12 million 24 months later. We had put sufficient financing in place to accommodate such growth, or so we thought.

By the next year, Canadian book sales were softening significantly. Chapters stores, overburdened with unsaleable inventory, were ordered to clean house. Books came back by the skid, more than our distributor, the University of Toronto Press, could handle, or quickly process. The skids sat in their warehouse, unprocessed, a mountain of dead inventory. When they were finally processed and credit notes were issued, Chapters stopped paying. That left the UTP with insufficient cash flow to honour its existing contract terms with us, which were based upon payment in full, net 90 days from the end of every month. To cope, the UTP proposed unilaterally changing its payment terms in a direction our cash flow couldn't endure.

Dramatic, and painful, moves confronted us. We resigned the distribution of Orion, effective at the end of 1998. And we broke from our UTP distribution agreement, accepting an offer from Jack Stoddart's General Distribution Services to move our books there, effective January 1, 1999. Jack offered distribution at an acceptable rate and cemented it with an equity investment in D&M of $150,000 to secure the arrangement.

Jack was conceptualizing his grand plan to assemble a number of Canadian houses into a single large entity, one capable of standing up to the growing multinational companies making editorial inroads in the country. Investment Canada had been grandfathering in the established multinational companies, rather than using the forced ownership-review mechanisms of the Baie Comeau policy to support the growth of Canadian-owned companies. Ottawa turned a blind eye to international corporate consolidation. The dreams of the 1980s to build a sustainable Canadian-owned book business of scale had died.

Resigning Orion took a great toll. By contract, they were not required to take back any books, and they didn't. Not even a single book was transferred to their new Canadian distributor, a painful slap in the face. Worse, their response to negotiating more lenient payment terms for our outstanding amount owing was churlish. They threatened legal action. My suspicion is that they were well underway with their negotiation to sell the company to Hachette, which was finalized later that same year. The last thing Orion wanted on its balance sheet was returned inventory. Our consequence was writing off almost $1 million of unsaleable books. We had grasped the tail of a shooting star and been scorched.

—

Having been badly burned by the changes in the distribution business, we resigned all distribution partnerships except Farrar, Straus and Giroux. M&S had done the same thing in the 1960s, and its proprietary publishing had more than made up for the loss of distribution income. Our passion and skill set was publishing authors, not managing the mechanics of fulfillment and a functioning back office. And we had the advantage of no warehouse with a fixed overhead.

Patsy Aldana tried to persuade me to drop FS&G along with all our other distribution partners, but following an uncomfortable telephone conversation with her from a phone booth in LaGuardia Airport, I insisted on going ahead. The Orion lesson necessitated another trip to New York to negotiate with FS&G. I arrived full of dread. When I proposed changing the newly signed contract from firm sale to consignment, with full return privileges, I braced for the worst. To my very great relief, the change was agreed on the spot. It took some months for the practical details of the consignment agreement to be worked out, which also gave us the gift of some months of free financing.

My stress on that trip must have been showing. When I unexpectedly ran into a publishing colleague from Toronto in my New York hotel, he later confessed that he felt I looked very uncomfortable in my own skin. He was right.

The scale and quality of the FS&G programs, both adult and children's, turned out to be a perfect fit for us. Even following Roger Straus's sale of his company to the German Holtzbrinck Publishing Group in 1993, he remained firmly in command, and our relationship flourished. Any conversation in his office was a graduate seminar in publishing as it once was, punctuated with strikingly graphic language. His judgement could be scornfully derisive, particularly about colleagues, but it was always entertaining.

Led by company president Jonathan Galassi, FS&G also had a group of the most experienced and savvy literary editors in New York, including Sarah Crichton and Elisabeth Sifton. Talking books and authors with them, while actually selling our own books, became a treasured part of my publishing year. What grew into a 17-year relationship with the house gave us the opportunity to license some of their important authors for Canada (always, in the grumpy words of Jonathan Galassi, "paying competitive international royalty advances").

For all the Sturm und Drang of the decade, our publishing program strengthened during the 1990s. We passed sales of $12 million in 1996 and remained there.

That year was our 25th anniversary, and some celebration was in order. The plan included a national media tour by me to tell the company's story. The primary purpose of the trip was to emphasize D&M's emergence as one of the largest remaining independent Canadian-owned publishing houses. My introduction to that fall's catalogue summarized the company's journey:

> Statistics tell part of the story — over 900 authors; 1,500 titles issued; three successful publishing divisions; millions of books sold around the world . . . publishing entities reflect the values and shared passions of all those people associated with them; and we have been blessed . . . with 35 people in two offices, and senior publishing colleagues Patsy Aldana and Rob Sanders. The path has been deeply rewarding . . . I hope everyone reading this message will take a moment to salute the dedicated crew, not least of which are authors and artists, who have made our adventure possible, and so worthwhile.

It was instructive to endure the intense, odd experience of encountering a cross-section of the country's media directly, on occasion as early as 5 a.m. Some of the people who interviewed me had actually prepared for the moment; most had not. In some quarters on the other side of the Rockies, there was still skepticism that a British Columbia–based entity could make national inroads, let alone be seen and heard outside the province. I felt a new kinship with those authors we had thrown to the wolves over so many years.

Growth meant we were finally able to install stronger administrative backup. It was long past time that the company had a professional managing money. We had financed our growth with a multi-million-dollar operating line at a very supportive Bank of Montreal. Collateral mortgages on our home were needed to secure the operating line. Stretched cash flow was a constant sword of Damocles over my head as the only shareholder on the hook in case of financial disaster. We had always made do with a senior bookkeeper, rather than a qualified CFO. For years, I had generated detailed annual cash flows myself from sales estimates provided by the publishers. It was never a pleasant task and always exhausting, as it pitted editorial fantasies against market realities, a self-inflicted wound for any book publisher.

We embarked on a careful process to hire a CFO, and got lucky. When David Cater, a chartered accountant with CFO experience, entered our boardroom in April 1996 for an interview, it seemed we had found the right match. He felt the same way. Over the next 17 years, he was in the office very early each morning, seamlessly handling all financial issues. To my immense relief, that included cash flow. David exuded a Zen-like calm while making things look easy.

One remaining cornerstone was finding someone experienced and committed to handling operations. Our legal arrangements had been handled for some years by McCarthy Tétrault out of its Vancouver office. Having worked closely with both Rob and me, one day a McCarthy partner, Karen Gilmore, called to ask if we might be interested in her joining us in-house. Taken aback at the gift such a possibility suggested, we arranged a lunch. She was serious, and after reciting my usual litany of caveats, she remained engaged by the cultural achievement that D&M represented.

A second lunch was required to discuss terms. Compensation was going to be an issue. When it came time for me to put a package on the table, the blood drained from Karen's face, even though she'd expected it would likely not be munificent. Still, she accepted, and we welcomed one of the most accomplished executives ever to grace the company.

Karen became vice-president, operations and corporate and legal affairs, a title she sardonically suggested gave her responsibility for "everything nobody else wanted to do." She engaged that broad portfolio selflessly, working long hours and calmly cutting through tough issues. Her patience, and focus, was a godsend.

—

One final evolution over that decade of change was a move to larger and brighter quarters. We had outgrown our rather shabby combined office and warehouse space on Venables Street in East Vancouver, and with the move to General Distribution Services, we no longer needed a western warehouse.

There were other reasons. The necessity of preaching caution to our warehouse staff to avoid used needles covering the ground in our back alley each morning had worn thin. More than once, as the lead contact, I had been awoken in the middle of the night to drive across town in response to smashed front-door glass from an office break-in. Once, in predictably cavalier fashion, I abandoned caution to waltz into the warehouse. I was not alone. A police officer, accompanied by a ferocious dog, was responding to the blaring alarm. She suggested being more cautious next time. Her language was not diplomatic.

Rob led our search for new space, with fine results. In March of 1999, we moved into splendid new quarters in Mount Pleasant, then not the trendy high-tech neighbourhood it has become. Our address was on Quebec Street, which nicely reflected our federal perspective.

The move to new quarters was more than symbolically important. The offices were bright, with large, north-facing windows and generous open spaces. Previously they had been occupied by an architectural practice, so we inherited some stylish enhancements, including a large, intimidating reception desk. It didn't leave room for chairs and other normal welcoming fixtures. Corky was tasked with fixing that, adding posters and some semblance of comfortable seating and lighting.

Two energetic D&M managers, managing editor Terri Werschler and production manager Kim Lyons, were charged with choosing the colour scheme. They erred on the bright side, choosing a rich yellow matched with a strong purple. Initially, it seemed out of character for a publishing house, but when the walls had been painted, the reviews were exemplary. When the movers were unloading our furniture to cart it into our new spaces, one of them audibly exclaimed, "You're moving that junk into this space?"

The social centre of the new office was an elevated counter where staff could deposit baked goods and other edibles to be shared. Those plates were always empty by the end of the day they arrived. Many a Friday afternoon a few bottles of wine appeared, usually from my cellar at home. When authors were in the neighbourhood, they joined us. People were encouraged to abandon their offices for a visit to that counter according to their whims.

—

Between 1987 and 2010, all of D&M prospered, including Groundwood Books and Greystone, together publishing about 75 new books a year plus 50 backlist reprints. We enjoyed a growing national reputation and had the necessary resources to support a stronger program. A steady stream of bestsellers ensured that the market accepted our presence as a national publishing house of reputation. Old prejudices had all but disappeared. That meant D&M could focus on its core strengths, which were still shaped by my personal passions (though not entirely) — accomplished non-fiction and fiction voices from British Columbia, Canadian politics, Canadian art and architecture, Indigenous art, issues, and justice, Canadian military history, and food and wine.

10

SHARP WORDS

Journalists on Canada's West Coast had a well-earned reputation for pushing comfortable boundaries. The media environment was brash and irreverent, with independent voices unconstrained by cautious owners. A cynical Toronto editor once proposed a theory: When you reach the far side of the Rockies, the air molecules are further apart.

Vancouver's accomplished journalism community was anchored by the *Vancouver Sun*, BC's self-styled "newspaper of record." It was then a first-rate newspaper, independent in voice and ownership and committed to quality journalism.

Its tone was set by a rat pack of acerbic writers — Marjorie Nichols, Allan Fotheringham, Jack Wasserman, Jack Scott, Paul St. Pierre, Simma Holt, Robert Hunter, Barry Mather, and Denny Boyd to name a few — all granted sufficient editorial independence to write with a free hand. Union battles ensured that they were paid well. Their potent voices were so central that the *Sun*'s marketers, never shy, once orchestrated a city-wide billboard campaign using the slogan "The *Sun* has the writers."

Cheeky defiance was the rule of thumb. The newsroom was chaotic, opinionated, full of smokers and drinkers, bottles of booze and packs of cigarettes in every top desk drawer. And the denizens all valued books —

I first met them as a publisher's rep for M&S towing around writers of reputation, and I was always welcome.

The steady stream of national figures accompanying me promised good copy, and good company, often continued off the premises. Later D&M was to become the beneficiary of that manic energy, as old alliances offered future opportunity. Several of the best of them — including Marjorie Nichols — joined the Douglas & McIntyre list in the late 1980s and early 1990s.

Two other influential voices of the time were Jack Webster and Jack Munro. Webster, originally a journalist at the *Sun*, became Canada's leading talk-show host, while Munro, a sharp-tongued labour leader, echoed the outspoken opinions of the day.

———

"Write a book? I can't even fucking read."

Jack Munro was a hard man to ignore. We were in an elegant restaurant, and the sound bite carried to neighbouring tables.

Jack hadn't warmed to my suggestion that he write a memoir. We were there because Jane O'Hara, a D&M author, had indicated that she was prepared to ghostwrite such a book, if Jack could be cajoled into agreeing to the project.

I had first crossed paths with Jack at a dinner honouring Jack Webster, immediately realizing that he was a seminal figure in the BC labour movement with an important story to tell. He was the right guy to cut to the heart of the fraught union-management relations at that time, which were tearing the province apart.

A large man in every way, including physically at 6'5" and 265 pounds, he was no shrinking violet. He had been the long-time leader of the International Woodworkers of America and had a temperament that was a perfect match for the rough-and-tumble battles that then characterized labour relations in British Columbia. He was a Prairie kid who had grown up on a farm in Alberta, which he described as "a godforsaken hole," and had dropped out of school in Grade 10. He had an unmatched skill at terrifying his opposition with blunt profanity, effectively delivered.

In 1983, what became labelled "Operation Solidarity" had been formed to fight Premier Bill Bennett's "restraint" program, which included massive cutbacks to government programs. Jack was the leading, and the loudest, naysayer. Five months later, when he became part of the solution, helping negotiate what became known as the "Kelowna Accord," he was disdained for being a wimp and a sellout. Such was the edgy state of labour relations in a union province.

Once, when confronted during a union organizing drive in Newfoundland by a testy local with a shotgun, his colleagues fled. He just stood his ground with the words: "You couldn't knock a hatpin up my butt with a sledgehammer." When Prince Philip once suggested that Canadians were always complaining about something, Jack responded, "Well, that's bullshit."

As is so often the case with larger-than-life men, vulnerability hid just beneath the surface. He had a heart to match his stature. And he was very good at his core priorities: boosting union wages and working conditions. Jack Webster had an answer. "After you get past Munro's deleted expletives, you find the best #@*!!@#!! labour leader in Canada."

Jane O'Hara had once been a professional tennis player, moving into journalism as a sportswriter. Comfortable in a world of male ego, she tamed the lion. The result was 1988's *Union Jack: Labour Leader Jack Munro*, another D&M bestseller, with sales passing 10,000 copies. When I wrote a letter of recommendation supporting Jane's application for a Southam Journalism Fellowship, I used the anecdote about Jack's disparagement of his own ability to read, with the language unchanged. She won the fellowship.

However intimidating Jack could be to his adversaries, he was unfailingly gracious with me. I suspect he felt that anyone crazy enough to be a Canadian book publisher was never going to be a threat to anyone. When I hand-delivered his large first royalty cheque, I couldn't resist asking how he intended to spend it. "I'm going to buy a new Harley-Davidson," he replied.

When he died of cancer at age 82 in 2013, the province lost one of its most abrasively effective fighters. The Harley had been well used.

—

A memoir from Jack Webster was widely acknowledged as one of the great potential catches in the Canadian media world. Of course, I pursued him relentlessly, but he remained coyly distant. My competition was Anna Porter, never to be underestimated when guile, cachet, and Toronto glamour might become determinant.

Finally, he declared himself ready. The price was going to be steep, but I was absolutely determined that we would not lose to Anna, as we had lost Allan Fotheringham.

As the dollars escalated, my determination grew. Rob was in charge of the negotiation, but at the investment level being considered, I was heavily involved.

As the deadline for landing the book neared, I was in Montreal with my son, introducing him to McGill, which he was soon to attend. We were in a hotel room when the phone rang. It was Rob asking how high we should go in offering Jack's royalty advance. It was going to have to reach six figures.

My response was unequivocal: "Whatever it costs, just get it."

Winning the right to publish Jack's story strengthened what was already a warm relationship. With money out of the way, cordial behaviour returned.

Jack's face was all expression: jowls capped by thick eyebrows in a face seemingly made of putty. His distinct, wide mouth could be used at will, to devastating effect, emphasized by a raw Glaswegian burr that was perfect when theatre was required for effect.

The epithets people threw at him, including "Oatmeal Savage," were all earned the hard way. His bluster was balanced by the skills of a hard-nosed beat reporter with an uncanny ability to read the moment, adjusted for the degree of angst any guest was revealing.

He was a Clydeside boy who had grown up rough on a seedy side of Glasgow. He left school as a young teenager to try his luck as a journalist on Fleet Street and made his mark, once sharing a desk with Ian Fleming. When World War II broke out, he began a six-year stint in the British army, serving in the Middle East and rising to the rank of major.

Arriving in Vancouver in 1947, he soon made a name for himself as a *Vancouver Sun* reporter. Radio beckoned, where his unmistakable bluster was unavoidable and helped define what open-line radio was to become. Over 40 years, he kickstarted a new form of radio and changed his adopted country for the better while never compromising his standards. His program had the largest and most loyal audience in the city, averaging 200,000 listeners.

Jack never forgot his roots and retained a genuine soft spot for the disadvantaged. He was always up for a fight to defend those he felt had been wronged, but heaven help anyone arrogant enough to exude privilege. And God save any politician who tried to pull rank or mutter pablum while evading honest answers. When Pierre Trudeau was his guest, often the only media appearance Trudeau would consent to in Vancouver, sparks flew. Both of them relished the repartee, and the town loved it.

His autobiography, *Webster!*, was written in partnership with Ian Mulgrew of the *Vancouver Sun*. It opens with revelatory self-analysis. "Sometimes you forget: all the world isn't a talk show. Jack Webster doesn't have to growl at the world all the time!"

With fingers crossed, we were confident the book would fulfill our hopes. It did, earning out its six-figure advance, selling some 25,000 copies by its first Christmas.

Jack's greatest gifts to us all were his overwhelming humanity and, of course, his provocative tongue. When he died in 1999, the memorial event was packed. His legacy has been properly honoured by many accolades, not least of which are the Webster Awards, established in 1986 to recognize excellence in all genres of British Columbia journalism.

—

Marjorie Nichols was the feistiest of a scrappy lot of writers, a dominant voice writing about the zany excesses of Social Credit politics. If she had ever endured prejudice because of her sex, it never showed. She was a tall poppy amongst the well-staffed Victoria-based press corps of the era. The W.A.C. Bennett regime, and the party he bestrode, had dominated British Columbia politics since the early 1950s, winning several majorities until being briefly defeated by Dave Barrett's dreaded "socialist hordes" in 1972.

The Bennett government was populated by characters not far removed from their rural constituencies, including many of its ministers, who seemed mystified by the nuances of urban behaviour. Marjorie and her colleagues had a romp with their pens.

I knew Marjorie had a book in her. My first thought was a sardonic overview of the odd state of BC politics, what cynics beyond the mountains dismissed as "Lotus Land." Such a book might dispel convenient myths while probing the historical roots of the province's peculiar brand of hinterland politics. She accepted, and began work.

As a columnist, Marjorie was accustomed to fixed deadlines triggering short bursts of potent writing. Months passed, and nothing appeared. My courting turned into nagging. Finally, Marjorie responded with an outline and a chunk of manuscript. When I read the material, it was clear that what she proposed could not be shaped into a publishable book.

Marjorie was then living in an apartment just off Granville Street on Vancouver's west side. I chose to deliver the message in person and entered her apartment full of trepidation at the news I had to deliver. What I encountered was an almost empty space that a tornado seemed to have just swept through, hollowing out all signs of permanent habitation. Following my news, the tornado reappeared. We parted civilly. To my great relief, the friendship survived.

Marjorie Nichols was a Red Deer girl, born and raised on an Alberta farm. Her university degree was from the University of Montana, and she began her journalism career with the *Ottawa Journal* in 1967. She was just 23 years old, the youngest member of the Ottawa Press Gallery. Any lingering timidity, of which there wasn't much, quickly disappeared. She regularly matched wits with Pierre Trudeau, Brian Mulroney, John Turner, Patricia "Pat" Carney, and a host of other terrified politicians. She always held her own.

By the time Marjorie joined the *Vancouver Sun* in 1972, her pen was very sharp, a perfect weapon for her new beat. Her new friends Allan Fotheringham and Jack Webster discovered they had met their match. Alcohol was the friend she gave up. Cigarettes, never. Judy LaMarsh understood: "Marjorie is the clearest eye that ever held a pen." Fotheringham seconded the motion: "The toughest journalist I have ever met."

Tough, but with a heart of gold for her friends, of whom I remained one. When she returned to Ottawa to join the *Ottawa Citizen* in January 1987, her apartment there was no more elegant than the one she had abandoned in Vancouver. Having given up alcohol, she would proudly open the refrigerator door to prove that it contained two bottles of beer — one for Fotheringham and one for me. I drank mine. Her review of Ottawa was flinty: "A cold, grubby little granite town." Marjorie warmed it up.

Her lifestyle caught up to her in 1988, when she was diagnosed with inoperable lung cancer. It barely slowed her down, but the dark rider was on the horizon. The last time I visited, she looked waxen, doing her ironing, slowly, on an old-fashioned ironing board. We laughed a great deal about Ottawa and the shenanigans of its inhabitants. I was worried by how she looked, but needed to get to the next thing. A few days later, when Jack Webster saw her, he took her straight to the hospital.

Trying to persuade Marjorie to get to "that book" had always been central to our conversations. In 1990, she declared herself ready. She persuaded Jane O'Hara to help her. The required royalty advance had escalated, but I was confident it would earn out. *Mark My Words: The Memoirs of a Very Political Reporter* was published two years later, becoming a great bestseller.

But time had run out for Marjorie. She died before the book was published. With a heavy heart, I flew to Calgary to attend her memorial service. Fotheringham gave the eulogy. Emotions ran high.

I choose to believe that books such as the ones we published by Jack Munro, Jack Webster, and Marjorie Nichols made a difference to the political crosswinds that blew across the province. Unfortunately, they seldom made an equivalent impact in Ottawa and Toronto, cities that remain securely comfortable in their belief that they occupy the centre of the Canadian universe.

At the time, British Columbia had neither an illustrated history nor an encyclopedia that did justice to the province's legacy. An encyclopedia would require significant funding, ideally from government, analogous to what the province of Alberta had offered Mel Hurtig of Hurtig Publishers for his audacious *Canadian Encyclopedia*. I knew that Howard "Howie" White of Harbour Publishing had been contemplating something for some years. To Howie's credit, Harbour published its encyclopedia on British Columbia in 2000, at over 800 pages and with 4,000 entries, edited by Daniel Francis. A magnificent piece of publishing, it well deserved both its bestseller status and its ongoing digital life.

Knowing an encyclopedia was underway, we turned our attention to developing *The Illustrated History of British Columbia* in 1998. After much discussion, we settled on Terry Reksten to write the text. She was passionate about the province's history and had a deep knowledge base, the time, and the discipline. The project had a distinguished editorial advisory board, including Tom Berger, Peter C. Newman, Doris Shadbolt, and bookseller Jim Munro. It was a monumental undertaking, doubly challenging as I was in the midst of handling other crises. We made it work.

As usual, fundraising to cover the extraordinary costs fell to me. It was a challenge, ultimately blessed by good fortune and good timing, characteristic of many of our large projects. Initially, Credit Union Central of British Columbia was intrigued, and for a moment we thought it might spring for the entire $200,000 needed. Ultimately, members decided such a number was a stretch, although they wanted to keep their hand in.

I had been pursuing Robert "Bob" Williams for a book, and as he had become chair of ICBC, I felt he might help. We talked, and ICBC was in. BC Hydro was the next logical choice. Its new chair, Brian Smith, had a history degree, and I had met with him a few times during the years D&M Educational was developing its Explorations social studies program. The two of them happened to run into each other in the Helijet terminal, and Bob was clearly persuasive. Hydro was in, although the next management layer down was grumpy, suggesting that the chairman had overstepped his bounds. The chairman prevailed. Soon thereafter, Telus joined the parade, and our target had been reached.

The last piece was finding a way to use the extraordinary visual resources of the BC Archives, which then were being managed, for profit, by a stand-alone division of the BC government. We were going to need hundreds of images, so we needed to blunt the potentially exorbitant rights costs by luring BC Archives into becoming a sponsor. The building momentum, and the stature of the other sponsors, tipped the balance.

The writing and image-gathering took almost two years. The work was going well when, unhappily, Terry became very ill. She would need help finishing the last two chapters. Our editorial director, Saeko Usukawa, who had anchored our department for over 30 years and was a published author in her own right, wrote the final pieces. Saeko's skill with words and images, enhanced by her fierce dedication, justified the faith so many had placed in the project. And it was superbly manufactured in Canada by Friesens.

The book's first printing, 15,000 copies, sold out quickly at an ambitious suggested retail price of $60. Scale, and risk, had once again been rewarded. The book, unlike many popular histories up to then, centred First Nations in the province's history and highlighted the injustices they experienced at the hands of settlers.

—

Hugh Brody's second book with us, *The Other Side of Eden: Hunters, Farmers and the Shaping of the World*, likewise pushed the boundaries of traditional historical accounts of Canada's past.

The book was a long time in gestation, following *Maps and Dreams* by 19 years. It embraced an equally challenging idea. Buttressed by recent scholarship from linguists, anthropologists, and historians, Hugh suggested that stewardship of the land has been more responsibly handled by hunter-gatherer societies than by intrusive agricultural "settler" societies. Hugh was nervous, anticipating critical scholarly reception.

Human possibility shone through the writing. Mary Simon, then Canadian ambassador for circumpolar affairs and now Canada's Governor

General, noticed: "As an Inuk who has been active in many of my people's struggles and victories, I was captivated. Hugh Brody's profound understanding of the importance of language in the shaping, sharing and survival of Indigenous cultures is both moving and motivating."

Hugh needn't have worried. The book was taken by Farrar, Straus and Giroux in the US and by Faber & Faber in the UK, securing space within both the popular and academic worlds. To honour the imminent publication of *The Other Side of Eden*, Hugh brought an extraordinary white burgundy to celebrate. It was his last remaining bottle. Hugh and I were rhapsodic; Corky, not so much.

Hugh and I enjoyed the wine during a long dinner at our home. Savouring a fading summer twilight sitting on our front deck, in an absent-minded moment Corky poured lemonade into our glasses, still half full of the gifted ambrosia. Hugh felt obligated to comment in a personal note to me, "It is the only moment in 33 years of our friendship when time stopped in its tracks by shock, disbelief and a realization that dinner with a publisher might, after all, be susceptible to certain strains . . . And it is of course the greatest possible tribute to all the relationships at that table: only the strongest could have survived such a crisis! . . . My debt to Scott and Corky is beyond reckoning . . . In the years to come, as we sit and reminisce about what great publishing means, we can try again."

—

In these decades, D&M published many groundbreaking books bringing attention to the Indigenous cultures of British Columbia. Two stand out.

In the early 1990s, I read a deeply disturbing personal cri de coeur in the *Vancouver Sun* by Stó:lō leader Ernie Crey. Four generations of his family had been torn apart by residential schools, followed by time in foster homes. With the untimely death of his father, he was summarily arrested by the RCMP, spent a week alone in a jail cell, then was told he was to be shipped off to Brannan Lake Industrial School on Vancouver Island, cut off from his family, friends, and culture. He had been part of the notorious "Sixties Scoop," when provincial social workers were empowered to enforce federal law. Even in outline, his life chronicled an outrageous betrayal of trust.

I wrote to him suggesting that he had important things to tell the country, and if he ever thought about writing a book, D&M would publish it.

When I came to know him, I discovered that Ernie was a gentle man with a warm smile and the laugh of someone who had become comfortable in his own skin. I could not imagine the dark side of his personal journey. Several years later, when he partnered with Vancouver journalist Suzanne Fournier to tell his story, we were offered the book.

In 1997, we published *Stolen from Our Embrace: The Abduction of First Nations Children and the Restoration of Aboriginal Communities*. Based on interviews with survivors of the system, it was a heartbreaking account, one of the first books to reveal the truths of a repugnant system. It concluded on a hopeful note, became an award-winning book, and remains in print to this day. I like to think that it nudged reconciliation along before it became a compelling national issue.

The same might be said of *A Stó:lō–Coast Salish Historical Atlas*, which came to us by accident. In 1993, we had partnered with the Nisga'a Tribal Council to publish a lavish photographic book, *Nisga'a: People of the Nass River*, partly to honour the imminent conclusion of a century of land claims negotiations with BC and Canada. That book was seen as a model for other groups seeking a moment in the sun, which led to a delegation from the Stó:lō nation paying a visit to our offices.

The thought of another photographic book, however skillfully done, held little appeal, but the delegation was so young and enthusiastic that I asked if they had anything else that might be of interest. The very engaging young woman who seemed to be the spokesperson diffidently offered the thought that they "were working on some maps" but didn't think they would be of interest. The few pages of material they had brought were extraordinary. It was obvious that the working group of Stó:lō who were gathering the material and making the maps had assembled a distinguished collection of scholars, authors, and artists, all working under the guidance of a strong editorial board of Elders.

We were in. When the atlas was published in 2001, it was instantly recognized as a distinguished work of scholarship, including much unknown material about the early years of Indigenous and white settlement in the Fraser Valley. Images, detailed maps, and charts including a massive amount of data told us more about the Indigenous and settler heritage of the lower Fraser Valley than had ever previously been gathered in one place. The book's oversized pages, 10.5" x 14.5", made the perfect canvas, allowing the images to breathe. The Honourable Steven Point contributed a foreword.

The implicit message, of course, was that the Stó:lō Nation owned most of Metro Vancouver.

The Stó:lō Nation and the University of Washington Press both took generous co-editions, allowing the first printing to reach 10,000 copies. When the book won that year's Vancouver Book Award, with ironic tongue in cheek I was able to point out that an atlas demonstrating that all the metropolitan area of Vancouver was Salish territory had been honoured by the city that, theoretically at least, had therefore to hand itself over to new governance.

—

It was around this time that Justice Thomas "Tom" Berger walked into my office with a manuscript that I'd almost lost hope of ever seeing. For many years I'd been pestering Tom, a long-time D&M author, to write about his important First Nations legal cases from a more personal perspective. Typical of Tom, he arrived in my office with a finished draft, encased in a thick, three-ring binder, tucked under his arm. No belligerent financial negotiation; no contract in place; just a promise. Another way of doing business, entirely indicative of the man. The book reflected upon his legal career of four decades and focussed upon 12 seminal cases — all important, all groundbreaking.

In 1974, Tom had been appointed commissioner of the Mackenzie Valley Pipeline Inquiry by then-minister of Indian Affairs and Northern Development Jean Chrétien. No one knew what to expect. Nor did anyone fully appreciate his determination to fully engage with "the voices of the frontier." In 1977, when Tom wrote to Warren Allmand, the minister of Indian affairs and northern development, to introduce a critical report, he stated: "We are now at our last Frontier . . . Profound issues, touching our deepest concerns as a nation, await us there."

He spent his time listening, travelling to 35 small communities along the proposed pipeline route, often by dogsled or canoe, patiently drawing out the quiet voices of people unaccustomed to being heard. Trust is not easily won in such communities. Tom's gentle manner earned him more than his share. Some of the people he met claimed him as their own: "The judge will look after us."

The Mackenzie Valley Pipeline Inquiry became the most successful government report in the country's history. It was published under the title *Northern Frontier, Northern Homeland: The Report of the Mackenzie Valley Pipeline Inquiry*, and sales exploded. It sold some 200,000 copies. His uncomfortable core recommendation was that the pipeline be, at the very least, postponed for a generation, and government was compelled to listen. By empowering voices that had been in the shadows too long, he offered hope. This was personal for Tom: "I have put everything I have into this."

I met Tom for the first time in the mid-1980s. His deceptively calm manner was disarming to me, as it was to so many of his adversaries. For someone once feared as a "Young Turk," his round face, warm eyes, modulated voice, and understated manner defused expectations. There was no demonstrative ego, never any bombast. But his clarity of voice and focus could, and did, win in court.

Tom was born in Victoria in 1933, the son of a Swedish-Canadian RCMP officer and the grandson of a police judge and a baroness living in Gothenburg, Sweden. Tom's father understood courage. Newly arrived in Canada during the early years of World War II, a defining scar was witnessing the internment of Japanese Canadians, without cause or due process, their property unilaterally confiscated without recompense. Many were Canadian citizens. He passed that memory on to his son. It established Tom's defining credo: "the overriding impulse . . . to be of service; to help the people who believe they need my help."

He also inherited an innate stubbornness. On more than one occasion, he put serving the law, and confronting power, ahead of his career. He spent time as a federal NDP MP, followed by a term as leader of the party in British Columbia, stepping down when the NDP was unexpectedly defeated by the wily tactics of W.A.C. Bennett.

He accepted an appointment to the Supreme Court of British Columbia in 1971, where he served for a decade. He publicly opposed Prime Minister Pierre Trudeau, insisting that the rights of Indigenous Canadians and women be included in Trudeau's proposed Charter of Rights and Freedoms. Rebuked by the Canadian Judicial Council for his publicly expressed opposition, he resigned on principle and returned to private practice.

When his spirited Irish law partner, Tom Hurley, died in 1961, Hurley's equally strong-willed widow, Maisie, offered an opinion: "Now, Tommy, you will have to defend the Indians." "Defending the Indians" became the cornerstone of Tom's legal practice.

Tom's first book, *Fragile Freedoms: Human Rights and Dissent in Canada*, had been published by a Toronto publisher. I hoped to lure him to the D&M list. One result was that in 1988 we were able to publish a newly revised edition of his Mackenzie Valley inquiry, *Northern Frontier, Northern Homeland*.

We fell into the habit of getting together for an occasional lunch in a French bistro not far from the Bergers' new home in Kitsilano Point. After assessing the state of the world, and his wise take on the country's archaic legal structure, stories would flow.

I was soon pressing him to pursue the book that I intuited he had long wanted to write. With regular prodding, in 1991 we were able to publish the result, *A Long and Terrible Shadow: White Values, Native Rights in the Americas, 1492–1992*. My persistence had matched his. "My other books about Native people and Native rights were the product of inquiries into specific issues. My object was to enable Native people to speak for themselves. This book is my opportunity to speak for myself."

In Tom's own voice, it was a powerful account of trust betrayed and genocide in action. It opened with an account of the doomed efforts of a 15th-century Dominican priest, Las Casas, to push back against the wanton destruction of the Indigenous peoples Europeans had encountered in the "New World."

The work of Las Casas triggered an unsettling debate amongst Spanish royalty in Valladolid in 1550, echoing the ethical issues Tom encountered during his travels in the Canadian North. Since being first raised by the Spanish priest, they had hardly evolved over the intervening centuries.

Tom's cases increasingly set legal precedent. Two of the most notable were what is now known as the Sparrow case and the court battle that established the legal groundwork for the Nisga'a Treaty.

The Sparrow case tested the legal limits of the time. Two Indigenous hunters had been arrested for hunting out of season. But it was not quite that simple. Perhaps they had historical rights. With diligent research in the bowels of the BC Archives, Tom's team dug up "conveyances" covering the "understandings" between the First Nations of southern Vancouver Island and the Hudson's Bay Company, then theoretical owners of all the land west of Hudson Bay.

In simple language and barely legible handwriting, the chief factor of the company, James Douglas, soon to become governor of the BC Crown colony, had papered informal arrangements in what are now known as the "Douglas Treaties." Amongst their seemingly innocent precedents, they had granted fishing and hunting rights to the Indigenous occupiers of the land "in perpetuity." The apparent abrogation of white procedure was the reason the case had first come before the courts. Conventional assumptions had been challenged. Berger's win in court changed the narrative.

Tom's more important victory was laying the foundations for the eventual Nisga'a Treaty, which settled a century-long debate with the Crown (the Government of Canada) over unceded territory in northern British Columbia. Its grinding and difficult passage through the Supreme Court laid the groundwork for the Nisga'a settlement, which eventually provided a measure of justice after a century of promises. Initially, it was a loss in the Supreme Court, but the legal principle of Aboriginal title as valid in Canadian law had been upheld. Legal floodgates had been pushed open, and a critical precedent had been established. The Nisga'a had prevailed.

Another of Tom's books published by D&M, *One Man's Justice: A Life in the Law*, ends with a biblical proverb: "The path of the just is as a shining light, that shineth more and more unto the perfect day."

—

Douglas & McIntyre was in the right place at the right time. We were able to play a small role in the revival of cultures once discriminated against. To echo Claude Lévi-Strauss, a cultural heritage that "was so close to dying . . . made its entry upon the great stage of the world."

Michael Audain, while engaging the deep spirituality of many pre-contact Indigenous masks, once told me that to understand the art, he had to read Douglas & McIntyre books. He recently added, "The books you bravely published about the history of our beloved province and those who created it, played a crucial role in my love of British Columbia art." These are huge compliments, coming as they do from one of Canada's most accomplished and generous cultural patrons.

This was a matter of personal conviction for me. The fact that all these books travelled internationally, carrying an important message that was then ahead of its time, was doubly satisfying.

11

A VISUAL WORLD

Although art books are considered a risky category of publishing, they separated Douglas & McIntyre from most other Canadian houses and remained a linchpin. Through trial and error, we learned that gallery relationships and corporate partnerships brought us projects of scale, some of them accompanied by healthy guaranteed purchases that solved any perceived risk. These purchases allowed us to successfully publish monographs on many of the country's leading contemporary artists.

Art books bring their own cocktail of high emotion, perfectionist artists and curators, and a requirement for very high printing standards. Commercial constraints, certainly those of any publisher, are often pushed aside. But when things go right, as they most often did for us, remarkable books can result.

In the late 1980s, Doris Shadbolt and I met to discuss our next Emily Carr project. Preoccupied by our conversation, we failed to notice that her husband, Jack, had slipped back into his studio. While we talked, Jack painted. An hour or so later, he offered the finished work at a generous price. He had conjured up a vibrant butterfly, one of his signature images, turning the half-finished work on his easel into an accomplished painting. Corky and I happily accepted it.

The combination of Jack's reputation as an important artist and his long-standing contributions to Canada's cultural community suggested to me that it was time for a book of appropriate scale about Jack himself.

The Shadbolts contributed hugely to the vibrancy of Vancouver's cultural fabric. They embraced the reality of the Vancouver of the time and worked to enliven it. As the city lacked any vibrant urban core, gatherings in people's homes anchored social cohesion. This was the case for an unruly assemblage of artists and architects, friends all, who developed their own cultural scene. It included Jack and Doris Shadbolt; Jessie and Bert Binning; George and Inge Woodcock; Gordon and Marion Smith; Lawren and Bess Harris; Arthur Erickson; Cornelia and Peter Oberlander; Abraham Rogatnick and Alvin Balkind; plus an assortment of others as visitors came and went, often lured by the community's surprising international reach.

The Shadbolts' parties were legendary: full of music, animated conversation, and, occasionally, wayward guests from afar. One night, Igor Stravinsky was found passed out under someone's kitchen table. Creating community as well as art was always the implicit intent. Vancouver was a tough date then. In Alvin Balkind's sardonic words: "Instead of buying a painting, in this town you put in a window."

When we got to work on the Jack Shadbolt book, we had a simple imperative: to create an art book without compromise, an artifact worthy of Abrams, then considered the finest art book publisher on the continent. Hemlock Printers was again onside. Jack proved a sympathetic collaborator.

We commissioned a leading art critic to write the text, but the process dragged on well past the agreed deadline. When we were finally offered a first draft, we judged it unpublishable. We had no choice but to reject it.

We next approached Scott Watson, then curator of the Morris and Helen Belkin Art Gallery at UBC. He turned out to be a perfect choice. Scott's critical text sensitively probed the inner psychological turmoil underlying so much of Jack's work. His text stripped Jack's soul bare, so successfully that Jack acknowledged he had learned new things about himself when reading it. It takes real authorial skill, and guts, for a critic to write with such perception about a living contemporary.

Jack Shadbolt was published in 1990 as an outsized hardcover, printed on the highest-quality art paper, with two gatefolds doing justice to Jack's multi-panel large works, French flaps for the dust jacket, and an astutely curated selection of his best images. Jack and Scott, working together, chose wisely from Jack's huge archive.

We printed 5,000 copies at an initial retail price of $85, another risky gesture. The book sold about 1,500 copies its first season, which I found greatly disappointing. When I complained to my colleagues at Thames & Hudson about such a meagre initial sale, the response was simply that I was crazy. No European single-artist monograph (beyond perhaps Picasso or Matisse) could have sold so well at that time. We didn't fully appreciate the new ground we were breaking.

As part of a plan to soften the financial risk of undertaking such publishing without institutional support, we created a signed limited edition of the book, with an original Shadbolt watercolour as a tipped-in frontispiece. Leather-bound in a slipcase, with an appropriately signed and numbered colophon page, it sold for $475, and we eventually shipped the entire edition of 146 copies. The Vancouver Art Gallery let us use their mailing list gratis, and an elegant promotional brochure was printed by Hemlock as a further gift.

Jack had volunteered to hand-paint the tipped-in watercolour that would grace the front of each book, theoretically justifying its value. Only later did he sheepishly confess that, when applying watercolour paints to the printed drawings we had supplied, the paper had rippled. He spent a weekend ironing each image flat with a steam iron, in his kitchen. That is goodwill and dedication of a high order.

All copies of both editions sold out. It took almost 20 years for the trade edition to work through its first printing, but it remained an active backlist title during all that time. We had honoured Jack's bold, sometimes abrasive, always perceptive career.

Limited editions were often created as add-ons to help underwrite the absurdities of publishing high-end art books for the Canadian market. We had first tested the waters in 1981, when I suggested an extravagant limited edition for *The Art of Emily Carr*. Doris acceded to our hope, with great reluctance. She personally loathed what she considered artificial aberrations pandering to a commercial market. She later softened her view, suggesting that if it would help us diminish the financial risk we were taking, she would "hold her nose" and accept the folly.

The limited edition of *The Art of Emily Carr* was over the top. It sat in a handcrafted cedar box with a faux-argillite medallion of Emily Carr embedded on its front (the medallion was created by a Vancouver artist working in a Granville Island studio who did work for the British Museum). An elegant portfolio of continuous tone reproductions of six Carr charcoal images sat atop a fully repackaged trade edition, with all the colour plates tipped in on outsized pages. We sold out of 250 copies at the elevated price of $900 apiece. Copies have held their value, appearing from time to time on auction sites, with an asking price still approaching $2,000.

—

Beginning in 1991, when the Vancouver Art Gallery initiated a project, we became the publisher of choice. First, with Doris Shadbolt then extending through subsequent directors Willard Holmes, Luke Rombout, and eventually Kathleen Bartels and Daina Augaitis, we established preferential relationships. Sharing a deep commitment to the art of British Columbia, we jointly created 23 art books. Our relationship allowed us to create ambitious books based upon the lives and work of BC's iconic artists, amongst them Gordon Smith, E.J. Hughes, and Fred Herzog.

There were always financial issues to work through, and it took several years to overcome inherent skepticism amongst directors and curators about any publisher not based in Toronto or New York. A number of pieces needed to fall into place, including printing and distribution.

Starting in 1976 with Ulli Steltzer's *Indian Artists at Work*, we'd built a working relationship with printers based in Hong Kong. Asian manufacture then cost about one-third of the cost in North America.

Over many years, we built a strong working relationship with C&C Offset in Hong Kong. The chairman, Charlie Lo (in Cantonese Lo Chi-Hong), who had led the company's expansion into the English-speaking world, became a friend. We had invited him to Vancouver for an event, and I spent one Saturday morning helping him unpack boxes of books for Sino United Publishing, his company's new Vancouver bookstore. Such personal gestures are seldom forgotten.

For several years, at Charlie's invitation, we had been requesting production quotes from his printing company in Shenzhen, not far from Hong Kong. But they would badly miss the mark. When I complained, he quietly said: "Send those requests to me." Dramatically preferential pricing resulted, with generously extended payment terms. That company's service and quality became impeccable. We felt guilty choosing C&C over Friesens, but as business pressures mounted, pragmatism was necessary.

Over time, however, nationalism tempered our choices, and with supportive Canadian manufacturers, notably Friesens in Manitoba and Hemlock in Vancouver, we tried to print as much of the program domestically as possible. Granting bodies nudged us in that direction.

The final piece of the puzzle was winning international distribution through Prestel Publishing, an art book house of distinction headquartered in Munich, with offices in London and New York and sales representation around the world. The English-language operation was run by an old friend of mine from my Thames & Hudson days, Andrew Hansen. We had reconnected while ducking the rain waiting in line for a party in Frankfurt. Discussions unfolded from there, and while negotiating the arrangement took some years, the contract was finalized in 2010. Dangling the arrangement in front of curators and gallery directors was far more effective than any actual sales results. In the art world, cachet matters.

When VAG's senior curator, Ian Thom, began work on a major Gordon Smith retrospective, we were commissioned to publish the accompanying book, *Gordon Smith: The Act of Painting*. English-born, Gordon had immigrated with his family to Winnipeg in 1933. Between 1935 and 1939, he studied art there, settling in Vancouver following the end of WW II, where he had been badly wounded fighting during the invasion of Sicily. For the next 75 years, he was a much-loved fixture in Vancouver's cultural scene as an educator, collaborator, and, above all, painter. Gordon spent time in the studio adjacent to his idyllic West Vancouver house every day. His images became increasingly intricate and accomplished, eloquent love letters to the landscape that surrounded him.

A sweet, unfailingly generous man, as well as an artist of stature, Gordon always made time to give back. Mentoring several generations of young students, he left an enduring mark on the community. While he was shy in crowds, his innate kindness became part of Vancouver's social fabric. The book was an overdue homage to a lifetime of contribution.

To help ensure that the necessary money was raised, Michael Audain was brought on board. As chair, Michael had built his Vancouver real estate development company, Polygon, into an important anchor of the city's development scene. He had followed his personal passion to become an influential collector of the art of British Columbia, including the province's extraordinary Indigenous art. Sitting at the distant end of a long table during an initial fundraising meeting, he seemed an intimidating presence. It was the first time I had met him. It was not to be the last. Michael's generosity, personal and corporate, became a cornerstone beacon of hope in a town not famous for its commitments to the arts.

In 2002, Ian Thom told me he was in the midst of pulling together a major E.J. Hughes retrospective. We would receive an accomplished critical text, plus fresh photography for over 100 of Hughes's images spanning the breadth of his career.

Hughes, a BC artist of refined vision, had an unerring eye for the seascape and landscape of the province. Born and raised in BC, he stayed home and lived a quiet life in the small town of Duncan in the Cowichan Valley.

I had previously pursued him for a book, without success. He had a close friendship with Patricia Salmon, his trusted assistant, who was also at work on a Hughes biography. After seeking Doris Shadbolt's opinion, I turned her manuscript down. The door was firmly shut.

But Hughes's images were so compelling, such perfect expressions of the province's maritime inheritance, I could not excise them from my imagination. I was determined that, somehow, we would find some way to honour his work. Better still, a group of patrons was willing to provide the necessary financial backing. This one had angels on its side. Collectors, notably Jacques Barbeau and Stephen Jarislowsky, stepped up, as did Dick Kouwenhoven of Hemlock Printers in Vancouver, ensuring that a book of exceptional quality could be manufactured in BC. Everyone involved put their hearts into it.

E.J. Hughes ranks amongst our most accomplished art books, with superior editorial, design, and manufacturing standards. Happily, market success matched the expectation. We sold several thousand copies, at the stiff retail price of $75 a copy.

—

In 2007, when the Vancouver Art Gallery organized a major show of Fred Herzog's work, we published the catalogue. It became a local bestseller, quickly exhausting several printings. That led to Andy Sylvester of the Equinox Gallery deciding to represent Herzog around the world.

With new opportunities provided by digital scanning, Herzog's thousands of boxes of Kodachrome transparencies were given a new life. The world noticed, and Herzog is now widely recognized as one of the pioneer urban photographers working in colour in the 1950s and 1960s. Once, while guiding me through his one-man show of photographic prints in the Equinox Gallery, Fred gripped my elbow and exclaimed, "Look at those reds. They're bright again!"

I first encountered Fred when we licensed reproduction rights to 30 of his images for *The City of Vancouver* book in 1976. We chose a selection of his informal photography reflecting the less polished side of the city. We did discuss a more ambitious book project, but neither of us was ready.

Born in Germany, Fred had arrived in Vancouver in 1953, armed only with a dated camera, a strong work ethic, and a residue of irascible determination. Scrambling to make a living, he joined a maintenance crew on one of the CPR steamers then serving the coast.

In 1957, he became a medical photographer at St. Paul's Hospital. Fred spent spare moments wandering the city, recording what he found along the downtown streets of what remained an overgrown lumber town. He was an engaged amateur, wanting to "take pictures" while adjusting to life in the unsophisticated town he had discovered. He had no money, so shot his thousands of images in Kodachrome. He couldn't afford the processing costs of ordering prints from Kodak. His images languished on film.

"I loved the city for its grittiness. I was not a journalist. I did not have a chance to become that." He just took pictures.

He chose to work in colour, then not in fashion for serious photographers. On his first roll of colour film, he photographed the original CPR Pier B, swathed in a hazy fog. The Marine Building hovers in the background, ghostly in a thin fall sunshine. In the foreground are the rhythmic ochre freight sheds of the old pier. It was the building where my father spent his working life. That light evokes the deepest memories of visits I made in childhood. A print of that photo now sits on a wall in our bedroom.

His 1958 image "Black Man, Pender" showed a father and his daughter, with the family dog on a leash, walking briskly toward the camera. The father is in a pinstriped suit, his daughter in a stylish powder-blue coat set off by white socks and black patent leather shoes. Pride bursts out of the image. What had been renewed was a vibrant patch of red-orange in the immediate background. It made the picture pop while enshrining a moment in time, perfectly captured.

In 2011, I finally commissioned a large book of his work, *Fred Herzog Photographs*, with essays from Claudia Gochmann, Sarah Milroy, Jeff Wall, and Douglas Coupland. It turned into another bestseller, racing through 15,000 copies. Herzog's photographs, revealing his distinctive spirit and unpretentious eye, became a huge influence on what is now known, to their dismay, as the Vancouver School — Jeff Wall, Ian Wallace, Stan Douglas, Roy Arden, Ken Lum, Rodney Graham, and Vikky Alexander.

International publishers understood. Two monographs were published by the German art book publisher Hatje Cantz. His work is now sought out by curators around the world. Fred had emerged from the shadows. Bemused by the belated attention, he retained his "endearing skepticism," in the words of Sarah Milroy, until he passed in September 2019.

—

Emerging as Canada's leading publisher of art books, we spread our wings across the country. Other Canadian publishers were forging similar partnerships, but our program was the largest, and the strongest. The international partners we could bring to important projects were often a critical factor.

The commercial template for such relationships was straightforward. I had "borrowed" the concept from colleagues Paul Gottlieb at Abrams and Eva and Thomas Neurath at Thames & Hudson. When the books were also catalogues for important shows, the sponsoring institutions undertook the necessary research, commissioned text (usually from their own curators), assembled and photographed the art, cleared all necessary copyrights, then purchased an agreed number of copies at a preferential discount for their own use.

It was a win all around. D&M provided professional editorial, design, and production advice and negotiated preferential printing costs. The gallery avoided the complexity of coping with the finicky process of shaping intricate projects. Working with an experienced publishing house expanded market reach and media impact for the accompanying show. Royalties from North American and international sales generated ongoing revenue. The risk of the gallery overprinting, leaving cartons of unsaleable books in its basement, was greatly diminished. As a bonus, government and private-sector funders welcomed such partnerships.

One of these early projects was *Our Boots: An Inuit Women's Art*, by Jill Oakes and Rick Riewe of the University of Manitoba. The research and writing were underwritten by Sonja Bata. Sonja was quintessentially Swiss, sharp-witted, respectful of intelligence, well travelled, and energetic. She was passionate about three things: her family's business, the high arts, and her museum, Toronto's Bata Shoe Museum.

She and her Czech husband, Thomas, had moved to Toronto in 1946, determined to rebuild the family shoe manufacturing business, which had suffered greatly during WW II; after the war, Communist governments in Eastern Europe had nationalized all the company's remaining assets. The Batas quickly embraced their new country. The international Bata Shoe headquarters was re-established in Canada, and the company was rebuilt, literally from the ground up.

Sonja had trained as an architect, combining a shrewd eye for business with a perceptive eye for good design. Their new Canadian headquarters was evidence. She was generous about supporting young scholars and had become enraptured by the skills of Canada's Inuit at making warm clothing and footwear out of animal skins.

The museum housed a masterfully curated collection: 14,500 shoes from around the world, historical and contemporary, famous and quirky. Queen Victoria's ballroom slippers, Robert Redford's cowboy boots, Terry Fox's running shoe, Elton John's monogrammed silver platform boots. Sonia's collection of Inuit footwear from across Canada's Arctic regions was superb.

From my first meeting with Sonja it was clear, to me at least, that we could work well together. I doubt she suffered fools gladly, but I was engaged by her determined energy. She wanted to ensure that a large book extolling Inuit survival skills was well published. That was our challenge.

Following our first meeting, which included a visit to the basement of the museum to pull rare treasures out of their careful cocoons, we soon agreed to do the book. We would need a subsidy, of course. Because travelling to meet was unrealistic, my financial request had to be made by cell phone. Sonja was driving up the Don Valley Parkway when I mentioned the number, and I feared for a moment she was going to drive off the road. She accepted.

Robert Keziere was commissioned to undertake the critical photography of the boots. His images empowered them, in an eerily anthropomorphic way, as living and breathing evidence of a thriving culture.

We felt the book was worthy of international co-editions. At that time, I was courting Paul Gottlieb, publisher of Abrams, hoping to win his Canadian distribution. That led me to his New York office, carrying our elegant dummy of *Our Boots*.

Visiting Paul's office meant enduring a certain amount of theatre, as minions came and went seeking approvals for cover designs and other issues requiring his attention. I don't think his desk was actually elevated on a dais, but it seemed to be. When the room cleared, I showed the polished dummy, and he committed on the spot to 4,000 copies. That was still the way things were done in the 1990s.

We lost winning Canadian distribution for Abrams to the Manda Group. As the VP of marketing told me when delivering the news, "Those guys could sell *anything*, even pots and pans, and you're a *publisher*."

Our Boots, published in 1995, became a great success. Abrams confirmed its quantity for the US; Frederking & Thaler took a German-language edition; Thames & Hudson took it for the UK; and we enjoyed a first printing of some 15,000 copies. For a book about *boots*!

My relationship with Sonja and Thomas strengthened, and my visits to Sonja's "shoebox" of a museum, an exquisite small building on Bloor designed by Raymond Moriyama, became frequent. On one occasion, we were to meet in the York Club. I wanted to talk to Thomas about his time in the "Hasty P's," the Hastings and Prince Edward Regiment, of which Thomas was honorary colonel. He was taken aback that I knew anything about the regiment, until I admitted that I had read Farley Mowat's regimental history. I wasn't wearing a tie, so we were relegated to an informal back room. Yet another establishment club had felt compelled to turf me.

When Asia-Pacific Economic Cooperation (APEC) was meeting in Vancouver in 1997, we invited the Batas to our house, wanting to welcome them to our city. Unfortunately, the security cordon around the Bayshore hotel, where the delegates were staying, was so strict that they couldn't escape the compound.

Corky and Scott McIntyre (SMc) in Club Vagabond, Leysin, Switzerland, Christmas 1969. Toronto behind us, this was our last stop before going home to Vancouver.

J.J. Douglas Ltd. staff, 1977. From left to right: (top row) SMc, Jim Douglas, Caroline Schroeder, Don Sacks, (bottom row) Heather Douglas, Marilyn Sacks, and Catherine Kerr.

SMc with D&M's editorial director, Saeko Usukawa, mid-1980s. Her authors named her the "Great One."

D&M all-staff retreat, Grouse Mountain, 1994. Top row, centre: Patsy Aldana (in an orange coat), Rob Sanders (on Patsy's left), and Susan McIntosh (on Rob's left), three senior executives in D&M. Patsy, a director, had founded and continued to run our children's affiliate, Groundwood Books; Rob, publisher of Greystone, a division of D&M; and Susan McIntosh, national director of sales and marketing.

SMc, American publisher Tom Woll, and Jon Beckmann, the director of Sierra Club Books, in Paris on the way to Frankfurt, 1979.

SMc with Peter Mayer, then CEO of Penguin Books, on publisher David Godine's island off the coast of Maine, July 1990.

Greg Gatenby (founding artistic director of Toronto's International Festival of Authors), SMc, Margaret Atwood (famous as an author by then), and William "Bill" French (book editor of the *Globe and Mail*) celebrating Bill's retirement at Centro, Toronto, April 3, 1991.

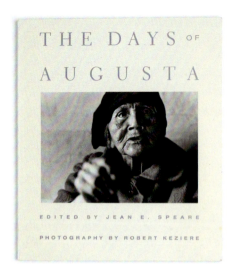

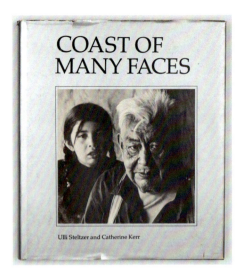

The Days of Augusta (edited by Jean Speare, photography by Robert Keziere, 1973). The *Smithsonian Magazine* commented, "This little book achieves the stature of a contemporary classic of oral literature."

Coast of Many Faces (Ulli Steltzer and Catherine Kerr, 1979). Steltzer at her best. Portraits and memories from people living in small port towns along the full extent of the British Columbia coast.

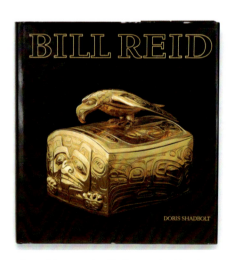

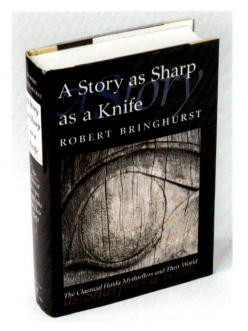

Bill Reid (Doris Shadbolt, 1986). Claude Lévi-Strauss: "Thanks to [Bill Reid] the art [of the Northwest Coast] makes its entry upon the great stage of the world; it begins to converse with the whole of mankind."

A Story as Sharp as a Knife: The Classical Haida Mythtellers and Their World (Robert Bringhurst, 1999). Bringhurst's masterwork is one of the most important books I ever published. Margaret Atwood called it "one of those works that rearranges the inside of your head."

Photographer Ulli Steltzer and SMc at the installation ceremony for Bill Reid's sculpture, *The Black Canoe*, in front of Arthur Erickson's new Canadian embassy in Washington, DC, November 19, 1991.

Doris Shadbolt and SMc at a show in the Bau-Xi Gallery in Vancouver, 2001. Doris became a close friend. Her wisdom was a cornerstone of our art-book program.

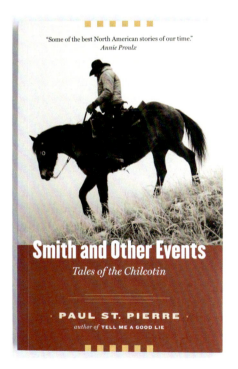

Smith and Other Events: Tales of the Chilcotin (Paul St. Pierre, 1995, under licence from Doubleday). St. Pierre: "If there is a moral in this book, it is not my fault."

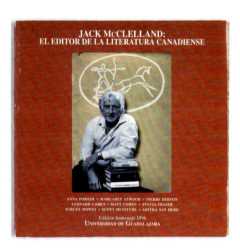

The "Homage Edition, 1996" cover of *Jack McClelland: The Publisher of Canadian Literature,* published by the University of Guadalajara as part of that year's Guadalajara International Book Fair program.

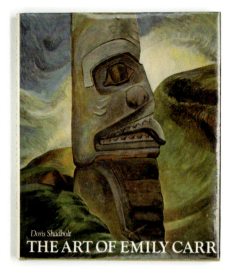

The Art of Emily Carr (Doris Shadbolt, 1979) was the company's first major art book. Its first printing, 30,000 copies, sold out by Christmas that year.

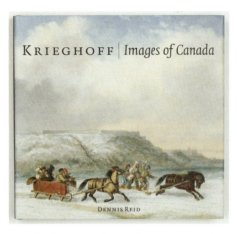

Kreighoff: Images of Canada (Dennis Reid, in association with the Art Gallery of Ontario, 1999). Chapters wanted to buy the entire first printing of 25,000 copies. We said no.

Fred Herzog: Vancouver Photographs (Grant Arnold and Michael Turner, in association with the Vancouver Art Gallery, 2007). The beginning of Herzog's recognition as one of the great urban photographers of the 20th century.

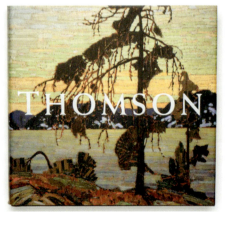

Tom Thomson (edited by Dennis Reid, in association with the Art Gallery of Ontario and the National Gallery of Canada, 2002). An example of our flourishing partnerships with major national cultural institutions.

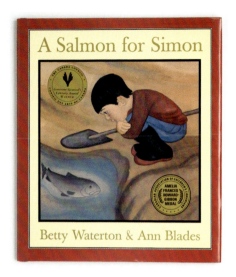

A Salmon for Simon (Betty Waterton, illustrated by Ann Blades, 1978). This was the company's bestselling children's book and an international success.

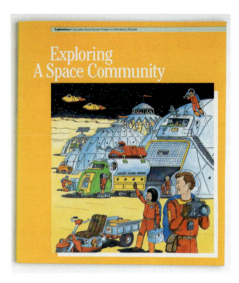

Exploring a Space Community (Hugh Gordon/Scott McIntyre, 1983). This Grade 2 textbook was a part of Explorations, D&M Educational's social studies program. It sold 100,000 copies nationally.

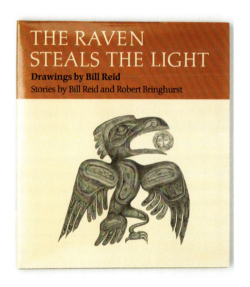

The Raven Steals the Light (Bill Reid and Robert Bringhurst, 1994). In Bill's sardonic words, "a good selection of bestiality, adultery, violence, thievery and assault, for those who like that sort of thing."

Red: A Haida Manga (Michael Nicoll Yahgulanaas, 2009). Initially, I turned the book down but had the wit to re-approach Michael and apologize. He forgave me.

SMc and Anna Porter at the Giller Prize, 2007. Anna and I have been competitors, friends, and co-conspirators for over 50 years.

SMc, Corky, and painter Gordon Smith in his West Vancouver studio, February 2016. Gordon was so generous that any visit resulted in a "gift." Our house is full of such gifts, including a superb painting from his pond series.

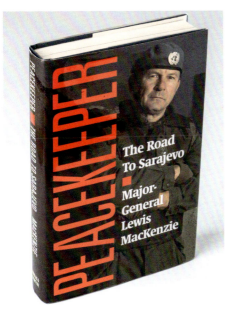

Peacekeeper: Road to Sarajevo (Major-General Lewis MacKenzie, 1993). When I took a rough of the cover design to him for approval, his wife found us on the floor of his garage poking around in one of his Formula Fords.

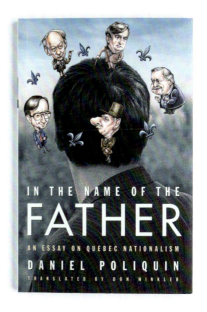

In the Name of the Father: An Essay on Quebec Nationalism (Daniel Poliquin, translated by Don Winkler, 2001). It was originally published in French by Les Éditions du Boréal in 2000.

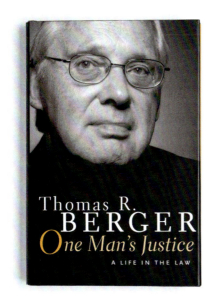

One Man's Justice: A Life in the Law (Thomas R. Berger, 2002). Tom's summation of why Canada must reconcile with its Indigenous peoples: "It is our destiny."

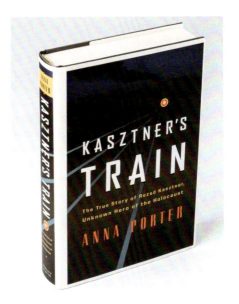

Kasztner's Train: The True Story of Rezso Kasztner, Unknown Hero of the Holocaust (Anna Porter, 2007). Anna's first important book for D&M. Thomas Keneally said, "It will become a classic of the times it deals with."

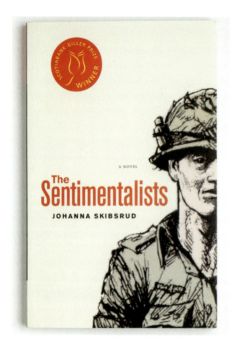

The Sentimentalists (Johanna Skibsrud, 2009, under licence from Gaspereau Press). This Giller Prize winner sold 130,000 copies.

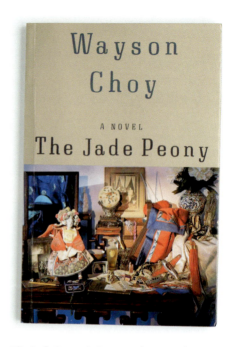

The Jade Peony (Wayson Choy, 1995). The most successful novel in the company's history, a vivid reminiscence of three children from an immigrant family.

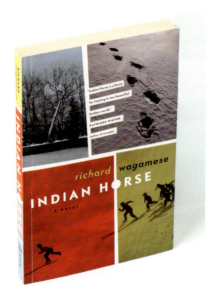

Indian Horse (Richard Wagamese, 2012). A kindness I offered some years before led the author to us, and this book became the second most successful novel in the company's history.

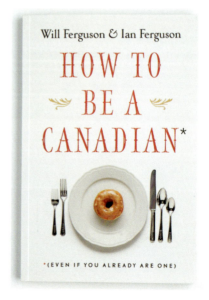

*How to Be a Canadian *(Even If You Already Are One)*. Will Ferguson and Ian Ferguson's 2001 book was a huge bestseller, with sales now approaching 250,000 copies. Margaret Atwood first suggested the idea to Will.

Canada was the first country to ratify the UNESCO Convention on the Protection and Promotion of the Diversity of Cultural Expressions, Montreal, November 23, 2005. From left to right: SMc, co-chair, Coalition for Cultural Diversity; Liza Frulla, minister of Canadian heritage; Line Beauchamp, Quebec minister of culture and communications; Pierre Curzi, co-chair, Coalition for Cultural Diversity; Prime Minister Paul Martin.

Elizabeth McClelland, SMc, and Elizabeth's daughter, Anne McClelland, at the Giller Prize award ceremony on November 6, 2007. Jack McClelland kicked Canadian publishing into high gear. My parting words: "I wouldn't have missed McClelland & Stewart for the world."

SMc (right) visiting author Farley Mowat (left) and his wife, Claire (right), at their home in Port Hope, February 12, 2014. My relationship with Farley mirrored the arc of my career.

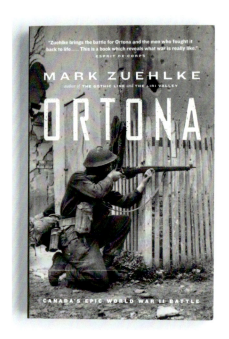

Ortona: Canada's Epic World War II Battle (Mark Zuehlke, 2003). The first book of Zuehlke's "Battles" series, now more than 13 books, is the essential record of Canada's distinguished military record during WW II.

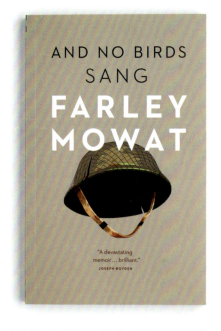

And No Birds Sang (Farley Mowat, 2012). A reprint of one of his 13 backlist titles we committed to re-issue. The book that inspired my conviction to launch a strand of the D&M program honouring Canada's military history.

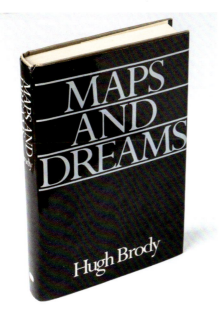
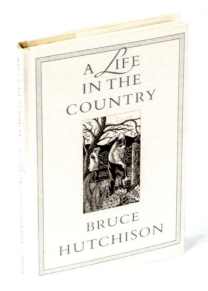

Maps and Dreams (Hugh Brody, 1981). A groundbreaking introduction to Indigenous approaches to life: how two ways of living, and two ways of thinking about maps, collide. Paul Theroux called it "superb anthropology."

A Life in the Country (Bruce Hutchison, 1988). The gentle side of Hutchison, one of the great journalists of his time.

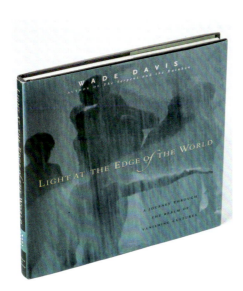
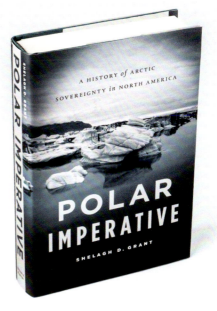

Light at the Edge of the World: A Journey Through the Realm of Vanishing Cultures (Wade Davis, 2001). National Geographic and Bloomsbury UK took substantial co-editions, allowing a first printing of 20,000 copies. It has since been translated into Basque, Macedonian, Serbian, and Malay.

Polar Imperative: A History of Arctic Sovereignty in North America (Shelagh D. Grant, 2010) was awarded the Lionel Gelber Prize for the world's best non-fiction book on global affairs.

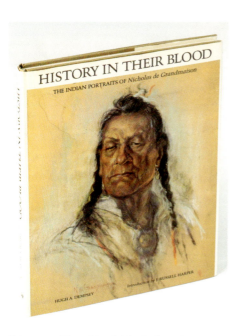

History in Their Blood: The Indian Portraits of Nicholas de Grandmaison (Hugh Dempsey, 1982). The only time in my career when a handshake put $700,000 at risk.

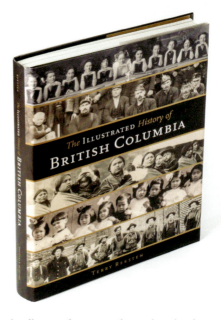

The Illustrated History of British Columbia (Terry Reksten, 2001). The first illustrated history to truly capture the province's legacy.

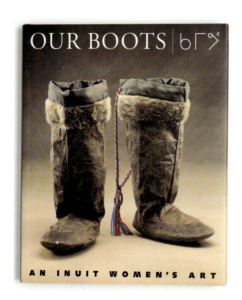

Our Boots: An Inuit Woman's Art (Jill Oakes and Rick Riewe, in association with the Bata Shoe Museum, 1995). My first encounter with Sonja Bata. Abrams and Thames & Hudson co-editions pushed us to a first printing of 15,000 copies, for a book about *boots*!

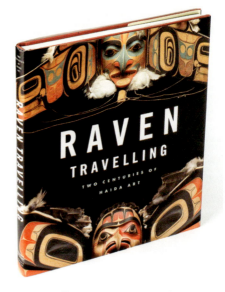

Raven Travelling: Two Centuries of Haida Art (2006). One of D&M's many collaborations with the Vancouver Art Gallery. Finally, the achievements of Haida art were being recognized as art, not anthropology.

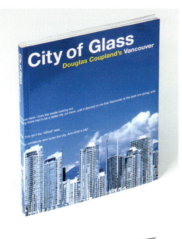
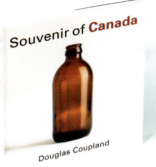

LEFT: Author Doug Coupland's bestsellers: *City of Glass* (2000) and *Souvenir of Canada* (2002). RIGHT: Coupland at the McIntyres' for dinner, April 28, 2017, with Gathie Falk's painting on the wall behind him.

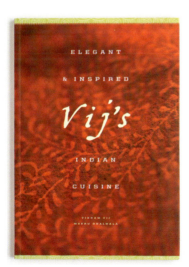
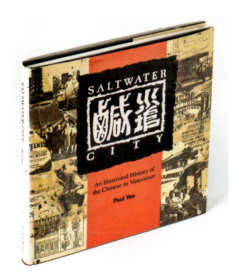

Vij's: Elegant and Inspired Indian Cuisine (2006). Chef Vikram Vij's cookbook sold 45,000 in its first season and won a Cordon d'Or Gold Ribbon.

Saltwater City: An Illustrated History of the Chinese in Vancouver (Paul Yee, 1988). An early declaration of our commitment to Vancouver's Asian inheritance.

SMc in front of stacks of D&M books at his retirement party, Equinox Gallery, February 27, 2013.

SMc speaking after being "blanketed" by the Squamish Nation during his retirement party. In the Indigenous world, being blanketed is a high honour.

Sometimes, the Canadian book market failed to share my enthusiasm. In the early 1990s, Thames & Hudson announced that it would publish two posthumous Roloff Beny books. The books — *Visual Journeys* and *People: Legends in Life and Art* — would appear a year apart, in 1994 and 1995, and both anthologies would be shaped out of the Beny archive. A Canadian partner was deemed essential, and two companies were considered: D&M and Key Porter.

Up against Anna Porter, my competitive ego came into play but so, too, did my early enthusiasm for Beny's extravagant tomes. Roloff's *A Time of Gods*, printed in lustrous gravure, had been published in 1962. In the middle of my Vancouver project with Bob Flick, it stuck in my imagination with its extraordinary combination of the velvety, deep-black images gravure printing allows, thick art paper, and the light of Greece. Beny's books were over the top, but before his later books became increasingly indulgent, they epitomized a newly flourishing postwar art-book world.

When *Persia, Bridge of Turquoise*, the first of two sumptuous Beny books lauding Iran, appeared in 1975, it was published simultaneously in seven foreign co-editions, with a total first printing of 75,000 copies. It was a true international co-production: It was led by M&S, typeset in Toronto, and printed and bound in Italy, with a print run shared by publishers in each country. Beny had reached the pinnacle of the postwar golden age of international art-book partnerships. Lorraine Monk, head of the stills division of the National Film Board, and queen of that world, weighed in: "[Beny] made the whole western world begin to see photography as an important art form. He made everyone, even royalty, feel it was a privilege and an honour to possess photographic books."

When it came to *Visual Journeys* and *People: Legends in Life and Art*, the critical question was, Who would offer to buy the most copies for Canada: D&M or Key Porter? Logic flew out the window. Knowing better, I committed to far too many copies of each.

Sales were extremely disappointing, leaving skids of leftover books in our warehouse. Jack McClelland came to the rescue as chair of the Roloff

Beny Foundation. Asking what might be done with so many books, and wanting to avoid seeing them remaindered for pennies on the dollar, Jack suggested I come up to his family's Lake Joseph cottage for the weekend to discuss the possibilities. I jumped at the invitation.

I arrived on a Saturday, in time for a swim and dinner, with an invitation to spend the night. After a warm and collegial dinner, I walked by Jack on my way upstairs to the guest room. He was staring into the distance, gazing at the horizon. There was an eerie silence in the room. He seemed an old sea captain remembering things past. In the guest room, above my bed there was a black-and-white photograph of the motor torpedo boat Jack had captained during the war. I sensed a legacy of diminishing memories. I was to drive back to Toronto in the morning to catch a plane home to Vancouver. I had no plans to sleep in, but Jack's sharp, clear "Scott" would have awoken anyone. The moment took me back to my days at M&S. The command was as undiminished as those he issued back then on a regular basis.

True to his word, Jack ensured that the Beny Foundation solved our inventory problem. It bought all our remaining copies of both books, for a reasonable price. The bonus was a weekend in a cottage that over the years had become part of the mythology of M&S.

—

When we struck up an important relationship with the Art Gallery of Ontario, Jessica Bradley, a senior curator, opened the door. Director Matthew Teitelbaum allowed us to go through it.

The most successful of our collaborations with the AGO was *Krieghoff: Images of Canada*. Ambitious and groundbreaking, with 360 pages and 150 colour plates, it became our lead book in fall 1999.

Krieghoff's palette, with its snow and hues of winter light, was difficult to print. In this case, Friesens of Altona, Manitoba, which over the years had become our ever more valued partner, was up to the task. Curators were always skeptical of Canadian printing, but we held our ground. My trusted friend and colleague Marc Laberge took a substantial French-language edition for his Montreal house, Trécarré.

Echoing the old marketing tricks of M&S, we announced a first printing of 25,000 copies, carrying a retail price of $85, with an organized sales strategy of suitable scale. We launched it with a high-level presentation event for Indigo executives. Senior AGO and D&M people jointly made a personal pitch.

When the Indigo buyers asked about the quantity commitment we were seeking, they thought we were asking them to buy the entire first printing. We tactfully demurred. Indigo did commit to an initial order of 7,500 copies. Our theatre had been effective.

The entire first printing sold out.

A second AGO project of consequence, undertaken jointly with the National Gallery, grew out of a major Tom Thomson retrospective. Dennis Reid of the AGO and Charles Hill of the National Gallery coordinated five curatorial essayists and chose 140 Thomson paintings from a broad assemblage of galleries, collectors, and public institutions across Canada. It was to be a show of great curatorial panache and historical importance.

Friesens was again trusted with the printing, and the designer, Mark Timmings, put heart and soul into a very complicated endeavour. The first printing of 20,000 copies, priced at $65, sold out.

—

Art books remained mainstays of the D&M program. We shed timidity to pursue projects of scale. Partnerships blunted the necessity of finding fresh capital, allowing us to successfully publish some 200 art books.

Kathleen Bartels, the VAG director with whom I had worked for many years, once spoke these gracious words:

> We thank you for your insatiable love of that undeniable object of the book — the old-fashioned type that we can touch and smell and feel the weight of in our hands, and return to again and again as old friends . . . Art books have never been particularly viable financially . . . they simply had to be made . . . A community's strength and significance is

in large part due to its most creative thinkers — its writers, architects, designers, filmmakers and visual artists . . . A community and a country's strength is also due to its fearless publishers . . . Thank you, Scott, for this remarkable legacy.

Amongst our many important art-book successes were Roald Nasgaard's *Abstract Painting in Canada*, 500 pages representing a lifetime of scholarship (and a partial sponsorship for which I personally persuaded David Thomson to step up); Iris Nowell's *Painters Eleven: The Wild Ones of Canadian Art*; and *Indigena: Contemporary Native Perspectives in Canadian Art*, which introduced us to Gerald McMaster and the Canadian Museum of Civilization. McMaster's overview was the first book of national consequence to showcase new work from Indigenous artists.

An art book led me to my first, and only, encounter with Prime Minister Jean Chrétien. We had struck an arrangement with the National Gallery for a book to accompany a newly curated Joe Fafard retrospective, opening in 2007. Fafard was an accomplished Saskatchewan artist and sculptor, known for his humorous depictions of politicians and other animals. The curator for the show was Terrence Heath, a D&M author, and because we could pay him an advance as "author" while the gallery could not, the gallery was happy to let us initiate the project.

The opening event in the gallery was very high profile. Chrétien was there to formally open the show. I was there as well and happened to be wandering through the show right behind the prime minister's party, at about the same pace. We both stopped in front of a wicked caricature of John Diefenbaker standing on a red chair. I lingered to have a look. Chrétien grabbed me by the arm and said, "I'm in the show, too, you know," and led me across a crowded room to where *his* bronze was standing proudly.

—

It was also an art book that led me to Arthur Erickson.

After our first meeting in the late 1960s, when Bob Flick and I had the audacity to propose a large book on his design for SFU, we had crossed paths at a distance when I was a fine arts student in pre-architecture at UBC. Thanks to Alvin Balkind, we had also spent time in his house. But I doubt he remembered any of that.

Concrete was Arthur's muse, "the marble of our time." He used it to subtle perfection, shaping its rectangular contours to his will. An international colleague once suggested that Arthur was the only architect who could be sufficiently trusted to design a new building for Venice. Several Middle Eastern kings and princes shared that view and could afford his dreams, although none of their commissioned buildings ever saw the light of desert sun — including, more's the pity, his audacious plan to reshape Babylon.

If people couldn't find the front doors to his buildings, and roofs occasionally leaked, that was irrelevant. Frank Lloyd Wright, once dealing with an outraged client complaining about water dripping on his head through the ceiling of his new (and extraordinarily expensive) dining room in Fallingwater house, had the answer: "Then move your fucking chair!" Arthur would never have been so crass, but I suspect he would have endorsed the sentiment.

Canada was gifted with more than its share of Arthur's serene buildings. To my eye, the Museum of Anthropology at UBC is his best. There were many others: Simon Fraser University (*Architectural Digest* called its main concourse "the grandest enclosed space since the Romans"); the Canadian Pavilion at Expo '70, brightened by Gordon Smith's multicoloured swirls; Thomson Hall; Robson Square; and many elegant private homes. He melded a Japanese aesthetic with the imperatives of the West Coast landscapes in which his buildings were situated, often defined by Cornelia Oberlander's harmonious plantings of native species.

It was essential that D&M become his publisher. When such a project was offered to a select handful of publishers by a Toronto agent in 1987, I pounced. Our competition was M&S, with its new publisher at the time, Adrienne Clarkson. We won publishing rights to the book and found great success in Frankfurt that year, with Harper & Row and Thames & Hudson committing to substantial co-editions.

Well aware of how precise and demanding Arthur could be, we were careful during every step of the publishing process. We showed him a detailed, full-sized mock-up of the entire book, with all images in place, to secure his presumed blessing. He granted it, or so we thought.

As is so often the case with brilliant, preoccupied people, Arthur hadn't focussed on details until the last possible moment. The book was being printed when he carefully examined the final pages. He was dismayed at the treatment of his line drawings. Some had been enlarged or reduced to facilitate the design process, and to Arthur's eye they'd been arbitrarily and irresponsibly handled. The lines of his renderings had become inconsistent in width, unacceptable for a purist.

I was decompressing one Saturday morning after an exhausting trip when the phone rang. Arthur was not happy.

As the conversation dragged inconclusively on, in desperation I suggested that Arthur go through the book carefully, marking up everything to which he objected. We would make all his corrections when the book was reprinted. He accepted the offer, and *The Architecture of Arthur Erickson* was published in 1988. The book was never reprinted, and the issue disappeared.

The friendship survived. We continued to have lunch in Arthur's preferred Kits Point Italian restaurant. He always raised the memoir he was in the midst of writing, and I was always encouraging. He was writing it longhand, "mostly on airplanes." Expecting that it might never be finished, and ducking the large advance request he kept hinting at, I declined to bite. To my knowledge, the memoir was never quite finished, although the family claims it does exist in draft, and it would be a great service to this country's cultural legacy if it ever could be published.

D&M made up for it with David Stouck's fine biography, *Arthur Erickson: An Architect's Life*, in 2013. It, too, attracted some controversy. We sent the manuscript to Phyllis Lambert hoping for a jacket blurb endorsing the book. Phyllis is the founder, and funder, of the Canadian Centre for Architecture and is a brilliant gift to Montreal, her city, and Canada.

Phyllis, Sam Bronfman's daughter, is intense, articulate, favouring black as her defining colour, mistress of all she commands. Upon reading the manuscript, she called me one day, unannounced, with the sharp judgement few people can match. She was clear: "You can't publish this!" This was not an opinion with any nuance. Phyllis felt that the author had misrepresented some salient architectural details. As a consummate defender of Arthur's legacy, she demanded changes, although not specifically spelling them out.

I got on well with Phyllis, having successfully worked with her and the Canadian Centre of Architecture on several projects. I endorsed her standards. As a compromise, she recommended a knowledgeable reader, expert in architectural matters, to correct the perceived flaws. Her nominee, a distinguished professor of architecture at McGill, went through the manuscript and, after considerable delay, suggested only a few minor changes.

David Stouck was vindicated. The book was shortlisted for six literary awards, including the RBC Taylor Prize, the UBC Library's Basil Stubbs-Stuart Prize for Outstanding Scholarly Book, and the City of Vancouver Book Award.

This was my curse. Whenever an art book of stature, scale, or high financial risk was imminent, strong emotions erupted. Because I cared so much, too much in fact, such episodes were unfailingly painful. Whenever brilliance reaches the light, the knives come out. It's been that way since the Renaissance, and probably long before.

12

PEACE AND WAR

My determination that D&M would play a part in overcoming the prevailing ignorance about Canada's military record came from a surprising source — Farley Mowat.

Prior to the late 1970s, I had a romantic notion of Canada's military past. I had only one uncle who had served in Europe, and he returned unscathed. When I was growing up, my father would regale me with tales about his childhood summers in Duncan, BC, decidedly "Kipling country," populated by "black sheep" from British aristocratic families and retired army officers from the Raj. Their surnames, and sometimes their titles, tripped off my father's tongue, tinged with nostalgia for his own cherished memories.

The most accomplished storyteller was an old warhorse, Colonel Maxwell Edward Dopping-Hepenstal, CBE, DSO, Croix de Guerre, late of the Gurkhas. He had served everywhere: India, China, Aden, Burma, Afghanistan, France, and Mesopotamia, but had retired to the gentle world of the Cowichan Valley. Short, wiry, and animated, he had remained a bachelor, distinguished by a mound of snowy hair, bushy eyebrows, and skin the weathered texture of old shoe leather. To emphasize a point, he would cut and slash with one of his personal collection of kukris, those terrifying short knives used by Gurkha regiments. He was a character straight out of *Boy's Own Annual*. And he was a master spinner of tales.

One day, in the midst of sharing memories, Dopping-Hepenstal presented me with a surprising gift. It was a Ceylon tea tin, fire engine red, decorated with images of parrots in cages. Inside was his collection of old coins picked up on his travels, some stretching back to the 18th century. The largest of the coins was scorched, bent double from severe heat. A casualty of the 1857 mutiny, he said. No further embellishment was offered.

With no personal experience to understand the reality of war, these shards of Empire fired my impressionable imagination and kindled a serious collecting passion. It turned out I had some talent at, and patience for, painting 54mm models, which most of the world identified as toy soldiers, but which collectors dignified with the label "military miniatures." Passionate about this new interest, and with the support of my father, I joined a group of Vancouver collectors, mostly retired military officers, some of high rank and battlefield distinction.

Tales from two club members lodged in my imagination. Commander Nicholas Beketov was born in 1891 in St. Petersburg, Russia, to a well-known architect of noble blood. He attended the Imperial Naval College in that city and survived the Bolshevik revolution, later emigrating to Canada, where he served as a naval officer in both world wars. He commissioned me to paint a model in the dress uniform of the Hussar regiment in which he had once served.

Captain Van Oudenallen had a flushed face, thinning, slicked hair, favoured a stylish monocle that emphasized the mischievous sparkle in his eye, and indulged a nip out of a hip flask from time to time — "doctor's orders." He seemed sent from central casting and told memorable stories in a distinctive, soft Dutch accent. They touched upon his time serving in the Dutch cavalry, including, in his telling, a role in one of the last cavalry charges of World War I. His descriptions were precise, with sufficient veracity to be almost believable. His ribald advice about how to enjoy Paris as a young man caught my attention.

Farley Mowat's 1979 book, *And No Birds Sang*, disabused me of all my fanciful notions. Its blunt authenticity shook me. Ortona was hell. There must be many accounts of such power; this one truly hit home. Coming from a friend and, eventually, an author, Farley's searing memories had real impact.

—

Mark Zuehlke became the most prolific author for this strand of the program. Now considered Canada's most important popular military historian, he had dedicated himself to chronicling our distinguished military record in WW II, and beyond.

The first book in his ambitious Battle Series, *Ortona: Canada's Epic World War II Battle*, was published in 1999. The battle for Ortona, over Christmas 1943, was vicious. Confronting elite German units, the Canadians liberated the town, at a huge cost in lives. The *New York Times* described the battle as "Little Stalingrad." Such desperate, heat-of-the-moment innovations as "mouse holing" — moving from room to room by blasting through the walls of contiguous houses — became a tactic adopted by other armies. The CBC's Matthew Halton described the physical and emotional exhaustion of both sides lapsing into "the quality of a nightmare . . . the men in there are as if possessed." That same intensity had impelled Farley Mowat to write *And No Birds Sang*.

Ortona turned into a bestseller, establishing the template for a series that has now reached 13 books. Mark's determination to set the record straight has given Canada the most well-researched and emotionally resonant narrative of any single army's fighting record during WW II.

His singular devotion was eventually rewarded. In 2014, he won the Governor General's History Award for Popular Media, also known as the Pierre Berton Award, adding to his hometown's City of Victoria Butler Book Prize for distinguished non-fiction. In 2024, he was awarded the Order of Canada.

—

Pierre Berton steered us to a book with a much more personal edge. His recommendation was compelling: "Of all the reading I have done on the war in Northern Europe this is the most memorable." The author, Sgt. Charles D. Kipp, a volunteer from St. Catharines, Ontario, was typical of those volunteers who stepped up when duty called.

Because We Are Canadians: A Battlefield Memoir, published in 2005, is an unadorned front-line account, told in plain words. Kipp was with the Lincoln and Welland Regiment from D-Day through the slog that followed. He was wounded nine times during the cruel push north through endless gumbo, and once unknowingly endured a battle while in the midst of a heart attack.

The fight for the Scheldt estuary was wet and murderous. Kipp was in the centre of it at its nastiest, the Battle of Bergen op Zoom. After the battle was over, and Kipp was safely settled in a friendly basement, his Dutch colleagues, toasting the victory, asked why their hands were trembling, yet those of the Canadians were not. "Because we are Canadians."

———

When Lewis "Lew" MacKenzie's *Peacekeeper: The Road to Sarajevo* was offered to publishers by Linda McKnight, Lew's Toronto agent, it was clear that the circumstance would be highly competitive. It was a remarkable memoir.

A Canadian major-general who had served in the Middle East, Cyprus, and Vietnam, MacKenzie was caught up in the violent breakup of Yugoslavia during the Bosnian War. In 1992, he was tasked with establishing and commanding Sector Sarajevo, a 30-nation "peacekeeping" force under the jurisdiction of the UN, identified by the clumsy acronym UNPROFOR. Its urgent mandate was to open the airport, which was essential to allowing desperately needed food and medical supplies into the besieged city. Using words and media interviews, "the only weapons I had," Lew was attempting to get a compelling message out to an indifferent world. "If I could convince both sides to stop killing their own people for CNN, perhaps we could have a ceasefire."

The manuscript had been scribbled in pencil, often under fire, during the two years MacKenzie led the fraught, impossible-to-fulfill mandate. With the encouragement of Martin Bell of the BBC, his scribbling in a mingy diary, primarily to record expenses to satisfy UN bureaucrats, began to assume greater importance.

Between Christmas 1992 and May 1993, the diary grew in size. Lew expanded the narrative to include episodes from his earlier tours on peacekeeping missions. The storytelling had surprise and bite, evidence of a natural penchant for narration. His terse dismissal of policing Sarajevo's "suicide alley": "How do you fight people who are not afraid to die?"

Lew demonstrated the character and audacity that epitomize the Canadian army at its best. And he was not shy about breaking rules when necessary. This didn't endear him to his UN masters, but his soldiers loved him.

The obvious house for such a book was HarperCollins, then being run by Nancy and Stanley "Stan" Colbert, who would have scooped the book up for more money than we could afford. But they had recently sold their literary agency to Linda McKnight and Arnold Gosewich. One of the strictures was that the Colberts were disqualified from competitive bidding for anything Linda had on offer.

Having read just a short sample, enough to gauge the power of the story, it was clear that it was a perfect fit for D&M. The deal was done from a public pay phone in a damp, cold phone booth on top of Vancouver's Little Mountain, during a break in our company's Christmas party.

I offered an advance well into five figures, normally out of character for us. We had our lead book for the next fall, one I believed was destined to become a high-profile national bestseller.

Nancy Colbert immediately made a handsome offer for HarperCollins to acquire mass paperback rights, which the terms of her contract allowed her to do. Numbers had suddenly become reassuring. That's how the business once worked in New York. Seldom did equivalent windfalls unfold in Canada.

We published the book in fall 1993, and it fulfilled all our expectations, becoming an immediate number-one bestseller. We shipped 35,000 copies between publication date and Christmas. Lew's national tour generated massive media coverage, punctuated by tearful recent immigrants turning up at autographing parties to tell stories of how they had been rescued by Canadians. Inevitably, the daily media schedules became overstretched. Our Calgary sales rep shared an anecdote: Running late one day, Lew suggested he take over driving her car. She was flabbergasted: "I didn't know my car could do things like that." Lew's other passion is driving Formula Fords as a competitive race-car driver.

Lew's record was not without controversy. His sharp tongue was not always his greatest asset. He was cursed by a suspicion of siding with the Serbs, and accused — most specifically in Carol Off's 2000 book, *The Lion, the Fox and the Eagle* — of being willfully ignorant of the Bosnian political situation. He disputes the evidence, but it must have been painful to endure.

The Bosnian War was an ugly episode in a bitterly fragmented place, with all sides and two religions trying to score points in world opinion. My own view is that Lew dealt with an impossible hand fairly. His Order of Canada, and retirement record, speaks for itself. A film based on his memoir, *A Soldier's Peace*, won a New York Film Festival Award in 1996.

Sarajevo was not the only casualty of the fighting that tore the former Yugoslavia apart. The proud town of Dubrovnik, once the city-state of Ragusa, a defiant jewel in the heart of the Venetian empire, was caught in a pincer of ongoing shelling from Serbian artillery. The Western press suggested that not much damage had been done, but many roofs of buildings in that centuries-old town had been shattered.

Dubrovnik is a special place for us. Corky and I spent our honeymoon there in 1967. Returning 50 years later, we were greeted by a wholehearted welcome, and a population now fluent in English. Sharp reminiscences about the internecine wars first greeted us during our taxi ride from the airport. Hearing our story, the driver whipped out his ID from the war. It showed a photo of a much younger man. One day he was a researcher in a university, beginning his life; the next he was in uniform.

When I suggested that surely those days had passed into history, he pointed to the mountain rising directly behind us: "They are just over that hill, and they'll be back. It's just a matter of time."

Canada's Afghanistan involvement began in late 2001, extending through 2011 with a lingering, reduced role training the Afghan army. Over the decade, given twice-annual rotations, some 45,000 Canadian troops and police served in the theatre.

One of them was an idealistic doctor from Sudbury, Capt. Ray Wiss. An emergency medicine doctor with previous military experience, he was a reserve officer responding to the call of his country when he volunteered to return to the field in late 2007. Expecting a relatively safe posting to the main base near the city of Kandahar, he ended up on the front line. He was seconded to what was euphemistically called a Forward Operating Base (FOB), "outside the wire," in one of the most dangerous places in a dangerous country, the Panjwai Valley. The nickname for such places was "hellhole."

To maintain his sanity and stay in touch with home, Ray began a diary that became *FOB DOC: A Doctor on the Front Lines in Afghanistan*, which we published in 2009. Ray's intent was straightforward: to spread word about a cause in which he fervently believed, "the first moral war since WW II."

It was entirely in keeping with Ray's unselfish motivation that he insisted all royalties be donated to General Rick Hillier's Military Families Fund. In that spirit, the coda to his book is a portfolio of "The Fallen," portraits of those Canadian soldiers killed during his tour.

The editorial process for the book was conducted via satellite telephone in between medical emergencies. During one such call, loud popping sounds disrupted our conversation. "Those are the UK guys defending our position lobbing mortar shells at the Taliban." Conducting an editorial consultation in the middle of an active war zone was a new experience.

During Ray's national publicity tour following publication, a generous Vancouver couple organized a dinner in his honour. Toward the end of it, a seemingly innocent question about why this mattered provoked an intensely emotional response. He talked about how many thousands of young Afghan girls were going to school for the first time, and how many young women had been protected from extreme measures. Before leaving, he bowed gently and presented our hostess with an elegant Peshmerga scarf, purchased in a Kandahar marketplace.

The book sold well enough to encourage us to accept a sequel, a diary from Ray's second tour, *A Line in the Sand: Canadians at War in Kandahar*. Terry Glavin caught the diary's spirit: "Wiss has never compromised in his brave and distinctly Canadian idealism . . . this is a gripping, heartbreaking and inspiring book."

The gift to us was Ray Wiss's humanity. When his wife tragically drowned while on a well-deserved vacation in the Caribbean in 2012, leaving him a widower with two young children, it broke my heart. His spirit had deeply touched me, and his service in that difficult, never-ending war had somehow been a beacon for the country's distinguished and unselfish military record.

Words from Desmond Tutu make an appropriate coda to Ray's motivation: "If you are neutral in situations of injustice, you have chosen the side of the oppressor."

—

When the Canadian War Museum was finally opened in 2005, D&M won the right to create a book paying homage to it.

The man who envisioned the museum's physical form was Raymond Moriyama, a Japanese-Canadian architect. He'd spent much of his childhood in an internment camp in Slocan Valley, British Columbia, during WW II. He and his family had been deemed "enemy aliens." Raymond's father, refusing to be separated from his pregnant wife and young children, was arrested and sent to Ontario. The family remained apart until after the war.

Moriyama's first architectural experiment was a treehouse he built as an escape and a private refuge near the Slocan River, fashioned out of leftover wood donated by sympathetic neighbours. For him, the deprivations of war were real.

He survived with his innate decency intact. Moriyama's buildings exude an understated, serene quality, reflecting the ideals of democracy and hope. The War Museum building is a metaphor for the nature of war: raw concrete, exposed steel, patinated copper, disconcertingly angled walls, and narrow spaces suggesting the "devastations of war," culminating in bright, open spaces hinting at redemption. It is a building shaped by "controlled imperfection," appearing to emerge from a scarred landscape, and pays tribute to Canada's distinguished military legacy.

Getting it built was a struggle, fraught with controversy, too often the case in Ottawa. Even with champions Sheila Copps, Adrienne Clarkson, and Jack Granatstein, it took Herculean efforts to raise the necessary money.

Moriyama was a gentle presence to work with. The process remained calm from beginning to end, seldom the case when working within Ottawa's usual strictures. We published *In Search of a Soul: Designing and Realizing the New Canadian War Museum* in 2006. The book became so successful that we hoped to work with Raymond on a second project, a personal memoir. Disappointingly, we never quite got there.

At the 11th hour of the 11th day of the 11th month, a shaft of sunlight shining through a window in the Canadian War Museum's Memorial Hall frames the original headstone of Canada's Unknown Soldier. To experience that moment is profoundly moving, a culmination of the architectural and storytelling power of the place and its creator.

13

GOOD TASTE

We lingered, finishing a long lunch. We were there to negotiate the contract for Umberto Menghi's next cookbook, but our focus had wandered, distracted by good conversation and better wine. Still, we wanted the deal finished.

Our solution was to draft the contract directly on the elegant tablecloth covering the table in front of us, adding decoration poured from our glasses. Umberto was being pursued by other publishers, so some mildly humorous comments were scribbled along the edges. Even if it was an enjoyable occasion telling stories, I hadn't lost my focus. Settling the business arrangements remained essential. When it came to money, I didn't doubt Umberto's focus matched mine.

For the tablecloth to become a legal document, it required the signature of a witness. Pino Posteraro, then working in Umberto's kitchen, was summoned to officially bless the deal with his name. Years later, when it became his turn to sign a contract with D&M, he cited that moment as determining that he would sign only with us.

The contract for *Toscana Mia*, Umberto's love letter to the lifestyle of his native Tuscany, was worked out on that tablecloth. For many years, it retained pride of place in the company's archive.

When I was growing up, the food culture of Vancouver was unsophisticated. It had barely evolved beyond a collection of saloons and hotels with dining rooms. My Anglo-Scottish family retained a skeptical view of Europe's gastronomic excesses. Asian cuisine was terrifying. When my father was invited to meetings in Vancouver's Chinese restaurants, he ordered bacon and eggs.

Food is as much a cultural expression of place as the other creative arts. It was inevitable that D&M would embrace its Vancouver evolution. Beginning in the 1970s, a small group of European-trained chefs, many with experience in the world's best restaurants, were seduced by Vancouver's landscape and lifestyle. They were all well trained and passionate about food. Many became determined to put down roots in Vancouver.

Umberto might fairly be considered the Godfather. Those chefs who followed, many of whom initially supported themselves by working in his kitchen, discovered the extraordinary quality of local produce. They became a band of brothers. A distinct food culture began to flourish, one based on fresh, unadorned ingredients. We published books from most of that first wave.

Umberto's story is a good one. Intuitively rebellious, at age 12 he ran away from home to escape becoming a priest. His parents found him a few days later and relented, eventually consenting to his attending a cooking school in Rome. By 1967, he was working in a London kitchen. His eye caught an ad from Canada House for a job posting at Montreal's Expo 67, and he scored an interview. He was judged "perfect," which included a ticket to Montreal.

His wanderlust unabated, he made it to Vancouver a few years later. Planning to cross the country by train, he acquired an 8mm movie camera and set out to record what he expected was going to be a grand adventure across the Wild West. Herds of buffalo, cowboys, "Indians," perhaps even some train robberies. He acquired appropriate gear: cowboy hat, jeans, and a holster, with two cap guns to fend off expected dangers. The only thing this disguise achieved was an arrest by the RCMP while he was exploring Winnipeg. Guns in a holster were dimly viewed. The arresting officer thought he was crazy. After hearing his story, the officer let him go, only confiscating the cap guns. Umberto's legendary charm served him well, as it has ever since.

In 1973 Umberto found a way to turn downtown Vancouver's "little yellow house," owned by a wedding dress designer, into a restaurant. The result, lovingly prepared Italian food, was a revelation for the city.

My first memories of Umberto are mixed. While always charming, he could be skeptical of someone who might just be the next salesman. I trod gently. Over time, with five beautiful and hugely successful cookbooks behind us, our partnership warmed. But I would not have wanted to work under his mercurial eye in the kitchen.

Umberto's passion for good food was authentic, his eye for creating hospitable space unmatched. The rooms in his restaurants were beautifully orchestrated, every detail just right. Combining a warm welcome with very good wine, the restaurants became the place to be seen.

Umberto's Kitchen: The Flavours of Tuscany was our first collaboration. I assembled the creative group that was to produce it, including photographer John Sherlock, in what we referred to as the dungeon, a room in the basement of D&M's offices. My imperative was simple. We'll give you the resources to produce a cookbook to international standards. It was published in 1995, our first high-end cookbook. It has since sold some 35,000 copies and remains in print.

The string continued in 2000 with *Toscana Mia*, Umberto's love letter home. It was birthed by that tablecloth contract and embellished with superb photographs of the Tuscan landscape. His five cookbooks have all become bestsellers, and in 2020 he was awarded the Order of the Star of Italy. Not bad for a kid from Pontedera.

—

John Bishop added a sense of refinement to Vancouver's culinary scene. Instinctively dedicated to flawless service, he found his way into the kitchen as a teenager. Born in Shrewsbury, England, he grew up in Wales, learning his craft in London. When he was considering a career in the Royal Navy, "to see the world," his mother vetoed the idea. She cited his grandfather, who had returned from the navy "with tattoos and a drinking habit."

Instead he got a job in the kitchen of a London hotel and was soon hooked. He moved from kitchen to kitchen, including a brief stage cooking on the RMS *Queen Mary*, before following a friend to Vancouver and falling in love with the landscape. After experimenting with farming in partnership with his new wife ("hippie stuff"), he entered Umberto Menghi's kitchen, where he spent the next 10 years cooking. He also played "the straight guy" to Menghi for over 100 episodes of Umberto's early TV show.

The recession of the early 1980s changed everything. Menghi's new comptroller began to aggressively assert control. Finally, during an argument, he threw John out, a very unplanned exit. Devastated, and unsure what to do next, John was persuaded by a former customer offering financial help to take the leap of opening his own restaurant. Bishop's launched in 1985, with Expo 86 on the horizon.

Bishop's became a quiet refuge for patrons. The cooking echoed the man: understated, accomplished, and elegantly presented. The white walls of the restaurant's compact, congenial space were covered with art from John's friends, amongst them Jack Shadbolt, Gordon Smith, and Alan Wood.

Corky and I came to think of Bishop's as a safe haven, a respite from chaos. John was the ultimate host, gliding as though floating on air through the understated spaces. With John's unlined face, calm demeanour, and designer glasses, a journalist once suggested his countenance was more that of a modernist architect than a harassed restaurateur. The restaurant, widely considered the best place to eat in Vancouver, deservedly attracted a legion of food lovers from Boris Yeltsin and Bill Clinton to Jacques Pépin and Hugh Johnson.

It was obvious that John should be persuaded to write a cookbook for D&M. His first, published in 1997, was simply titled *Bishop's: The Cookbook*. It was followed by three others: *Cooking at My House*, *Simply Bishop's*, and *Fresh*. All became bestsellers.

John's generosity affected a generation. Many of those now considered amongst Canada's top chefs — Michael Allemeier, Adam Busby, James Walt, Andrey Durbach, Carol Chow, Rob Feenie, and Vikram Vij amongst them — spent time in his kitchen. They all absorbed John's lessons of grace and shared knowledge. When it was announced in late 2020 that John would be retiring, and the restaurant would close, it cast a pall over the city.

—

John's legacy continues. On a chaotic evening during Expo 86, my wife and I were having dinner with friends. A new, very nervous waiter confused our orders. He seemed so flustered that we accepted what appeared and happily ate it. The waiter was Vikram Vij, and he never forgot the kindness. He felt that he was going to be fired (not likely with John). Vikram didn't tell me that story for years, adding that it had tilted his decision to sign with D&M.

Vikram, born in Amritsar in the state of Punjab, was another wanderer who had discovered Vancouver, first arriving at the Banff Springs Hotel in 1989 following apprenticeships in Salzburg and Vienna.

When his eponymous restaurant first opened in a tiny house on Broadway, it had no gas hookup, no liquor licence, and just 16 seats. Vikram's parents spent the first three months doing the cooking in their home and busing it to the restaurant.

Lineups were soon appearing. The city had embraced South Asian food. With Vikram's then wife, Meeru, running the kitchen and Vikram radiating charm in the chaotic front of the house, the restaurant was becoming widely known. A no-reservation policy was strictly adhered to; it seemed counterintuitive, but it worked. Even Adrienne Clarkson, as governor general, had to wait, delegating one of her RCMP guardians to hold a spot in line.

When the possibility of a book finally arose, Vikram and Meeru visited our offices. Vikram was ebullient; Meeru was utterly focussed. It was clear that no nonsense would be tolerated. We survived initial intensity and forged one of our happiest and most successful publishing relationships.

When *Vij's: Elegant & Inspired Indian Cuisine* appeared in 2006, sales exploded. The book quickly sold 45,000 copies. Mark Bittman of the *New York Times* declared Vij's "easily among the finest Indian restaurants in the world." The book won Cuisine Canada's Gold Award for Best Cookbook, and a Cordon d'Or Gold Ribbon.

The couple's hospitality equalled their accomplished cooking. As a gesture of appreciation for our staff, they invited everyone to dinner in their home. They cooked, and their daughters served. It turned into an extraordinary evening.

Five years later, we published a second book, *Vij's at Home: Relax, Honey: The Warmth and Ease of Indian Cooking*. The awkward title followed an hour-long debate in my office, with me trying to persuade them both that "Relax, Honey," while of personal importance to them, was not a workable main title. It was squandering their "brand." Our words became so heated that anxious staff asked what had been going on. Peace was restored. The second book, with a slightly altered title, matched the sales success of their first.

—

The first time Rob Feenie tried cooking, he almost burned his house down. As a 13-year-old attempting to roast potatoes, he had let soccer practice take precedence. Forgetting the oven was on, he smoked out his family's new kitchen. He swears he never let it happen again.

Rob is a beacon for a new, homegrown generation. An athlete as a young man, he became fascinated by cooking. A year in Europe as an exchange student confirmed his passion. Back in Vancouver, studying at the Dubrulle Culinary Institute led to a stage as a sous-chef in Whistler and an extended apprenticeship at Michel Jacob's Le Crocodile. Jacob recognized the innate talent and persuaded Rob's father to let him continue working in the restaurant rather than joining the Burnaby fire department, where his father had spent his career.

Soon enough, his imperative was trying something on his own. His first restaurant, Lumière, launched in 1995, soon followed by its more casual next-door neighbour, Feenie's. Lumière reinforced the growing belief that high-level, elegant cooking could work in Vancouver. The restaurant was extraordinary, worthy of a Michelin star or two and soon blessed by being awarded Relais Gourmands status, a rare distinction in Canada.

A relationship with a publisher was in the cards, and as two local boys, we had much in common. International quality from local roots resonated with me. We published Rob four times as his reputation grew and his career thrived.

Rob Feenie Cooks at Lumière appeared in 2001. It was intended to push boundaries, and our hope was fulfilled when Ten Speed Press out of San Francisco, known for its sophisticated cookbook publishing program, bought the US edition. We overindulged in the design, wrapping our hardcover edition in a rather self-conscious parchment paper. Still, it worked, as did the less ostentatious *Feenie's*. Our third collaboration, *Lumière Light*, was less successful, and I share the blame for giving it a title that, while perhaps amusing, proved too clever by half.

Rob was a comet in the food world. Still young, in 2005 he became the first Canadian to win *Iron Chef America*, defeating Masaharu Morimoto, Japan's iconic iron chef. As a chef consultant, Rob restructured the menu for La Régence, the signature restaurant in the Hotel Plaza Athénée in Paris, and was invited to join *Iron Chef Canada*.

Unfortunately, Rob linked up with a business partner of less-than-stellar instincts. He eventually lost both his restaurants, and his business.

But it is difficult to keep good chefs down. After a decade guiding the menus of Cactus Club, he was ready to reengage his dream of an independent, high-end restaurant. In spring 2024, Rob returned to Le Crocodile as owner and chef, allowing Michel Jacob to retire. The refurbished restaurant reopened in June of that year as Le Crocodile by Rob Feenie.

A palm reader on a back street in Yorkville first divined his path: "In a past life you were a chef. Auguste. You're going to be a chef again." The young man was just 12 years old, visiting his brother in Canada. Destiny was playing trickster.

Pino Posteraro was raised in Lago, a hamlet in Calabria, Italy, inheriting a cherished family tradition of honest cooking. His path in life was not untypical for someone from a small town, even from a family with noble pedigree. He enrolled in a medical school on a scholarship, but encountering depressed patients ended his dream of becoming a heart surgeon. "I wanted to be around happiness. I told my mother I was going to become a chef instead. I went back home."

He began at the bottom in local restaurants, washing dishes, eventually graduating to cooking in famous establishments, some with Michelin stars. Travel and cooking became his passions. Ultimately anointed by Hollywood after cooking for an event in Frank Sinatra's Palm Springs home, he was lured by Umberto to Villa Delia in Tuscany, then to Vancouver in 1996.

Three years later, with deep-pocketed friends to help, he took the extreme risk of opening his own restaurant, Cioppino's Mediterranean Grill & Enoteca. He soon won an enviable international reputation as one of the 50 best Italian restaurants outside Italy. In 2023, Gambero Rosso, Italy's equivalent to the *Michelin Guide*, awarded Pino its highest honour, a Guardian of Tradition Award.

When the moment was right, a cookbook was in order. Pino had never forgotten signing Umberto's tablecloth. Our contract was on paper, signed the old-fashioned way. Gérard Boyer of Les Crayères in Reims contributed the foreword, with recipes all embellished with personal anecdotes. When I hand-delivered the first copy of the book, I was gifted one of the finest lunches of my life.

The world moves on. In mid-2024, Pino announced that, after 25-plus years, the restaurant would be closing and he would be retiring. His business partner, Ryan Beedie, summed up his legacy: "[Chef Pino] is a magician. He left a mark, and blazed a trail, and made an impact not on just this city, but on Canada."

The food culture these idealists created transformed the scene. In Vancouver, it has tilted to Asian cuisines now, given the mix of new arrivals and international fashion. Sushi restaurants are ubiquitous, but Chinese restaurants still rule, as in truth they always have. The Cantonese restaurants of unpretentious character that characterized Vancouver's Chinatown in its formative years are back, notably Carol Lee's Chinatown BBQ.

Mandarin restaurants of newer provenance have proliferated. The passion for locally grown produce has increased, with a network of producers dedicated to elevating standards. Refusing to be intimidated by history is the mantra. Finally, the culinary heritage of our Indigenous cultures is being rediscovered.

Educated patrons, sophisticated cooking schools, land and adjacent water that can produce superior products, empowered ethnic diversity, and that magic ingredient, passion, has transformed the local food scene. Without a "national" cuisine deeply rooted in history, except in Quebec, Canadians have been reluctant to honour what they have. That is changing now. Even mighty, arrogant Michelin has succumbed.

14

THE POWER OF STORIES

The instincts of any publisher are drawn to the power of gifted storytelling. Our hesitation about embracing fiction partially stemmed from Jim's concerns about saleability. Author sensitivity also requires gentler handling. Jim had less patience with this than I developed as the company grew.

Into the 1980s, sales of new Canadian fiction remained underwhelming, although M&S and Macmillan were both publishing writers whose books were beginning to break out. Margaret Atwood, Margaret Laurence, Robertson Davies, and Mordecai Richler were becoming bestsellers. Still, even writers of such stature were usually published first, or at least simultaneously, by US or UK houses of reputation and stature.

In 1987, we felt ready to establish a small fiction presence. This was not a business necessity, but rather an expression of our belief in the traditional ideals of the book world. We launched a small program mixing new writing with reprints, all paperback originals, modelled on the enormously successful Vintage Contemporaries, which had exploded with Jay McInerney's 1984 debut novel, *Bright Lights, Big City*. Under Patsy Aldana's overall guidance, with Saeko Usukawa as a western ally, we planned a modest program of five to seven books a year. The first lists included Malcolm Lowry, Sharon Riis, Robert "Bob" Harlow, and W.D. Valgardson.

Sales were disappointing. Our reputation at that time didn't extend to national reviewers. We didn't have the resources to outbid larger houses, nor did we have an established fiction track record. We remained undeterred.

Over the next 20 years, the D&M fiction program was built quietly, without fanfare, and guided by careful judgement. We published Paul St. Pierre and some of the best emerging Asian-Canadian and Indigenous writers. Patsy and later Chris Labonte extended our reach by bringing young writers to the program, amongst them Gail Anderson-Dargatz, Michael Helm, Marina Endicott, Ian Weir, and Fred Stenson.

—

One strand of fiction was important to me: younger writers from Quebec. Perhaps I was overly influenced by my two years at M&S viewing, even if from a distance, Quebec's metaphorical coming of age. I'd warmed to the passion of Quebec's creative community, which believed that strong cultural engagement was essential nation-building, worthy of support at the highest political levels.

Before he entered politics in the early 1970s and becoming minister of cultural affairs in René Lévesque's cabinet, Denis Vaugeois was one of the founders of the publishing house Les Éditions du Boréal. Once, after I had wrapped up an impassioned speech in Ottawa pushing for stronger cultural protections and, of course, more money, Denis, not famous for his empathy toward English Canada, embraced me and uttered the word "camarade." I was touched. Coming out of the mouth of a Quebec nationalist, that word choice was a genuine compliment.

Almost 20 years of playing a role in the country's cultural politics — debating, negotiating with, and much of the time siding with colleagues from Quebec's cultural community — meant that I had friends in Montreal.

Pascal Assathiany, current owner and publisher of Denis Vaugeois's old company, tops the list. Pascal is a committed publisher of the old school. His company is considered by many to be the leading independent house in Quebec, with the province's most accomplished mix of high-quality fiction and non-fiction. As is essential for all successful publishers, he is also a careful, shrewd businessman.

I was always struck by his eyes: large, round, exaggerated behind thick glasses, full of mischief. It may have helped that our meetings unfolded over long lunches in L'Express. The restaurant exudes character. Home to the city's cultural shakers and movers, zinc-topped bar, check-tile floor, and a jar of cornichons on every table. It commands pride of place close to the corner of rue St-Denis at rue Roy, a neighbourhood reminiscent of Paris yet defiantly Montreal.

Our discussions often touched upon the frustration of building anything in Canada, and why English Canadian publishing remained so systemically dysfunctional. The structure of the publishing business in Quebec differs fundamentally from that endured in English Canada. Even though most French publishers are distributed in Quebec, as most American and English publishers are distributed in the rest of Canada, the overwhelming disparity of scale faced by English-language publishers is more extreme.

Quebec publishers enjoy several structural advantages. Returns are very low and, spared active literary agents, advances remain modest, in keeping with the realistic scale of the market. Independent bookstores in Quebec also enjoy legislative protection requiring schools, universities, and other public institutions to buy their books from "accredited" bookstores, in turn directing their business to Quebec publishing houses.

Pascal loved to excoriate me about the business excesses of English Canadian publishing, which has to function without scale and endure massive competition from imported books, yet is saddled with the competitive requirement to overpay author advances, many of which can never earn out. Another glass of wine was sometimes required to resolve the toughest issues. In L'Express, the wine was generically French, but superior. The essential bond was the inherent goodwill linking our two worlds.

These lunches led to building a strong editorial tie between our two companies. We bought English-language rights to the best of his fiction, then the highest-quality fiction coming out of Quebec. Thanks to the Canada Council, translation costs were mostly covered. We could indulge our idealism while building financially responsible bridges.

These books never sold as well as we had hoped, but I felt, as did Patsy, who had been instrumental in initiating the relationship, that such a measure of cultural defiance was an important expression of principle. We published all of Monique Proulx, reissued all of Dany Laferrière's novels (including the cheekily titled *How to Make Love to a Negro Without Getting Tired*), and fiction from Daniel Poliquin, Guillaume Vigneault, and Gil Courtemanche, whose first novel, *A Sunday at the Pool in Kigali*, had become an international bestseller.

Daniel Poliquin, a Franco-Ontarian writer and distinguished translator in his own right, joined the list in 1990. He was blessed with a thick head of hair turning a distinguished grey, an open heart, a beguiling smile, and a ready laugh. We were to publish him five times, including his Trillium Prize–winning novel *The Straw Man*, *L'Obomsawin*, and his Giller-shortlisted novel *A Secret Between Us*.

His mordantly witty, sharp riff on Quebec and Canada, *In the Name of the Father: An Essay on Quebec Nationalism*, equal parts novel and polemic, hit the highest note. It savaged the conventional wisdom separating the intellectual communities of Montreal and Toronto. As a *Globe and Mail* review suggested, he was "a writer who has never met a sacred cow he hadn't kicked in its lazy butt . . . his book is anathema to every federalist and every sovereigntist who doesn't want facts to get in the way of pet theories."

Closer to home, Paul St. Pierre was a man of his time who cherished the language, and the authenticity, of the inhabitants of his beloved Chilcotin Plateau in central British Columbia. "Here's to slow horses, fast women, gravel roads, and cheaper whiskey."

Paul was a character out of one of his own stories. He spoke in a stentorian voice, emphasized by a spiked crewcut and mutton-chop sideburns, his fierce countenance softened by a robust sense of the absurdity of the human condition. He had a wickedly defiant disdain for all things politically correct, including most government regulation. A colleague once suggested he could have passed for an Old Testament prophet. He might have been able to part the waters of the Red Sea, had he chosen to make that his file. Instead, he spent four years as a member of parliament representing the expansive riding of Coast Chilcotin.

Paul was a consummate yarn-spinner, with a clear eye when judging people. His short stories were lean and perfectly pitched: Annie Proulx called them "some of the best North American stories of our time." The *Denver Post* went further: "An unsung literary giant in the grand populist mould of Mark Twain, Bret Harte, and . . . William Faulkner."

Beginning with a regular column in the *Vancouver Sun*, his stories became the basis of several books as well as the early CBC-TV hit series *Cariboo Country*, starring Chief Dan George. One of them, *Breaking Smith's Quarter Horse*, was even adapted into a feature film starring Glenn Ford, further evidence of his ability to conjure up unforgettable characters.

I first met Paul in 1970 in Jack McClelland's hotel room, listening enthralled as Jack pitched Paul on becoming an M&S author. Newly back from Toronto, I was there with Jim Douglas, both of us wearing the hat of an M&S rep. Jack was successful, and *Chilcotin Holiday*, a collection of Paul's *Vancouver Sun* columns, appeared on the list. I inherited the task of working with a local illustrator to provide black-and-white drawings to enhance the book.

I was a huge fan of Paul's writing, so I wanted to duplicate the feat later at D&M. I persevered, and by the mid-1980s, D&M had become his publisher. We eventually reissued all his early books, and originated his last novel, set in Mexico, *In the Navel of the Moon*, published in 1993.

Paul had a checkered relationship with publishers. His bullshit meter was finely tuned, and he could eviscerate the lofty pretensions of the international publishing fraternity better than any author I ever came across.

I avoided greatly sinning. It didn't take long before we became good friends. Our lunches were animated by his increasing dislike for big government, and almost any regulation, and enlivened by much sharp-witted skewering of his Ottawa colleagues. The theatre was always worth it. Beneath the theatre, we had serious conversations about Canada, the world, and what had gone wrong (just about everything).

I last visited Paul in his Langley home shortly before he died. Seeing him after some years was a shock. His weight had ballooned, and his mobility was lessened accordingly. His family had just given him a new motorized wheelchair so he could get around, and he seemed a kid with a new toy. His passion for politics, the country, and freedom from intrusion was undiminished, but his health was fading. He died, aged 90, in July 2014. He chose these words for his tombstone: "This was not my idea."

—

Fred Stenson was Patsy Aldana's discovery, with coaching, I suspect, from her then husband, Matt Cohen, who was well connected in Canada's literary community. A third-generation Albertan from Pincher Creek, Stenson had grown up captivated by stories about Canada's old West. He spun those stories into some of the finest novels the country has been gifted about that part of our history.

We published Fred twice: *The Trade*, in 2000, and *Lightning* three years later.

The Trade was set in 1822, following the Hudson's Bay Company's swallowing of its bitter rival, the Northwest Company. Beaver pelts were the source of profits; the Piegan, Siksika, and Blood peoples the local impediment. The narrative digs into the ugly truths of the fur trade, a myth-busting foray into Canada's mid-19th-century expansion. It was shortlisted for the Giller Prize that year, winning both the inaugural Grant MacEwan Author Award and the City of Edmonton Prize.

Lightning took up the story after 1881. It reveals more truths about the unruly Canadian West, once a lawless territory inhabited by greedy traders, smuggled whiskey, cattle drives, vigilantes, and lonely men only occasionally able to experience the redemption of frontier love.

Both novels were successful, but cry out for cinematic treatment, which has so far eluded them.

Given the historic and geographic truths of British Columbia, publishing Asian-Canadian writers was a priority. In 1988, we published *Saltwater City: An Illustrated History of the Chinese in Vancouver*, a book shaped out of an exhibition of images and text organized by the Chinese Cultural Centre in Vancouver. It introduced us to Paul Yee. Paul was a third-generation Chinese Canadian from Spalding, Saskatchewan, who had grown up in Vancouver's Chinatown, where he had enjoyed "a typical Chinese-Canadian childhood, caught between two worlds, yearning to move away from the neighbourhood." His restrained, always calm manner had been shaped in childhood. He went on to write several internationally successful children's books for our Groundwood children's program.

In 1991, we took the significant step of publishing both an anthology, *Many-Mouthed Birds: Contemporary Writing by Chinese Canadians*, edited by Bennett Lee and Jim Wong-Chu, and SKY Lee's extraordinary first novel, *Disappearing Moon Cafe*.

The anthology was ahead of its time. It included 20 pieces from writers who have since become touchstones within their community, amongst them Jim Wong-Chu, Evelyn Lau, Denise Chong, Fred Wah, SKY Lee, and Wayson Choy. The title was from a Chinese expression describing someone who disturbs the peace, with an unleashed tongue breaking a long and self-imposed silence.

Jim Wong-Chu arrived in Canada from Hong Kong in 1953 as a "paper son," living with an aunt and uncle in Vancouver. Attracted to photography and design, he attended what was then the Vancouver School of Art before moving on to take creative writing at UBC. He ended up making a living as a letter carrier for Canada Post for almost 40 years until his retirement in 2013.

Jim's real passion was the history and literature of Vancouver's Asian community. That led him to help shape what became *Many-Mouthed Birds*. Five years later, Jim co-founded the Asian Canadian Writers' Workshop Society and helped fundraise for the establishment of an Emerging Writer Award. The society next launched *Ricepaper*, a literary journal. A few years later, he was instrumental in helping establish one of the first Asian writers' festivals in North American, LiterASIAN.

Disappearing Moon Cafe was SKY Lee's debut, a bitterly ironic excursion into the very mixed blessing of a childhood in "Gold Mountain," based on her experience growing up in mid-20th-century Port Alberni.

The novel broke new ground for a Canadian writer. It was nominated for both a Governor General's Award and the Ethel Wilson Fiction Prize and won the City of Vancouver Book Award. *Canadian Literature* called it a "landmark . . . a singularly core text in the canon of Asian Canadian literature." The *Washington Post* praised its "lively, often riotous spirit" and called it "a moving, deeply human tale about the high price of assimilation, the loneliness of being of two cultures . . . and the way in which the sordid secrets of the past can cast long, tragic shadows."

Aware of Jim Wong-Chu's commitment to his literary community, it was inevitable that I seek him out. Might he become a "scout" for us in the Asian-Canadian writing community? He agreed, but there was more silence than assembled writing samples. I finally extracted a batch of his most recent submissions to take with me on a vacation so that I could read them with a degree of calm, rare in my day-to-day life. Patsy was handling our fiction program, and Saeko Usukawa as editorial director was always influential, but I was curious to judge for myself the calibre of writing that Jim was discovering. My views would be added to the process.

Several of the pieces were stunning. One stood head and shoulders above the others: Wayson Choy's short story "The Jade Peony." An early fragment had been one of the gems in *Many-Mouthed Birds*.

Wayson Choy had lived a life common to much of Vancouver's Chinese community, with working parents — his father was a cook aboard the CPR coastal steamers, and his mother worked in a butcher shop. Growing up, he was cared for in a variety of households, absorbing the subtle kindnesses of a close-knit neighbourhood. His early dream was to become a cowboy. Instead, he entered UBC to study creative writing, the first Chinese Canadian to do so, and there encountered the indomitable Earle Birney. He also tentatively began "The Jade Peony."

We published *The Jade Peony* in 1995, 30 years later. By then it had grown into a full-blown intergenerational saga about one immigrant family confronting an alien culture. Its episodic structure and rich texture revealed "things not seen in the glare of daylight."

"Why would a boy catch a hundred fireflies and keep them in a jar? . . . So he could have enough light to study at night." An uncle is talking to his eight-year-old nephew in the late 1930s in Vancouver's Chinatown. The unexpected response is a surprise: Its gentle, sweet tone perfectly captures the essence of *The Jade Peony*.

It takes significant writerly skill to portray such a subject so deftly and so honestly, at a time when Asian-Canadian literature was just emerging from its cocoon.

The book quickly made its way in the world. It was joint winner of that year's Trillium Prize, won the City of Vancouver Book Award, spent 26 weeks on the *Globe and Mail* bestseller list, was published by Picador in the US (becoming an American Library Association Notable Book for 1998), was named in the *Literary Review of Canada* as one of the "100 most important books in Canadian history," became the Vancouver Public Library's inaugural "One Book, One Vancouver," and was determinant in Wayson receiving the 2015 George Woodcock Lifetime Achievement Award honouring his literary career. Many hundreds of thousands of copies later, it remains in print.

For all the book's prodigious success, what mattered most to me was my pride in having been involved in its birthing, even at a distance. Few of our books were quite so blessed, nor quite so influential, in breaking down cultural barriers.

The euphoria was not to last. At our suggestion, Wayson acquired a literary agent, and our relationship with that agent, Denise Bukowski, was doomed from almost the beginning. She had spent a short time as our editorial director. Her chutzpah, energy, and literary taste were superior, but her people skills were lacking. It soon became clear that this was never going to be a workable partnership. Our parting, at my instigation, was not pleasant.

In Wayson's case, with Denise as his agent, keeping him was not a battle we were ever going to win. Wayson was uncomfortably caught in the middle. I shared a final, bittersweet tea with him in the lobby of Four Seasons Hotel in Toronto, in hopes I might persuade him to stay with us. He left the decision up in the air. The inevitable outcome was clear: We had to settle for knowing that *Jade Peony* was his best book and remains his most influential.

Wayson never forgot. When I was travelling and couldn't attend one of his events, he sent an eloquent, touching message: "And so it came to pass — as they say about legends like you, Scott — that I'm among many hundreds who are grateful to you and for the firm Douglas & McIntyre. To you, above all, for enlisting the very best publishing and editing talent on behalf of your writers . . . I know you must always have had final approval — which just proves, in fact, how much you mattered to so many of us. Thank you. Thank you. Thank you."

―

We had always hoped to build an Indigenous fiction program, however modest. It would parallel the ongoing strand of the art-book program dedicated to the visual cultures of the Northwest Coast. But Indigenous writers had not yet emerged, and those who had were wary of entering an alien white world.

In 1997, Robert Bringhurst came to me with a passion project — a book honouring the great treasury of Haida oral literature. In Robert's sublime description: "The world of classical Haida literature is a world as deep as the ocean, as close as the heart and as elusive as the Raven, whose unrepentant laugh persists within it all. This is a tradition brimming with profundity, hilarity, and love."

I shared his view of the importance of the work and agreed that we would publish what resulted, initially expected to be a single volume combining context with translations of the two great Haida oral poets, Ghandl of the Qayahl Llaanas and Skaay of the Qqunna Qiighawaay. Robert selflessly pursued the work, with all the tenacity characteristic of his commitment to cultural discovery. He returned to the oral transcripts gathered by John Swanton and began the monumental effort of translating some of them. Any thought of a publishing schedule was abandoned, as what was initially to be an introduction to the two poets expanded into a book of some 500 pages, with maps and charts, photographs, and six appendices, including a guide to Haida spelling and pronunciation.

We published *A Story as Sharp as a Knife* in 1999. It is a masterpiece of scholarship, discipline, and perceptive cultural interpretation. It was followed by two companion volumes, one each for the two great poets, Ghandl and Skaay. Robert's insistence that the two poets be specifically named was an important milestone. They were granted copyright as individuals, high time that Indigenous voices were given their due.

I have always considered this trilogy amongst the most important books I ever published. I stand by that judgement. Of all the superb reviews from accomplished voices, Margaret Atwood's in the *Times Literary Supplement* and *New Statesman* was the most trenchant: "Bringhurst's achievement is gigantic, as well as heroic" and "a monumental labour of love and intellect; it is an astonishing and essential book."

Not everyone was quite so gracious. A small group of white academics, aided and abetted by some Haida in an era when the idea of cultural appropriation was beginning to grow teeth, focussed on what are now widespread concerns: that somehow "white" people cannot speak across cultural boundaries. The voices of dissent became loud, disrespectful of what Robert had offered, and ultimately destructive. I was tempted to retaliate, but a war of words was not going to accomplish anything. We were too busy trying to survive to tilt at windmills. Sales of all the books in the trilogy were modest, a huge disappointment to me.

I wrote to Robert in the middle of all this: "I wish I did not understand how much of your soul resides within this manuscript; it adds to both my pain at the exquisite agony of what you have achieved, and my enhanced obligation to ensure that we publish this well. Literature was ever a mixed blessing, I suppose."

In her introduction to the 2011 Folio edition of *A Story as Sharp as a Knife*, Margaret Atwood added: "Robert Bringhurst is a kind of genius . . . stubborn enough so he's not easily cowed. He has stood his ground. His book, he insists, is indeed a book of wonders."

As a final homage to his spiritual guide and friend, Robert wrote this dedication for the trilogy:

> In memoriam
> Bill Reid
> of the Qqaadasghu Qiighawaay
> of the village of Ttanuu
> whose names were
> Iljuwas, Kihlguulins, Yaahl Sghwaansing,
> 1920–1998

A Story as Sharp as a Knife was accorded a further honour in 2015 when the Folio Society in London published an exquisitely redesigned, reset, and handsomely slipcased limited edition. Try as we might, we were never able to sell rights in the US or the UK. With what I suspect was pressure from Margaret Atwood, we almost persuaded James "Jamie" Byng of Canongate Books and Morgan Entrekin of Grove into sharing an international run, but the book's length, and Robert's refusal to accept substantive cutting, eventually ended any such possibility.

The stories prevailed. Robert's Haida trilogy won the *Times* of London Literary Editor's Book of the Year Award. Erica Wagner, then still literary editor of the *Times*, told Charlie Rose on US national television that *Story* was the most important book she had ever read. When Haida leadership actually read the book, they wanted it on the shelves of their own museum in Skidegate. And Robert himself eventually sold a US edition to the University of Nebraska Press.

—

Richard Van Camp joined the list in 1996 with a raunchy, unpolished, very powerful first novel. He was just 24, and the first Dogrib fiction writer to be published. *Lesser Blessed* tells the story of a Dogrib (Tlicho) teenager, Larry, discovering life in Fort Simmer in the Northwest Territories. Sex, drugs, and rock and roll play their part. The protagonist has the wit, hormones, and self-conscious mix of bravado and vulnerability typical at age 16, exacerbated by his circumstances. He is growing up in the age of AIDS, disillusioned with Catholicism, in a remote northern village. It was a coming-of-age story with the edge of *Catcher in the Rye*. *Lesser Blessed* remains in print, and in 2012 was the basis for an award-winning feature film that toured the festival circuit in North America, including winning a slot at the Toronto International Film Festival.

Richard was a young writer of enormous potential, energy, and charm. He has since published children's books, poetry, and educational graphic novels. But we couldn't persuade him to embrace the discipline of making a second novel work. Several of us tried to convince him to work with one of our editors to fulfill his promise. It never happened, and he moved on. He continues to write and teaches creative writing with an Aboriginal focus at UBC and the Emily Carr University of Art + Design, while working with Musqueam youth. He is fully engaged in the world of Indigenous writing and publishing. I wish he had accepted the discipline we hoped he might embrace to write the novel we knew he had in him. He chose a different path but has returned to it with a new young adult novel published by D&M in 2024.

—

Unannounced, Richard Wagamese knocked on the outer door of the D&M office. I knew his reputation as a columnist, having declined to pursue a collection of his columns some years before, but nothing about him beyond that.

He was down on his luck, on the street. When I invited him in, he suggested his reason for knocking on our door was that ours was the only name in Vancouver he knew. I gave him all the money in my wallet, which wasn't much, and asked colleagues to suggest where he might turn next for help. The episode seemed little more than a kindness to a lost writer. I felt that was the end of it.

Richard had not forgotten. In 2005, he moved back to a place that for him offered salvation: a cabin in British Columbia's high country.

It gave him a measure of inner peace, and it unlocked his pen. "The sublime moments in life are like the first push of light against the lip of a mountain. You watch that pink climb higher, becoming brighter, slipping into magenta, then orange, and then into the crisp, hard yellow of morning . . . This book was born in the hush of mornings."

One Native Life, published in 2008, was a reflective journey back to his roots, written from an Indigenous perspective. It was forgiving of childhood agonies, even absolving Canada of its historical injustices. The *Globe and Mail* named it one of the 100 best books of the year.

Richard ran away from home at age 16 to escape his family. He spent years on the street, in foster homes, or in prison, struggling with alcoholism, drug addiction, and PTSD. He had grown up devoid of learning a word of his native language, Ojibwe. Writing was redemption. Louise Erdrich, a prominent Native American writer, saw it: "Richard Wagamese divined the secrets of human scars and knew that broken people are the strangest and most extraordinary people of all."

We published his next book in 2012. It was a painful cri de coeur, a novel he had been struggling with for several years, *Indian Horse*. The draft manuscript was an editorial wrestle, particularly for Chris Labonte, then leading our fiction program. Chris came to me in the middle of the process to express great frustration, suggesting the novel just couldn't be made to work and should be rejected. My response was unequivocal. This is a story from a writer of real talent, who is one of ours, balancing the trauma of residential schools against the joyful release of playing hockey. This is an essential Canadian story. Make it work.

Wagamese's mantra drove him. "I believe that storytelling in and of itself is a truly redemptive thing." Sales were initially disappointing, until *Indian Horse* was shortlisted for the CBC's Canada Reads competition in 2013. It was runner-up, and that national exposure catapulted it into the limelight. It has now sold almost 200,000 copies.

A new medium extended the book's life — a film adaptation, written by Dennis Foon (once a Groundwood author) and directed by Stephen Campanelli, with Clint Eastwood as executive producer. The film debuted at the Toronto International Film Festival in September 2017. It is a difficult movie to watch but tells such a powerful story that its longevity is assured.

Richard had a vulnerable soul, hardly surprising given his life experience. The medicine of living in a landscape he loved was restorative. I only met him in person twice. Each time I was touched by the expressiveness of his narrow face, and an edgy, yet gentle manner.

When Richard died in March 2017, Canada lost a powerful voice. But it wasn't silenced. His final novel, *Starlight*, was published the following year, and D&M has been able to shape more books out of those stories, reflections, and fragments of wisdom he bequeathed as a legacy. The most recent, *Richard Wagamese Selected: What Comes from Spirit*, spent weeks on the *Globe* bestseller list.

15

STRONG VOICES

In 2001, D&M published multiple bestsellers, including *How to Be a Canadian*, by Will Ferguson and Ian Ferguson, and Wade Davis's *Light at the Edge of the World*.

Will Ferguson had come to my attention in the mid-1990s when Saeko Usukawa suggested I take a recent over-the-transom submission to read over lunch. She found it wickedly funny and suspected it would appeal to my sensibility. The manuscript had been rejected by several Toronto publishers. Newly married and recently returned from Japan, the author was cobbling together a living selling Anne of Green Gables sightseeing packages to Japanese tourists visiting Prince Edward Island.

Will had me at the beaver. The sample chapter that accompanied the proposal introduced Canada's national animal with a gloriously caustic description: "A fat, bucktoothed, waddle-happy, tree gnawin', tail slappin', dimwitted, hard-workin', web-toed, no-longer-in-fashion, right royal pain in the ass." Perhaps a metaphor for the country? Will had a literary agent, and in his telling there was competition for the book. I was too convulsed with laughter to notice. This was his first book, *Why I Hate Canadians*, a sardonic dare. I loved it. We bought it.

The book launched the career of one of Canada's now most successful and admired writers. He was a delight to be around and seldom shy, and his Irish ancestry seeped out, as did memories of his small-town upbringing in the former fur trading town of Fort Vermilion, Alberta, 800 kilometres north of Edmonton. His parents split when he was very young, leading to a nomadic childhood. By the time we met, he had travelled widely and was easing into adulthood. The itch to write was becoming dominant. He had the right package: the eye, the energy, and the material.

Ever masters of timing, we published the book on the very day Lady Diana died in 1997. Sales started slowly, but momentum built as reviews poured in. The *L.A. Times* went over the top: "If Douglas Adams and P.J. O'Rourke ever had an extraterrestrial Satanic love-child, it would probably write like Will Ferguson. That is, it would be observant, attitudinal, occasionally offensive, and funny."

Following the success of *Why I Hate Canadians*, Will didn't rest on his laurels. He was scribbling two books a year, including 1998's *I Was a Teenage Katima-Victim*, a, sharp-tongued account of his time in Katimavik, the volunteer youth corps set up by the first Trudeau government in the 1980s. Katimavik was a creation in the Trudeau style, full of the young and undisciplined, a motley crew of Canadians exposing their idealism to a series of adventures, noble and otherwise.

Will was determined to write fiction, but we weren't the right house for it, so eventually he moved on. Before parting, we published *Bastards and Boneheads: Canada's Glorious Leaders, Past and Present*. Will was never diffident, at least not in print. His writing was getting more acute, his outrage at Canada's foibles deeper and more skillfully expressed, and his canvas more internationally focussed.

We wanted another of his Canadian books. I suggested a "Will treatment" of the eminently mockable Senate, but Key Porter had beaten us to the punch with another writer. As Will was a new father, I suspected that money was likely an issue and suggested to his agent that we leave that contract open. The money could be applied against his next non-fiction project, whatever that might become.

The gods smiled. Will had run into Margaret Atwood, mother superior to all Canadian writers, terror to cautious politicians hesitant about supporting cultural policy. Margaret had tossed off the notion that Will might consider writing a tongue-in-cheek guide to the exotic struggle of becoming Canadian.

He roped in his brother Ian as co-writer. The book's title was basic: *How to Be a Canadian *(Even If You Already Are One)*. The cover featured a Tim Hortons doughnut holding centre ice on an elegant porcelain plate, surrounded by five pieces of sterling silver cutlery borrowed from Birks. Our timing was again dubious: The book's formal publication date followed 9/11 by just a few days. The world apparently forgave us. The book spent 86 weeks as a national bestseller and over the next four years sold 175,000 copies.

By the time we released a new edition in a smaller trim size in 2007, there were several hundred thousand copies in print. We chose a smaller trim to allow a lower suggested retail price and give the cover a family resemblance to equivalent new editions of his other books. The cover image was a Mountie, in full dress uniform. The RCMP is very touchy about representations of their uniforms, and we weighed seeking legal advice to defuse potential issues. In the end we just pressed ahead. Nothing nasty unfolded, and the book continued to sell thousands of copies every few months. We never could decide which was the more effective Canadian icon: a doughnut or a Mountie. History can judge.

As Will's career moved on, and his deserved international honours piled up, I could only tip my hat at his extraordinary discipline and skill. His books have won three Leacock Awards, and he was awarded a Scotiabank Giller Prize in 2012 for the novel *419*.

—

I first met Wade Davis when he submitted some very raw writing inspired by his three years wandering in the jungles of South America. He and a friend were following in the footsteps of his mentor, the revered Harvard ethnobotanist Richard Evans Schultes. They lived rough, spending time with Indigenous people and gathering thousands of rainforest plants, some of them hallucinogenic and many new to science, for shipment back to Boston to be analyzed.

Our great editor, Marilyn Sacks, had read early notes, and in her inevitably gracious manner had suggested that Wade re-approach us when he had more developed writing to show. She must have been more astutely encouraging than usual. Wade still rhapsodizes about the importance of that moment. He has never forgotten such a gesture of support for a young, unknown writer.

Of course I wanted to meet Wade. We convened in what was then my new cramped office, so new that proper lighting had yet to be installed. Wade's exuberance provided sufficient wattage. By the time Wade departed, the intensity of the discussion left us virtually hanging off the dark ceiling.

Wade is not easily forgotten. Tousled hair, bright eyes, square jaw, all coiled energy, engaging rather than threatening. He is a born storyteller, with a perfectly modulated voice and a vocabulary to match. Words tumble out in polished paragraphs without breaks in between. The mystery is how he finds sufficient oxygen to hold the pace.

He is one of the extraordinary talents of our time. Born in West Vancouver and raised in Montreal, he spent time in the woods of Haida Gwaii as a park ranger, forestry engineer, and licensed river guide. No shrinking violet, he was accepted into Harvard, earning a PhD in ethnobotany there before embarking on his South American wanderings.

Building a publishing relationship with Wade was essential, although considering Wade's talent, and American reputation, this was always going to be a long shot. My pursuit was relentless, and while book contracts remained elusive, the friendship deepened.

We reissued an early collection of essays, *The Clouded Leopard: Travels to Landscapes of Spirit and Desire*, in 1998. It touched upon his experiences from rainforests to the mountains of Tibet, from the Sahara to the hallucinogens of Haiti and Peru, from the world of the Inuit to the dreams of Jaguar Shamans who travel the Milky Way.

Light at the Edge of the World: A Journey Through the Realm of Vanishing Cultures was an elegant credo for Wade's passions, combining his text and photography. *National Geographic* bought 10,000 copies for the US and several thousand went to Bloomsbury in the UK, allowing us to set a 20,000-copy first printing. When that sold out, we made a little paperback out of the text alone. It has travelled well, finding homes in many languages, amongst them Basque, Macedonian, Serbian, Japanese, and Malay.

—

Over the next decade, more bestsellers appeared. Douglas Coupland stepped up with two *Souvenir of Canada* compilations, followed by his emotional homage to Terry Fox, *Terry*, of which we shipped 75,000 copies prior to publication. Anna Porter's *Kasztner's Train* cemented her reputation as an accomplished writer, as well as a celebrated publisher.

I'd missed my first chance to publish Douglas "Doug" Coupland. Mac Parry, then editor of *Vancouver Magazine*, had run an article about Doug in the magazine. Oblivious to the zeitgeist, I sniffed and didn't pursue. That seed grew into his first novel, *Generation X: Tales for an Accelerated Culture*. When it was first offered, the enthusiasm of publishers was distinctly muted. It was finally sold to St. Martin's Press in New York for a small advance.

Publishers were slow to recognize what a new century had unleashed. Doug was just following his instincts. His invented expressions "Generation X" and "McJob" helped define the vocabulary of a new generation. His second novel, *Shampoo Planet*, was published by Pocket Books in 1992. It gave the world a new buzzword, "Generation Y."

By the time I woke up, Doug had a thriving career as a writer of fiction, half a step ahead of the world. By then, the D&M program was hitting its full stride. I stumbled upon a short piece from Doug about the Lions Gate Bridge, titled "This Bridge Is Ours," that appeared in *Vancouver Magazine* in 1994. It struck a chord and led me to track Doug down to ask if he had more such pieces, out of which we might shape a little book.

The idea of a "little" book about Vancouver constructed out of text and images intrigued Doug. It was an opportunity to convey the essence of his hometown for international friends. "I thought I was going to go mental explaining dim sum, the sulphur pits, and Kitsilano for the umpteen-hundredth time."

With Corky and me nudging him along, a structure only Doug could conjure emerged: an idiosyncratic portrait in words and images, arranged alphabetically. *City of Glass* was the result, still in print some 40,000 copies and two editions after it was first published in 2001.

The international press has adopted his invented moniker as the standard way to describe the city. I have suggested to Doug that if he could be paid every time a journalist stole his inventive title, he would be a rich man.

When the project was formally underway, I offered a generous contract in recognition of Doug's established reputation. There remained the issue of how we would handle the editorial process. Doug was skittish, and it was essential that we make him feel comfortable.

I agreed to handle the project personally. If Doug was ever unhappy about anything, or was feeling vulnerable, he could call me. Voicemail was preeminent, so voicemail it would be.

I should have been more careful about what I offered. When raw circumstances declared themselves, as is inevitable during the creation of all books, I would receive a scathing message from Doug. It was always followed a few minutes later by a warm mea culpa. I rode an emotional roller coaster of my own.

Out of this a friendship grew. Doug fell in love with our home, as we did with his. We both live in modest houses in the woods, his by the architect Ron Thom, ours by Robert "Bob" Hassell, underappreciated gems of West Coast modernism. Visits to Doug's sanctuary often involved feeding flocks of birds or a scurry of squirrels, regular recipients of his generosity. The animal freeway that passes along the creek beneath our house is usually out of sight, although not always. Over dinner one evening we were eyeball to eyeball with an obstreperous racoon of healthy girth glaring at us from high up in an adjacent cherry tree. The racoon got the fruit. We enjoyed the show.

Doug was inclined to work overnight in his home studio over the garage and sleep late the following morning. One evening, the studio was full of literary bits and pieces, mostly from the M&S world I remembered. Doug was finishing a commission to replace the iconic caricatures of Canadian authors by Andy Donato, which had once decorated a back wall in the old Rooftop Bar of Toronto's Park Plaza Hotel. Another evening had Corky and me stripping FrogTape off precise Mondrian-style images in primary colours, destined for a new show. When Doug commandeered us to build towers of Lego destined for a major retrospective in the Vancouver Art Gallery, I failed.

Doug has the most culturally astute antennae of anyone I have worked with. He simply notices things, fitting for someone with such an accomplished visual and literary eye. The world has also noticed. His fiction makes international bestseller lists, and his singular eye has led to distinguished curators commissioning shows of his painting and sculpture in Asian, European, and North American galleries. For D&M, Doug discovered his "Canadianness." He conjured up two books arranged around Canadian icons, from stubby beer bottles to poutine. "I wanted to give people a book that explains what it feels like to be Canadian. And I wanted to find a new way of doing this."

Doug's two pastiches of text and image, *Souvenir of Canada* and *Souvenir of Canada 2*, their covers dominated respectively by a stubby beer bottle and a double-headed Canada goose, ruled bestseller lists for weeks, each selling over 30,000 copies. When *Souvenir of Canada* was published in 2002, the defiant beer bottle on its cover ran simultaneously on the front pages of all three Toronto daily newspapers, to the great chagrin of competitive editors. The half-title page reproduced the cover of Bruce Hutchison's *Canada: Tomorrow's Giant*, 1957 winner of a Governor General's Award, his quiet personal homage to a distinguished journalist.

Our last collaboration was the most heartfelt, and the most successful. Doug called one day to say he had been invited by the Fox family to look at their archive of son Terry's audacious attempt to defy fate. The 25th anniversary of his cross-Canada run was imminent. Doug was insistent. You've got to talk to Terry's brother, Darrell, right now!

When Doug agreed to pull together a book, which became *Terry*, a handshake was all that was required. He did the rest, masterminding the blend of visual and text elements that was becoming his trademark for those books he was undertaking for us. We had the wit to let him run with any project, including supervising page design and conceptualizing the cover.

Terry is the pinnacle of Doug's ability to combine image, ephemera, and text to achieve maximum emotional impact. It was essential that we publish a book properly honouring Terry's quest. Our first printing grew to 75,000 copies, all of which were shipped in advance of publication. Doug, Corky and I, and the Fox family gathered in St. John's for a private homage, honouring the official launch event there on April 12, 2005. The mayor of St. John's, Andy Wells, spoke at the unveiling of a small, slate memorial stone marking the spot where Terry had first dipped his toe into the Atlantic in 1980. The next morning, we met to symbolically dip our toes into that icy water. Terry had done the real thing. His Marathon of Hope continues, with annual runs in some 100 countries. Hundreds of millions of dollars have been raised to help find a cure for cancer. Terry's 143 days and 3,339 miles of agony changed the world.

Having turned 60, Doug and his talent continue to accelerate; his international reputation increasingly secure. He is painting full time, every day, working from 3 p.m. to 11 p.m., leaving time for a daily visit to the gym. His art has become "collectible." He has entered the pantheon. "I have a real job now."

Anna Porter and I had circled each other for decades, and the path that led me to being her publisher in many ways echoed the precarious journey of Canadian publishing.

As spirited competitors, we inevitably tripped over each other editorially. Anna's charisma, her cachet from being a Toronto publisher, and fierce author pursuit kept me on my mettle. Key Porter snared Allan Fotheringham. D&M landed Jack Webster. We fought over Roloff Beny's final illustrated books. Key Porter published Jean Chrétien, which catapulted her into the front rank of Canadian publishers on the rise. We lured her international rights director, Polly Manguel, to cross the floor to join us, triggering much Porter-style faux theatre.

We had always thought about eventually putting our companies together. When Jack Stoddart's General Publishing filed for bankruptcy in 2002, a group of Toronto investors suggested we try to put D&M, Key Porter, and General Publishing together to form an independent Canadian player of sufficient scale to stand against the multinationals. Ottawa's assistance was essential. In the end none of it worked out. There was never enough time, nor sufficient urgent conviction. Soon, General Publisher's banks were in charge. Ottawa abandoned the file and, not knowing what to do, just hid.

A group of Vancouver investors led by Ron Stern then expressed interest in helping Key Porter and Douglas & McIntyre merge to form a publisher of scale. He was offering an opportunity to blend our two houses, with strong Vancouver and Toronto operations, into a functioning entity of sufficient size to increase competitiveness for both authors and market share. I spent a summer virtually chasing Anna around her holiday lake, trying to put specific shape on the idea.

In truth, my heart wasn't in it. Whether Anna or I were truly ready for the dramatic changes such a merger would have required was questionable, as was whether I was ready to be CEO of a larger company with offices 3,000 miles apart and different corporate cultures. The fact that it didn't happen was probably the best outcome for both companies.

What did remain possible was Douglas & McIntyre becoming Anna's publisher. In a rash move, Key Porter sold itself to its Canadian distributor, H.B. Fenn, in 2004. As Fenn's distribution business withered away, and the Canadian book market restructured, Fenn was pushed into seeking bankruptcy protection. Key Porter became ancillary roadkill.

Anna is not someone who allows life's vicissitudes to defeat her. In her soul, she is a writer. Beginning with a murder mystery, 1987's *Mortal Sins*, she had been writing on the side for many years, following in the footsteps of a revered grandfather. Freed from the demands of Key Porter, Anna reinvented herself. She had time to tell stories. One that had remained close to her heart for years was that of Jewish sacrifice and survival following Nazi Germany's destruction of the last vestiges of Hungary's supposed "independence" during WW II.

Its thematic centrepiece was a single train on which 1,684 extraordinarily fortunate Budapest Jews escaped incarceration in the death camps to the north. Peter Munk, who would go on to build Barrick Gold and found the Munk School at the University of Toronto, was one of those passengers. The singular devil's bargain had been brokered in a very cynical "blood for goods" deal between Rezso Kasztner and Adolf Eichmann. Kasztner was a proud Zionist, an astute politician, a loyal family man, and a genuine hero of the Holocaust, often compared to Oskar Schindler and Raoul Wallenberg. But imminent tragedy shadowed him. Voluntarily returning to Israel following the war, he was dragged into court as a traitor and ultimately assassinated by a zealot.

We published *Kasztner's Train: The True Story of Rezso Kasztner, Unknown Hero of the Holocaust* in 2008. Deservedly, it was welcomed with superb reviews, national media attention, major award nominations, and good sales. Thomas Keneally simply said, "It will become a classic of the times it deals with." Peter C. Newman added, "Every once in a long while a book comes along that makes history so real that it trumps fiction . . . it is Anna Porter's consummate art as a storyteller that makes this true tale so compelling."

We followed *Kasztner's Train* three years later with *The Ghosts of Europe: Journeys Through Central Europe's Troubled Past and Uncertain Future*, Anna's personal rediscovery of her homelands 20 years following the collapse of the Soviet Empire. She was again paying tribute to childhood memories, and the legacy of her larger-than-life grandfather, Vili Racz, a journalist and family storyteller.

This book ventured into new territory, addressing the political shifts in Hungary, the Czech Republic, Slovakia, and Poland. Few North Americans could have tracked down Václav Havel, Adam Michnik, Radek Sikorski, and Viktor Orbán in their respective lairs for interviews, sometimes in their own languages. Her conclusions were fraught, shining a light on the despotic instincts of the new breed of power. David Frum called it "intimate and insightful: an exile's poignant return home."

—

D&M ended the first decade of the 21st century on high ground, and, for the most part, authors with strong voices continued to justify the emotional investment. I first confirmed D&M's interest in Arctic issues in 2009 when we published Michael Byers's *Who Owns the Arctic? Understanding Sovereignty Disputes in the North*. Byers was a distinguished academic who had newly returned to Canada to join the UBC faculty as a Canada Research Chair in Global Politics and International Law. His book was a trenchant rebuke to prevailing wisdom. Shelagh Grant's *Polar Imperative: A History of Arctic Sovereignty in North America* stands out as a reward for patience and stubborn defiance, and Ian Gill's *All That We Say Is Ours: Guujaaw and the Reawakening of the Haida Nation* required equivalent determination.

Some years earlier, I had met Shelagh's husband, Jon, and much liked him. He was president of Quaker Oats and an advocate for preserving the natural environment. They were living in Peterborough, where his wife was a research associate in Trent University's School for the Study of Canada. Jon mentioned that Shelagh had written one book on the Arctic and was at work on another. Naturally, I suggested that D&M would be interested.

The possibility remained in limbo for some years until Shelagh submitted a manuscript in progress reflecting 30 years of research. It was a sweeping history of sovereignty in the Arctic, beginning in 3,000 BCE, well before the beginning of the usual overview of adventuring by the British Admiralty. Critically, it framed the long history from a Canadian perspective.

Shelagh's monumental work was a long time in gestation. It was clearly an important book, but as the months dragged on, Shelagh became fiercely possessive of every word in the almost 200,000-word manuscript. The words kept changing in the middle of our publishing process. We would have long conversations about our requirement for a shred of process. Shelagh would apologize and virtually nod in agreement. Then the next round of changes would arrive, even though the book was edited and at the printer.

My patience is not usually tried, but it was in this case. The book was being edited by a careful, quiet freelance editor, normally associated with UBC Press, who happened to be sitting in our offices when the final call from Shelagh arrived. I exploded. All within earshot seemed shocked when I ran out of Anglo-Saxon.

When the book was published in fall 2010, things improved. The following year, it was awarded the Lionel Gelber Prize for the world's best English-language non-fiction book on global affairs. Shelagh was the first Canadian woman to win it. It was a finalist for the Shaughnessy Cohen Prize for Political Writing, the Canadian Historical Association's Sir John A. Macdonald Prize for the best book on Canadian history, and a fistful of additional honours. The Gelber Prize was awarded in the Munk Centre, and I made a point of being there as a witness when Janice Stein announced the award.

The story didn't end there. Shelagh, Jon, and I stayed in touch, and when I was invited to spend some time as a visiting fellow in Traill College at Trent University, they took charge. Corky was with me, and they spent a day chauffeuring the two of us around Peterborough, ensuring we spent time in their other passion, the Canoe Museum. The day culminated with a party in our honour in their house, but only after Jon and I had broken ranks to watch the Super Bowl.

I dwell on this story because it emphasizes why publishing matters. We had helped "birth" a book that changed Canada's perception of its Arctic inheritance, while inserting a Canadian point of view into an international story too often told without our participation. And it survived a difficult birth, where patience, belief, and ongoing support had been critical.

All That We Say Is Ours was another of those projects that began well but encountered turbulent political waters. It seemed to be my editorial curse: noble ideas running into the buzz saw of the real world.

Ian Gill was an experienced journalist who had built a reputation for sharp, insightful commentary during his years with the CBC and

Vancouver Sun. He had persuaded me, with his advocacy, to join the board of Ecotrust Canada. In 2002, while I was on the Ecotrust board, Corky finally convinced me to have us both join one of that entity's sponsored sailing trips around Haida Gwaii.

A ship called the SV *Duen* was to be our home for two weeks. It was a "gaff" rigged ketch built of Norwegian pitch pine, and extraordinarily sturdy, having endured 30 years in the Norwegian commercial fishing fleet, then, in retirement, circumnavigating the world. We were confident it was safe, even traversing the notoriously treacherous waters of Hecate Strait.

Our approach meant flying to Sandspit, where we were to spend a night in the one hotel available. At about midnight, thunderous screeching woke us. A huge raven had landed on a nearby power transformer, blowing out all the electricity in the area. Encountering northern ravens for the first time, large and mysterious creatures covered in lustrous, midnight-black feathers, made clear the reason for their iconic stature within Haida mythology. We chose not to take the large carcass on the road outside our room as an omen.

Our destination was Anthony Island, SG-ang Gwaay Llnagaay (Red Cod Island), and its Haida ancestral village of Ninstints, now anointed as a UNESCO World Heritage Site. As we walked along the constrained path into the village through a narrow defile of volcanic rock, ghosts seemed to inhabit every shadow. The bones of the village's ancestors could be seen, abandoned now, with disintegrating mortuary poles gradually succumbing to winter storms and eroding cedar. A palpable spirituality lingered in the air. It is an extraordinary place.

On the trip back, the magic was interrupted as Ecotrust's Beaver airplane arrived, carrying Gidansda Guujaaw, also known as Gary Edenshaw, and his family. I was a great admirer of Guujaaw, an apprentice to Bill Reid, carver, dancer, and fighter for Haida land rights, every inch a Haida warrior. He didn't share the same view of me.

No sooner had the group boarded the *Duen* when Guujaaw noticed me, glanced at me fiercely, and ominously declared: "You! Bringhurst!" That was the extent of the conversation. His judgement was unequivocal.

His mood softened over the next few days. He invited Corky and me to visit the museum-to-be in Skidegate, with its newly installed poles and existing cultural exhibits. We accepted and made a plan to join him.

The trip back to Queen Charlotte City (now Daajing Giids) took us up the outer east coast of the South Moresby archipelago, now Gwaii Haanas — "Islands of Beauty" to the Haida. Amongst the abandoned villages, with the remnants of the cedar longhouses still visible through the moss, it was Tanu I wanted to visit. That was where Bill Reid had been laid to final rest. A modest memorial stone had been set up, almost at the edge of the sea, overlooking his spiritual home. Inscribed on the stone were the words Iljuwas and Yalth-Sgwansang, the latter meaning "The Only Raven," a name given to Bill by Florence Davidson.

I sat alone and in silence for several minutes, paying private obeisance. I had known Bill as a friend, a disrupter, and a respected author, and had spoken at his memorial event. It was only in that quiet moment that I fully realized how deeply the raven, the man, his art, and his stories had touched my soul.

We did join Guujaaw in the museum for a tour. All seemed well until, on a rack in the museum bookstore, he noticed a single copy of one of Robert Bringhurst's *Classical Haida Mythtellers and Their World* trilogy. He immediately picked it up from the rack and moved closer to my face. Waving the book in the air, he began to shout. Pointing to the effusive quotes on the back flap, he emphatically kept repeating, "The Publisher says . . . ," while jabbing his finger at the cover with such intensity that I thought he might break it.

Always sensitive to such accusations, all too often a gullible white guy, I was becoming defensive. Guujaaw was pressing his advantage. As I was in full retreat, and Guujaaw was in full rhetorical flower, Corky burst in with a simple request: "Will you two fucking five-year-olds please shut up!"

Guujaaw is not easily cowed, but Corky won that round. Total silence ensued. Then, as though a dark cloud had passed, Guujaaw led us into the museum and gave us a personal tour. He steered us out to a picnic table on the beach facing newly raised poles, not yet accompanied by the longhouses since added, and opened up about his dream for the expanded

Haida Gwaii Museum in Skidegate. It is now completed, one of the finest on the coast. It contains the remains of revered Haida bodies, some repatriated from museums around the world against great odds and following much diplomatic negotiation. It is a fitting final resting place for Haida ancestors, once feared warriors and aristocrats amongst coastal cultures.

It had become clear to me that the Haida quest for ownership over their lands, a struggle moving with glacial speed through the courts, was an important cause. As a determined leader in the fight, Guujaaw would be worth a book digging more deeply into the issue and its historical resonance, I felt. We commissioned Ian Gill to write it.

This depended upon Guujaaw's willingness to cooperate, and he agreed. The manuscript was completed and published in 2009. We secured blurbs from Wade Davis, John Vaillant, J. Edward Chamberlin, and Joseph Gosnell, amongst others. Shawn Atleo's endorsement went straight to the point: "In telling the story of a modern indigenous hero and his people, Ian Gill has captured a moment in the global resurgence of indigenous people. This book artfully bridges the vast gulf of misunderstanding that still pervades our society."

So far, so good. Not for long. Having theoretically blessed the manuscript (without having been given any right of editorial approval), Guujaaw finally read it closely, and strongly objected to a few of what I considered to be trivial issues. Some were personal, but some suggested cultural inaccuracies.

After some email exchanges, the issue escalated when Guujaaw laid out his objections in a multi-page rant. It reached me via fax in a New York hotel. The fax machine ran out of paper.

Upon returning to Vancouver, I agreed to join a meeting convened by Miles Richardson, a prominent Haida leader, to discuss the issues and how they might be resolved. It was to be held in the Bill Reid Gallery. I arrived ready to listen. Miles was on the phone to Haida Gwaii (obviously with Guujaaw on the other end), and we were to discuss what might be done. To my surprise, David Suzuki had also been invited. And because he happened to be carving in the gallery at the time, Jim Hart was quietly observing.

The conversation dragged inconclusively on. Increasingly frustrated, I suggested that if we were provided, in writing, with a list of things that were specifically culturally inaccurate or factually wrong, we would correct them. Expecting that nothing would happen, I was proven right.

We published the book with only minor changes, all blessed by Ian, a few months later. But upon leaving the meeting in the gallery, I did endure a stern rebuke from Suzuki for having caved, which in my view I had not.

The book's sales were disappointing. Was it Raven? Was it Haida word of mouth? Was it the luck of the draw? Was it the understated cover design and obscure title — *All That We Say Is Ours*? There are never clear answers to such dilemmas. I remain adamant that the book was an important addition to the literature of British Columbia and honoured our original intent: to elevate the Haida cause and, in doing so, pay homage to Guujaaw's leadership. It was recently reissued in paperback, confirmation of its importance and staying power. On April 14, 2024, the Council of the Haida Nation and the province of British Columbia signed the historic Gaayhllxid/Gíihlagalgang "Rising Tide" Haida Title Lands Agreement granting the Haida exclusive control of all the land of Haida Gwaii.

16

WARNING SIGNALS

Traditional wisdom suggests that the foundation of any successful publishing house is backlist (all books except those from the current publishing season) reaching 50 percent of total turnover, a measure of both achievement and stability. By the late 1990s, we had reached that coveted milestone.

As Douglas & McIntyre built the various streams of its programs, profitability remained modest, small for our dollar volume, but such a circumstance was endemic to all Canadian trade publishing. Yes, the grants made a difference. But sales mattered.

Groundwood Books emerged as the highest-quality children's publisher in the country, attracting a who's who of writers and illustrators and garnering an ever-expanding list of national and international awards. It became a house of choice for fiction and illustrated books, with an illustrious group of talent including Brian Doyle, Sarah Ellis, Jan Truss, Janet Lunn, Teddy Jam, Blair Dawson, Paul Yee, W.D. Valgardson, Welwyn Wilton Katz, Sharon, Lois & Bram, Ian Wallace, Tim Wynne-Jones, Thomas King, Marie-Louise Gay, and Shirley Hughes, plus highlights from a distinguished group of publishers for whose books Groundwood won Canadian distribution rights.

Patsy Aldana's passion for the Latino world was growing, and her connections in that world were impeccable. The combination led to her launching a Spanish-language children's fiction imprint in fall 1999. Patsy's international network was also attracting writers and illustrators of reputation, expanding Groundwood's reputation, and reach, in the US.

If there is now an established pantheon for Canadian children's and young adult authors and illustrators, Groundwood can rightly claim to have been present at the creation. Patsy's words on the occasion of Groundwood's 25th anniversary ring true: "When Groundwood was founded twenty-five years ago, there were very few Canadian-authored or -illustrated books for children. It was an act of optimism born from the belief that Canadian children were entitled to find their own lives and experiences in their books. I was also convinced that great writers and illustrators would emerge from all the people who make up this diverse and tolerant country, and they have . . . Continuing to publish the kinds of books we do is a political act."

Groundwood's anniversary unfolded in Toronto, but it seemed appropriate that Vancouver offer something to honour the occasion. Thinking about what to do had been left until the last moment. With time running out, the necessity increased. Late one night, with the deadline imminent, I lapsed into doggerel mode and scribbled a limerick:

> There was once a small mouse from Toronto,
> Who grew famous for quality, pronto,
> Her touch was sublime,
> Her awards all the time,
> The first 25 years esplendido.

We designed the words in the shape of a bookmark and had a Toronto friend deliver the message by hand, with a bottle of good wine, to each of the Toronto staff.

Patsy's response a few days later summed up our relationship: "What a fantastic gesture, — elegant and fun. And thanks for everything else . . . I wouldn't be here without you. It makes me feel teary to think about it, believe it or not. We are the odd couple, I guess but under it all I trust you entirely."

Greystone, too, hit its stride. Its illustrated natural history books were selling increasing quantities of co-editions, becoming the backbone of the American Sierra Club's publishing program. Our tie to the Suzuki Foundation lured authors of consequence confronting environmental issues, amongst them Andrew Nikiforuk, Paul Quarrington, Brian Brett, Charlotte Gill, and of course David Suzuki himself and his prolific output.

With the strong advocacy of Patsy and Rob, the company's US sales enjoyed a growing US market. It was increasingly self-evident that the small and fractious Canadian market was never going to be large or reliable enough to allow genuine comfort, certainly not for adventuresome publishing. I was the hesitant one, as my own abiding passion for Canadian culture always blunted my enthusiasm for pursuing the American market, however beneficial I understood that neighbouring pot of gold to be.

—

I'd learned that fighting to preserve Canadian cultural space was always problematic. The issue was deeply resented in the American corporate world. Canadian ideas — expressed in the country's books, magazines, television, movies, and music — are usually squeezed to the margins. The mechanisms of their distribution were, and remain, primarily controlled by American corporations. Profit is the primary concern. Nation building is of little consequence. Americans feel that Canada is *their* turf and have the commercial weapons to prevail.

In 1994, when the Free Trade Agreement was expanded to include Mexico — now inheriting a new acronym, the North American Free Trade Agreement (NAFTA) — cultural issues once again became an irritant, equally frustrating to the Mexicans as well as the Americans. During one of the toughest moments, Conservative Minister of Finance Michael Wilson weighed in, playing the constitutional crisis card, given events then unfolding in Quebec. "This is not a question of protecting an industry. It is a matter of preserving the soul of a nation at a crucial time in our history. We are defending a culture . . . The US will not get through NAFTA, what it failed to achieve in the FTA."

Pragmatism, and probably ennui, prevailed. The US finally acknowledged that "Canada was a special case." Better, our negotiators persuaded the Europeans not to seize upon the precedent. So far, they never have. A "cultural exemption," one of Canada's quiet, unacknowledged victories, remains enshrined in every trade treaty Canada negotiates.

The Americans remained poised to attack. When Canada attempted to protect its magazine publishers, claiming that such magazines as *Time* and *Reader's Digest* were "dumping" their American editions into Canada, siphoning off scarce advertising dollars, the Americans took the case to a World Trade Organization tribunal. In 1997, Canada lost, a profound shock. In 1997, Art Eggleton, then minister of international trade, rather wistfully asked the SAGIT if we couldn't offer government something better than the offensive "protectionist" rhetoric, which his international colleagues viewed as out of sync with the progressive world. In response, Peter Grant, senior cultural lawyer at McCarthy Tétrault, and a member of the SAGIT, suggested a new approach: What about a new international instrument dealing specifically with cultural issues, framed as protecting "cultural diversity"?

It was obvious that the business-driven WTO would never accept such a measure. Rather than bashing our heads against a stone wall, perhaps we could draft the bones of such an instrument in order to clarify the issues. It might have to be parked, in legal limbo, outside any formal trade agreement, but could exert moral suasion on public, perhaps even government, opinion. Peter himself took a crack at drafting an initial version of how such an instrument might work. It wasn't simple. He once confessed to me, sheepishly, "This *is* brain science."

The Cultural Industries SAGIT embraced the strategy, an audacious dance around conventional wisdom. Critically, it might offer Canadian cabinet ministers Sheila Copps and Pierre Pettigrew some useful ammunition to bolster their Sisyphean efforts.

In February 1999, the SAGIT delivered its report, unglamorously titled *New Strategies for Culture and Trade: Canadian Culture in a Global World*. It advocated the creation of a new international treaty with a refined focus, acknowledging the unique nature of cultural goods and services and suggesting how responsible trade disciplines might coexist with cultural measures. Its clear purpose was to blunt growing pressure to have culture ensnared within the dictates of WTO policy. To our surprise and delight, government accepted the idea.

International colleagues viewed the idea as something between unnecessary and loathsome. The French, however, felt otherwise. With their advocacy, it was eventually agreed that the United Nations Educational, Scientific, and Cultural Organization (UNESCO) was the best place for such an instrument to find a sympathetic home. While not our first choice, we needed allies and pragmatically endorsed the prospect.

At the same time, civil society had energized itself to work in parallel with government. The initiative became particularly well organized in Canada, led by strong Quebec voices. It resulted in the establishment of the Coalition for Cultural Diversity/la coalition pour la diversité culturelle (CCD) in 1998. The initial chair was Pierre Curzi, an accomplished Quebecois actor and a man of great personal charm, with the rhetorical skills of someone accustomed to the stage. But the coalition needed an English-Canadian voice. Because of my publishing association work, I was nominated to be co-chair, another voluntary tilt at a windmill.

As the idea for a new treaty inched its way through the international system, my involvement intensified. But UNESCO is a large, structurally unwieldy, sclerotic organization. Sometimes it makes progress. More often, it succumbs to the dictates of geopolitical reality. The draft convention's stumbling steps up the procedural ladder stretched out over two years. Its convoluted language was refined at a leisurely pace.

UNESCO Canada had been involved from the beginning, adding this country's clout to those emphasizing the importance of the cultural file. Max Wyman, another Vancouverite, was president of the Canadian Commission for UNESCO during those years. He ensured that Canada's voice remained influential throughout the highly charged negotiations, dragging deeply skeptical countries to support the convention. Progress was slow, but steady.

—

In 1999, with three energetic and successful publishing programs, I decided it was time for the company to clarify its overall structure in some way that emphasized the linkage amongst the three publishing units. This was a common solution in publishing houses with diverse imprints, and it made good business sense.

I proposed that we launch the "Douglas & McIntyre Publishing Group" as an overarching identifier. It would fully respect the established separate characters of the imprints while clarifying a close family relationship. I was not oblivious to the power of a brand.

Suspecting that Patsy would be skeptical, given her fierce determination to maintain Groundwood's independence, and facing the complexity that she had taken a year out so that she and her family could live in France, a face-to-face conversation was required. On my way to Frankfurt that year, I took a detour to Carpentras, the closest town of any size to the farmhouse Patsy and her husband, Matt Cohen, owned in the Vaucluse.

Patsy had booked me into the Hotel du Fiacre, evocative of so many buildings of a certain age that dot provincial France. It had cavernous rooms, walls covered by once elegant but fading pastel wallpaper, squeaky, well-worn wooden floors, and a no-nonsense matron laying down crisp guidelines. She provided a password to open the back door in case I returned late at night, which I did.

Patsy and I spent a day seated at a spindly table in my hotel room, talking through many things while re-establishing the rapport we always managed to rediscover when we were together. The idea of the Douglas & McIntyre Publishing Group, composed of three equal publishing units, was agreed. Then it was off to a fine dinner with Patsy, Matt, and their kids. I carried Patsy's young son Daniel on my shoulders to the chosen restaurant.

Our momentum carried into the new millennium, but rumours of General Distribution Services being in financial trouble began surfacing. Cash flow began to become unreliable. It seemed incredible to be confronting such a situation again, and so quickly. As Yogi Berra liked to say, "It was déjà vu all over again."

In 2001, GDS was pushed to file for bankruptcy. We were owed over $700,000, all our receivables out of the Canadian market. If misery loves company, we were in good company. GDS had attracted distribution, including invoicing and collections, for a range of important Canadian independent publishers, amongst them us, Key Porter, ECW, and several others of reputation.

This was devastating to an already reeling industry. Ottawa was obligated to take notice. Sheila Copps, minister of the Department of Canadian Heritage, and her senior bureaucrats understood that something had to be done. With Minister Copps's clout in cabinet, supported by those of her senior staff in Heritage still willing to take risks, there was an implicit expectation that companies owed money from GDS must somehow be made whole.

It took many trips to Ottawa, and much pressure, to turn what was implicit into reality. It eventually appeared the money would be flowing, but what strings might be attached remained a mystery. The form the support finally took was an "advance" against monies coming from the Canada Book Fund, to be clawed back out of amounts otherwise owing from the fund over five years. Not a gift, but better than nothing, and survivable.

During my many meetings with senior Heritage people, the one thing I pressed for was assurance that the amount of the "repayable loan" not be considered debt on our already fragile balance sheet. It had to be papered in such a way that our bank could consider it neutral, not affecting our debt-equity ratio. That was critical.

Unsurprisingly, at the last minute, Treasury Board weighed in unkindly. The outstanding part of the "loan" had to be handled on our balance sheet as borrowed money, therefore showing as debt. As our strong sales growth was continuing, we were able to make another unhappy financial circumstance work in the eyes of our bank. It was, yet again, a narrow escape.

The downside was that the circumstance caused the bank to move our account into something called "Special Unit." This signalled that it considered the odds against our survival long. The issue also triggered an enhanced level of scrutiny, with more frequent reporting, and another level of debilitating uncertainty.

Enduring time in a Canadian bank's Special Unit is like being forced to pause in purgatory on the way to hell. That is usually the result. When we managed to earn our way out of the dilemma, proving we were sustainable, one of our bankers cheerfully told me that we were one of the first companies he knew of to have survived the experience. I don't recommend it.

―

Our fiscal agonies never showed in the books, or in our programs. The combined D&M/Groundwood/Greystone lists remained at about 70 new books a year. Revenue held steady in the $10-million range. We survived because of the publishing — editorially high-quality projects resonant with our self-imposed mandate and blessed by frequent national bestsellers. But D&M's fragile finances were increasingly being undermined.

I'd turned 60 in 2004 with no pension, our house still at risk, no prospect of dividends, and even the equity in my life insurance policy, theoretically a retirement fund, tied up in the company. My rose-coloured glasses had finally fallen off. Canadian investors were not lined up to invest in book publishing, particularly given that the business community had chosen to notice the uncertainties of the industry's financial track record.

One solution was to take the path that so many companies had chosen in the past: dramatically reducing both overhead and publishing programs. That meant destroying the team in place and the model. I wasn't ready for that, even though it would have been the pragmatic business move. Operating in Canada, with a constrained number of large houses, ownership restrictions still on the government books, and neither merchant banks nor private equity tempted, options were scarce.

I was increasingly ground down by the constant drama, and the paucity of working capital. It was also beginning to cost us authors who were moving to larger houses for more generous royalty advances. There was nothing surprising about authors of achievement asking for more money. In a world of literary agents, it is inevitable. The ironic curse of small publishing houses is always that the better they are at launching and nurturing talent, the more such risk-taking pushes them into the wilderness of lost authors. In one late-evening conversation with Anna Porter, I confessed: "It doesn't matter what you do in Canadian publishing. It is never quite good enough." Anna responded that she had heard Jack McClelland utter almost identical words just before selling his company to Avie Bennett.

I'd been thinking about selling D&M or securing an alliance since 2002, when General Publishing proposed a merger with D&M and Key Porter. It was abundantly clear, to me at least, that the comfortable world of traditional publishing was quickly evolving. Publishing houses could be small, or large. There was little room left in the middle ground. Acquire deep pockets and play the game at a serious level, or return to the historical path of publishing, as it had been when scale was small, or family wealth determined possibilities. Canadian-owned publishing, and those idealistic dreams some of us had for so long espoused, was roadkill in this new world.

Avie Bennett's McClelland & Stewart, then still independent, remained a possibility. Such a marriage would have been both practical and emotionally resonant. I knew and liked Avie, and my M&S experience lingered in my blood. In 2003, the M&S board authorized Douglas Gibson, then the company's president, to approach Patsy and me about a purchase. We agreed to meet. The possibility offered great promise, but ended when M&S, after a seemingly good year, discovered the truth of their final numbers when the contingent liability of unprocessed returns was factored in. Still, Avie remained personally enthusiastic. I'll never forget his final letter delivering the unhappy news of M&S's withdrawal of interest concluding with the wistful words: "If I was five years younger, I'd do it tomorrow."

Something had to be done. I spent the next two years quietly sounding out possibilities with many people, including a Vancouver investor who remained seriously interested. Our size meant that we had outgrown possibilities with most Canadian companies, all of which faced similar constraints. Our sales had plateaued, our debt load was discouraging, and our profitability unimpressive. Solving this by the seat of my pants was absolutely the wrong approach. As we lacked a strong outside board and shareholders pushing, my innate optimism held the high ground.

I retained faith that, sooner or later, luck would hold and something would work out. It turned out to be quite different than I'd hoped.

—

One diversion was my work on the Coalition for Cultural Diversity/La coalition pour la diversité culturelle. In February 2003, I flew as co-chair to attend and speak at a gathering of European cultural leaders. UNESCO has never been shy about ponderous event names: This one was titled the Second International Meeting of Cultural Professional Organizations. There were 300 invited guests from cultural groups across Europe, joined by senior politicians and bureaucrats, including Sheila Copps, who was to be a featured speaker. The setting was the Carrousel du Louvre, with a stage full of European political and cultural royalty, including Raymond Chrétien, then Canada's ambassador in Paris.

Sheila Copps spoke brilliantly during the first afternoon, in French, English, and Spanish, offering a persuasive articulation of why culture matters. The speech was ignored in most of English Canada.

I had flown in overnight from Vancouver and been rewarded with an exploding wisdom tooth. I remained mired in toothache agony, hoping that Sheila, having finished speaking, would depart the gathering. My panel was to follow, and I made the mistake of letting Sheila know. Her answer was decidedly not what I was hoping to hear: "If you're going to speak, I'll stay to listen."

Preparation for the panel had been a last-minute "briefing" in a dark room deep in the bowels of the Carrousel. The French was rapid-fire, the air in the room reminiscent of the Black Hole of Calcutta. None of what I had been able to glean of the instructions made any sense. I stumbled onto the stage, convinced that this was probably as good a way as any to die.

My panel consisted of three speakers. I was in the middle, flanked by two senior French delegates: one a very wealthy video executive whom central casting had provided as an example of triumphant French culture, the other an avuncular senator who much relished the sound of his own voice. I had no choice but to pray that the pain would subside in time and speak with as much confidence as I could muster. Sheila Copps and Pierre Curzi were in the front row, and when I had finished, to my very great relief they nodded in approval.

The event proved to be an influential tactic capping much lobbying to win the support of UNESCO's General Conference for the proposed new convention on culture. But the US remained a troublesome outlier. In October 2005, when a finished draft of the convention reached the UNESCO General Conference agenda and was to be voted on, the Americans realized they had been outfoxed. US Secretary of State Condoleezza Rice played a last card. A personal letter under her signature was sent to ambassadors of all UNESCO members, darkly hinting that, should the draft agreement be accepted, the US might reconsider its recently renewed membership in the organization. That proved too little, too late.

The convention, clumsily named the UNESCO Convention on the Protection and Promotion of the Diversity of Cultural Expressions, was adopted on October 20, 2005, with 148 countries in favour, 4 abstentions, and 2 opposed: the US and Israel. As of summer 2024, it had been signed by 153 nations. The speed with which it had jumped all necessary hurdles was unprecedented, and Canada had been influential, stepping out from its all-too-frequent hiding place in the shadows.

A new trade agreement had survived, one that allowed nation-states to set their own cultural priorities with impunity while allowing any nation-state to opt out of any new, restrictive measures that might arise in the future. From Canada's perspective, it was a successful end run on American belligerence.

I had never intended to become so involved in obscure trade policy, but events led me there. On balance it proved to be worth it personally, for the industry, and, because it opened doors in Ottawa, for Douglas & McIntyre.

—

When it became clear that M&S was not going to pursue an alliance with Douglas & McIntyre, alternatives required my focussed attention. There was never any single, dramatic moment. The company had always lived on the financial edge, relying on borrowed money rather than equity. Never in the company's history had it paid a dividend. As the majority shareholder, holding 65 percent of the equity, I had remained comfortable with this, accepting the view that while it could provide a decent living, there was never any serious money to be made in book publishing.

Cash flow was always difficult, particularly during the months when lean spring sales, diminished by growing returns, bumped up against the investments of the late spring and summer months, when expenditure for new projects was at its peak. The shadow of insufficient cash flow constantly hung over the passions of acquiring the next book. The predicament was the same for both Patsy in Groundwood and Rob in Greystone, as D&M financed their programs.

On top of this, our growing bank operating line, which peaked at well into seven figures annually, remained partially collateralized by a series of mortgages on our house. Initially, Corky and I had held the house jointly. Several years later, when it first became clear that the risk was too great, the house was moved into Corky's name. Still, she had to co-sign every mortgage. She always agreed, although with increasing reluctance.

There was never any substantial support from minority shareholders, none of whom had any real money or appetite for risk at this level. I could hardly blame them. When I once confessed to an author that our house was totally at risk to finance the company, alone amongst the shareholders, his response was utter disbelief: How could anyone be so stupid?

My eternal optimism held the dark clouds at bay. A letter from old friend David Godine, himself an independent publisher based in Boston, was succinct: "I look forward to a visit to further inject some much-needed optimism into my seared and soiled skin. Someone once remarked that the only philosophically tenable position for anyone to remain insane enough to engage in this business of fools and folly was one of profound and unshakeable optimism." I never doubted things would work out.

Lack of adequate working capital was eventually going to catch up to us, and it was clear that things were not going to improve. The Canadian market was slowly eroding. Indigo was pulling in its horns, and while US sales were growing, they were not growing quickly enough to generate a safety margin. And there were no angels we knew of hovering in the clouds above.

—

Patsy Aldana saw things clearly, as she so often did. She felt that sooner or later we were going to run out of miracles, and her baby, Groundwood, was going to get caught in the middle.

Scott Griffin had by then bought the House of Anansi out of the ashes of the Stoddart bankruptcy and was investing in Anansi's future. As a successful businessman with a passion for books and ideas, he had met Patsy and expressed interest in buying Groundwood to add a distinguished children's imprint and broaden the base of Anansi's rejuvenated adult publishing. He embraced the possibility, and he had the money.

This was a devastating development for me personally, but I couldn't fault Patsy's survival instincts. With deep reluctance, I made uncomfortable peace with the inevitable.

Scott and I met in Toronto to negotiate the business arrangement. The discussions were congenial, and in the end we accepted a fair offer for the Groundwood inventory, and those copyrights D&M owned, for a mix of cash and a 20 percent equity interest in Anansi.

Not knowing Scott well then, I was struck by his composed manner. Patsy liked to refer to him as the Gatsby of Canadian publishing. Elegant in dress and habit, clearly handling his years well, he fit the description. It didn't hurt his image that he was a qualified pilot with his own plane, and a passionate sailor with proven skill on the water. In another era, he would have made the perfect gentleman publisher, combining civil behaviour with membership in the best clubs. Scott also had the advantage, one that eluded many old-guard publishers, of being very shrewd and successful in business.

The deal for Anansi to acquire the assets of Groundwood closed in 2005. The benefits to us included some cash and an alliance that held promise for the future. A final issue was the question of whether I should be elected to the board. We were, after all, going to own 20 percent of the company, and my publishing experience was potentially valuable. Scott was initially uncomfortable with the idea. With Patsy's advocacy, I suspect, I was granted a seat. It provided a fascinating glimpse into the evolution of a Toronto-based independent of modest scale (about half our size), with a backlist of literary reputation, strengthened by a perfect combination of fresh publishing energy and renewed financing.

Parting company with Groundwood was painful, as was losing its annual sales of about $1 million with modest profits, but it was another business loss we could absorb. D&M was holding its own financially in spite of all that had unfolded, including the bankruptcy of GDS, writing off almost $1 million of Orion inventory, and now the loss of Groundwood revenues. Our survival instincts had been well honed. The essential thing, our Canadian publishing, was still working, and the Bank of Montreal remained onside.

—

I escalated my quiet search for a solution to the trauma sitting on the horizon. I initiated conversations with several companies, including Random House, Quebecor, and Michel de la Chenelière's then very successful education enterprise, Les Éditions de la Chenelière. Our balance sheet, our location, and the size of our bank debt always interfered.

We had promising initial discussions with Simon Fraser University, as I offered to give the company to the university as a shortcut to their building a university press. The university had a respected program of publishing studies, initially designed with significant help from Jim Douglas. This suggested both historical and practical resonance. Michael Stevenson, then president of the university, was intrigued, but the board, aware of the prevailing rhetoric of the time that book publishing was a sinkhole for cash, quickly ended the initiative.

In 2006, an entirely unexpected possibility presented itself. I had spent some years in a small book club that included several literate, well-connected Vancouverites. One of the group was Mark Scott, an investment banker who had recently helped a Vancouver film and animation company go public. He had no ongoing involvement in the new entity, was an avid book collector with an engaging manner, and was seeking a new opportunity.

Mark raised the possibility of acquiring D&M. I responded with my usual caveat that our balance sheet wouldn't impress him, but after he had spent time reviewing recent D&M financials, his interest intensified.

Just before Christmas, Mark and his colleagues confirmed they were ready to offer. A bit stunned, I embraced the possibility. New investors with potentially deep pockets, strong community roots, and a genuine interest in what D&M represented seemed an ideal solution.

Mark was joined by two friends, both very successful private equity investors, who were willing to help. Rod Senft was co-founder and chairman of Tricor Pacific Capital, and a colleague, David Rowntree, the other co-founder and managing director of Tricor. Given their combined reputation, I never pressed hard to probe the extent of their passion, or their willingness to open further pockets.

A fully vetted, acceptable offer arrived on the table in early spring 2007. The three new shareholders, between them, would acquire 75 percent of the company's common shares, and I would retain 25 percent, with monies owing for my shares to be paid out over five years. All the existing minority shareholders — Jim Douglas, Patsy Aldana, Don Atkins, Mark Stanton, Rick Antonson, and Allan MacDougall — would be cashed out. Mark would become president while I remained CEO for two years, with Mark stepping into my shoes thereafter. Paperwork was completed, a new shareholder's agreement put in place, and initial cheques exchanged on April 30, 2007.

A month later, Corky and I welcomed the new arrangement with a dinner party on the deck of our home. The sun was low on the horizon, throwing off golden light. The new shareholders and our senior management had all gathered for a quietly emotional celebration. D&M was about to embark on a new chapter.

Corky and I breathed deep sighs of relief. We were out from under sizeable debt obligations, and the agreed amount I would be paid for my shares enhanced the possibility of a reasonable retirement. Reflecting upon the circumstance, we pinched ourselves. We had successfully pulled off what few Canadian publishing houses had ever before managed. It seemed a graceful exit, fair to shareholders, management, and staff, while accommodating my continuing involvement in helping shape the D&M program.

—

News of the sale made waves nationally, and internationally. Prevailing Canadian sentiment was best summed up by Timothy Taylor in a long piece written for the *Globe and Mail*:

> Let's start off with the big story (big for those of us involved in publishing, anyway). Last week, Douglas & McIntyre, the Vancouver-based independent publisher founded in 1971, announced that a group of investors had bought a controlling interest in the company . . .
>
> Rich folks from the outside world have bought into publishing before, of course. Still, this acquisition was notable because of what sort of money came calling . . . Private-equity investors. Read: high priests of finance who buy assets with a fairly strict view of making money . . .
>
> Mr. McIntyre and Mr. Scott met in a book club. And it's these sorts of meetings . . . between our creative and investment classes . . . that will be critical to realizing the

upside of our bullish feelings, and happier aspects of that Great City.

A telling response came from New York as well. Tony Schulte, then second-in-command at Random House New York, an elegant, courteous man who had become a friend over the years, was on the phone: "Scott, tell me it's not true." The sale had been noticed further afield than I had been expecting.

—

The optimism of the moment was infectious, but it was not to last. As is so often the case when things seem almost too good to be true, until they are not, this turned into an example of high hopes gradually fading in a marginal business under constant threat from a restructuring market.

Our financial results remained healthy, but it turned out that Mark was better at endorsing the *idea* of books than he was at rolling up his sleeves and addressing the day-to-day reality of running a publishing house. He never made time to grasp the truths of how book publishing worked.

His interest focussed on acquisitions and taking advantage of digital opportunities, both potentially bold initiatives for the time, both requiring access to significant capital. He proposed establishing a new entity, one devoted to gathering existing material into a database that would allow individuals to assemble custom-made books, taking advantage of print-on-demand technology and leveraging extensive existing content to break through one of the last barriers of publishing. We were hardly alone in contemplating such an initiative, though it appeared we might have a lead over potential competitors. We also had the theoretical advantage of being small and lean.

Accordingly, in 2008 we launched a new company, BookRiff Media, a promising innovation. In reality, we were too slow, too badly managed, and too undercapitalized for the scale of the initiative. Mark kept his distance from the rest of D&M, which mystified existing staff accustomed to a much more hands-on management style. I continued on as CEO past the originally proposed two years, becoming increasingly anxious to give up the CEO title, although reluctant to abandon shaping the D&M program. Rob, similarly, remained focussed on Greystone, with his list steadily improving.

With our new ownership, the board had been restructured, with one new outsider. But the board remained a perfunctory institution, lacking any hard-headed, experienced, results-driven new voices from the broader publishing community, people who understood the business's fundamental truths. This was not an unusual structure for small publishing houses, but it is not helpful when there are new, less knowledgeable shareholders not engaged in the core business.

—

So long as our Canadian publishing held its own, with stable sales revenues plus grants, incipient problems could be swept under the rug. But with Mark consumed by his digital initiative, my passion gradually diminishing, and the always problematic Canadian market continuing to entrench, ominous clouds were gathering.

Aggressive possibility still existed, as small companies were beginning to be offered for sale. Generational evolution was becoming imperative. One of those companies seeking an exit for founding shareholders was New Society, an idealistic, environmentally focussed publishing house based on Gabriola Island that had grown out of a 1970s food co-op. It had originally been funded by Renewal Partners, a Vancouver-based investment entity dedicated to socially responsible, sustainable business practices. New Society's declared mandate resonated perfectly with the idealism of Renewal Partners, and with its ongoing support, the company had grown to become very successful.

The founders and guiding lights of New Society, Judith and Christopher Plant, had decided they were of an age to retire and were seeking to make an alliance that would honour their idealism while offering a secure future. Human compatibility, combined with financial stability and a shared corporate vision, was an essential requirement.

The Plants had engaged a Vancouver corporate broker to manage the process. In early January 2008, I responded to a request for expressions of interest and met with Judith and a few of her colleagues. It was a very encouraging initial discussion. Pointing out that I was no longer in control of the company and could not take a lead position during any negotiations that might follow, I expressed my delight at the possibility and handed the file to Mark. Our worst fear was that New Society might be gobbled up by an American company, given the strength of their balance sheet and topicality of their brand.

The negotiations proved seamless. D&M purchased New Society later that year for an amount reaching into seven figures, in cash and all with borrowed money. In truth, the amount was more than our balance sheet could comfortably handle. We were becoming increasingly vulnerable to any shift in financial performance.

Discomforted by the scale of the additional borrowed money, I bit my tongue. My consolation was that if more equity might be needed to deal with reality, the new shareholders had our backs. It was, after all, now their company.

The purchase of New Society expanded the company's base to include four operating divisions, the three Canadian programs — D&M, Greystone, and New Society — plus Farrar, Straus and Giroux. Net sales were stable at about $10 million, and our EBITDA (a profitability metric) was approaching 5 percent, which is not impressive by business standards but healthy by what was possible in independent Canadian publishing.

—

Danger signals from a restructuring publishing world were escalating. BookRiff was languishing, suffering from insufficient human and working capital. In the digital world, languid pace is a kiss of death. I lost interest in remaining the resident Cassandra. And it was becoming increasingly apparent that Mark's two Tricor colleagues had offered a small amount of initial equity to help Mark as a friend, not as engaged investors dedicated to building a company. Fresh equity might be possible, but only as a last resort.

Mistakes began to accumulate. When I suggested to Mark that I didn't think Anansi was ever going to make decent money, Mark took it upon himself to negotiate selling our 20 percent equity stake. Scott Griffin took offence, and with some hostility made a lowball offer. Mark accepted. Even the modest amount of cash offered was by then welcome.

—

Things began to unravel in 2010. Quarterly financial results suggested we were falling into a hole. Climbing out was not going to be easy.

Then one last miracle unfolded. A first novel, *The Sentimentalists*, from a Gaspereau Press author, Johanna Skibsrud, unexpectedly appeared on the shortlist for that year's Giller fiction prize. Gaspereau was a tiny literary house based in Wolfville, Nova Scotia, dedicated to creating beautiful books printed in letterpress in very small print runs.

The prize was to be awarded on November 9. I was invited to be there, as I had been for several years. The Giller is the crown jewel of Canadian literary awards. Everything about its arrangements is stylish: highly coveted hand-delivered invitations accompanied by a fresh red rose and an elegant dinner in the old Toronto Four Seasons Hotel preceded and followed by an open bar. The announcement of the winner of the juried prize marks the evening's culmination following dinner, when the buzz of expectation in the room builds, fuelled by adrenalin and alcohol.

The Giller was established and funded by Jack Rabinovitch in honour of his late wife, Doris Giller, a former literary editor at the *Toronto Star*. Jack was a gentle, respectful man, deeply touched and, I suspect, utterly taken aback by what his extraordinary gesture had unleashed. He remains one of the great unsung heroes of Canadian literature.

Launched in 2004, its $50,000 prize was then the richest in the Canadian literary world. In its early years, it retained the feel of a community celebration. When Scotiabank signed on as lead sponsor in 2006 and CTV, then CBC, began broadcasting the event live, it grew in scale, exclusivity, and impact. But the early spontaneity and collegiality amongst the invited guests had diminished. It remained the highest-profile, most anticipated event of the fall publishing season.

The evening was in full flower, and token bets over who would win were being bandied about. Just to be devil's advocate, an impulse I can seldom resist, I put my money on Johanna Skibsrud. Then, from the stage, her name was announced.

We were about to be blessed by the Giller effect. There was an explosion of noise in the room. The win was about to unleash a tsunami of orders, vastly more than Gaspereau could possibly handle.

I had been blasé during the first blush of euphoria following the announcement of the winner. But when editors from several houses, large and small, began boasting about how they had spoken with the author and were confident they had lured her to sign with them, I hatched a plan to get in touch quickly, and directly, with the two owners of Gaspereau.

Corky and I had spent a wonderful few days with Andrew Steeves and Gary Dunfield in their print shop in Kentville, Nova Scotia, a few years earlier. I had visited as an ACP-sponsored "mentor." As I was a great admirer of their publishing, and their dedication to craft, we had stayed in touch.

My thought was that D&M might immediately license paperback rights. We could manage the imminent flood of orders. Early the next morning I tracked Andrew down, and we talked on the phone. The deal was done.

The critical piece was finding a printer that could print a great many books very quickly. David Friesen and I talked, and he was in.

We needed to crank up our machine quickly. As I was still in Toronto, Chris Labonte, my Vancouver-based assistant, took charge. Our sales team convened in our Vancouver office at 7 a.m. on the morning following verbal agreement with Gaspereau. Phones were worked. By the end of the day, we had advance orders of 100,000 copies. The book trade was desperate, starved of a book that customers were demanding.

I called Jack Rabinovitch at home to tell him we had solved the problem. All would be well within a week, when all the orders could be filled.

I couldn't be certain, but he might have had tears in his eyes. Given what a gracious man he was, and what an extraordinary gift he had given Canada, making that call was very special.

By Christmas, we had shipped 130,000 copies, adding almost $1.5 million to our revenue for the year. That single book had rescued soft sales and solved D&M's financial issues for another year. Luck, decisive behaviour, and perfect timing had won again.

17

THE END OF THE DREAM

For any book publisher dependent on the market, quarterly fiscal results are deeply discouraging. The first quarter absorbs bookseller returns from the previous fall season. The second quarter is neutral, which is disappointing because new spring books never enjoy the sales success of fall books, and backlist sales seldom make up the difference. The third quarter is full of promise as fall books are being shipped and beginning to sell. The fourth quarter promises redemption, as lead fall titles are beginning to sell and are reordered. The Christmas season makes or breaks most booksellers, and publishers. Prayers to the gift-giving gods are frequent.

As a business strategy, it is pathetic. As a cultural strategy, it is essential to civilized nations. The great English publisher Geoffrey Faber had the emphasis right: "Books are not mere merchandise. Books are a nation thinking out loud." That cornerstone aspiration is what drives the model.

2011 began with promise. John Furlong's collaboration with Gary Mason telling the story of Vancouver's 2010 Winter Olympics, *Patriot Hearts: Inside the Games That Changed a Country*, led the D&M program. At the book's launch, I introduced John with the words: "I'm going to call you things you've never been called before: author, and number-one bestseller." The next day, *Patriot Hearts* hit number one on the *Globe* bestseller list, where it remained for some weeks. We arranged for a flash mob of Olympic volunteers in their special-issue blue jackets to take over the SkyTrain the next day while brandishing copies of the book, with a media scrum to follow. The stunt worked. It became a lead item on the national news. The book quickly sold some 35,000 copies.

Carmen Aguirre's *Something Fierce: Memoirs of a Revolutionary Daughter* survived slow sales during its first year to win CBC's Canada Reads, propelling it to 50,000 copies in hardcover. Richard Wagamese's *Indian Horse* was runner-up for Canada Reads, pushing its sales to over 50,000 copies. Greystone had Charlotte Gill's multiple-award-winning *Eating Dirt: Deep Forests, Big Timber, and Life with the Tree-Planting Tribe*, also a number-one national bestseller, shortlisted for both the Hilary Weston Writers' Trust and Charles Taylor prizes for non-fiction.

But it was not enough. By early summer, sales were missing expectations. Quarterly results remained deeply disappointing. Sales for New Society were also diminishing, suggesting the likelihood of a significantly reduced annual operating profit. The bank was not going to be pleased.

—

In the middle of 2011, another possible saviour reappeared. Ron Stern's interest in the company had been rekindled. His passion for print was undiminished. A practising lawyer and successful investor, he had a significant publishing history, having helped establish both *Equity* and *Vancouver Magazine*, and with a partner buying both the *Winnipeg Free Press* and the *Brandon Sun*. Ron and I had danced for years around the possibility of his buying D&M, and I had always been intrigued. Circumstances had always mitigated against it. That spring, Mark Scott had visited Ron to discuss a potential investment in the company, and Ron had been receptive.

What Ron had in mind was not quite what Mark imagined. Ron's interest was in buying the company outright. His senior staff were deeply skeptical of his interest in such a theoretically marginal business, but his personal faith in the world of print prevailed.

During the course of detailed due diligence, which on D&M's side always seemed to fall on my shoulders, I grew to respect and like Ron's senior colleagues. When I once grumbled that I didn't have time for so many meetings, I was scolded for not fully appreciating the gift of the possibility. Thereafter, I made all the meetings.

With impressive speed, a fair, formal offer appeared. Given that the proposed transaction meant that Mark would no longer have a place in the company, I doubted it would be greeted with enthusiasm. Mark and the other two significant shareholders dismissed the offer out of hand, and they held the majority voting interest in the company.

—

My gnawing fear turned out to be prescient. Results for fiscal 2011 showed a significant operating loss for the first time in D&M's history. Such a result might have been manageable in more prosperous times, but eroding sales and growing bank debt had narrowed our options.

We had to right the ship, with very little time in which to do it. Even though this was not all my issue to resolve, in early 2012 I wrote a sharp memo to Mark, by then president, and senior management outlining what I feared lay before us. Urgent action was required. I also wrote Mark a confidential personal letter hoping to prod him into more aggressively taking hold of his company.

An albatross was sitting on my shoulders. When the sale of the company had been completed and my and Corky's personal guarantees had been released, Mark asked if I might match his personal guarantee to the bank, since I remained a shareholder and we were partners. The guarantee was smaller than it had been previously but was still of significant size. Stupidly, as ever optimistic and still flushed at the prospect of the company being in new, more financially stable hands, I agreed, something I had sworn never to do again. I matched his guarantee, on a joint and several basis.

Further demoralizing news arrived mid-spring 2012, when I took a phone call from Joy Isenberg, SVP of operations at Farrar, Straus and

Giroux, with whom I had dealt from the beginning of our valuable 17-year business relationship. I feared the worst.

A corporate decision within the Macmillan Group had finally been taken to move FSG's Canadian distribution to Raincoast Books as of the end of the year, when it would be reunited with the rest of the Macmillan (originally the Georg von Holtzbrinck) empire. We had remained the single holdout for several years, strongly supported by the FSG sales and marketing team. Administrative simplicity had prevailed. FSG sales had remained in the low seven figures, and had never been essential to our survival, but this was another blow, emotionally and fiscally.

—

Mark had engaged a veteran of the digital wars to run BookRiff while packaging it for sale to one of the US companies that had initially expressed interest. Such a sale would have solved our financial issues. This, too, proved to be too little, too late, and the most likely prospects declined. I suspected that those companies had their own equivalent initiatives underway, or perhaps the world had moved past what we had to offer. There was to be no gold at the end of that rainbow.

Refinancing from the shareholders didn't seem to be an option, and Mark seemed increasingly distanced from the urgency of the moment. The only answer in the available cards was rejigging publishing priorities, turning our editorial resources to chasing corporate and special projects. This required reimagining the company's management structure, most definitely not something I had expected to inherit.

In July of 2012, we moved forward with that demoralizing task. Without an active board, and after consultation with Mark, I recommended elevating Jesse Finkelstein, whom we had lured from Raincoast to become manager of international and digital rights, into the position of CEO. She was partnered with Trena White, whom I had hired from McClelland & Stewart and elevated to group publisher, overseeing both the Greystone and D&M programs.

When discouraging final results had been imminent in 2011, and it seemed clear that new equity was unlikely to be forthcoming from the new shareholders, I'd suggested to Mark that one possible solution was to approach HarperCollins to see if that company would buy D&M. David Kent, then CEO of HarperCollins Canada, had hinted in the past that he would support such a possibility.

HarperCollins Canada was thriving. It had been handling our distribution since 2001, including invoicing and collections. Compared with our previous experiences dealing with Canadian-owned companies, encountering the HarperCollins operation was a breath of fresh air. It was well financed, well run, efficient, Toronto-based, and staffed with people who understood and cared about D&M. Critically, we could rely on being paid on time.

But HarperCollins was a Murdoch company. North American operations were tightly run out of New York. Securing a deal was not going to be easy. David Kent was passionate about Canadian books and was engaged by the possibility, as he saw the value of adding D&M's Canadian sales volume to that generated by HarperCollins's Canadian program. He was willing to embrace the difficult odds and fight.

Beginning in April 2012, following a visit by Mark and me to Toronto to propose the idea to David, every aspect of D&M was exhaustingly scrutinized. To justify such a purchase, HarperCollins's New York management had to be persuaded, and our revenues were not of the scale they preferred. Sentimental nationalism wasn't a good fit with a Murdoch organization. Still, the investment in time and energy HarperCollins's Toronto executives committed was extraordinary, a huge gesture of faith and goodwill.

As negotiations with HarperCollins dragged on, and our bank's patience waned, there remained the high hurdle of the Investment Canada Act, which theoretically blunted any possibility of a Canadian company selling to an American company. It had been put in place to protect the sovereignty of Canadian-owned publishing houses but had in turn hurt the ability of Canadian companies to raise the equity necessary for expansion. A double-edged sword. The grant programs of Heritage and the Canada Council were supposed to provide an alternative, but stumbling government action is no match for a restructuring economy.

A visit to Ottawa to meet with senior Heritage people was essential. An approval, at least in principle, was required, and had to be based upon a legally drafted affidavit affirming that D&M was insolvent. A duo of a McCarthy lawyer acting on our behalf and a HarperCollins lawyer acting on theirs trekked with me to Ottawa.

We encountered a room full of bureaucrats from Heritage and other ministries. It was an uncomfortable meeting, as the Heritage officials were shocked. D&M was considered the poster child for a successful Canadian independent publishing house. We had even been called, behind our backs, the "crown jewel."

Selling to HarperCollins was not going to go down well within the Canadian publishing sector, nor with government bodies who had endured the rhetoric of cultural nationalists, including me, for many years. So many of the "majors" had disappeared that the old guard, many of whom had once enjoyed sufficient scale and political clout to impact government and the media, were no longer in the game. D&M being on the block was definitely not good news, nor helpful in persuading the Stephen Harper government to consider solutions.

Departing Ottawa, we concluded that the necessary blessing from Heritage would eventually be forthcoming. The higher bar was persuading HarperCollins New York to commit.

New York's initial answer was "no," devastating news to receive.

David and his colleagues took the significant personal risk of continuing to push. They persuaded New York to revisit the possibility. The bank was aware of the unfolding drama and was awaiting the outcome before taking draconian steps.

Finally, in late summer 2012, the long-promised "Letter of Intent" arrived. All basic terms, including the money involved, had been agreed and, we felt, accepted. Legal documents could be drafted. Prying a blessing, in writing, from Heritage was going to be the final step, and we were confident it would be forthcoming.

It had been an excruciating year. Beginning to believe some version of salvation was at hand, Corky and I travelled to L.A. in early October to spend a few days with our kids, and to escape the numbing stress.

It was not to be. We had barely settled in when the phone rang on our kids' landline, an unusual circumstance. David Kent was on the line to say that, at the very last minute, New York had focussed on what was unfolding and pulled the plug.

David was emotional, viscerally upset. For me, it was a devastating gut punch. This news would likely trigger the bank to shove us into receivership. One of my colleagues in the bank, someone I respected and had worked with for many years, had previously offered this cold advice: "CCAA is absolutely a last resort. The only people who recover any money are the receivers and the lawyers."

The starter's gun had been fired. On October 12, 2012, Douglas & McIntyre filed for creditor protection under the CCAA (the Companies' Creditors Arrangement Act). The Bowra Group, led by David Bowra, was appointed receiver, a prospect I had initially encouraged, as I had come to know David in another circumstance and knew he cared about books. A very bumpy road lay ahead.

—

Theoretically, there was still time to find a solution. A distinguished Vancouver philanthropist, Michael Audain, had in the past offered solace, and while he was not yet formally in the picture, early in the process I had arranged a conversation with him. Sitting on a couch in his office, my mood softened by a very beautiful West Coast landscape hanging on the wall, I suggested that I didn't think anyone would notice our disappearance. He responded, with some astonishment, that I was badly misjudging the circumstance. He was right. A burst of media attention erupted when the news broke, all of it agonizing to read.

There were a few surprising moments of grace amidst the agony. When Corky had been quite ill some years previous, the noted BC artist Gathie Falk had sent, as a gift, one of her small paintings of a glowing light bulb. Within days of our CCAA filing, Gathie wrote one of the most moving notes of my publishing career:

> As a friend, I sympathize with the business of the great and worthy and successful Douglas & McIntyre being in bad health. I wish I could do something about it. It did occur to me that if I made 10 or 20 lightbulb paintings a day and was able to sell them for $1000 each, the problem would not go away in a week, but could be solved in time.
>
> I've done the math . . . I know it is a chancy thing, but I have done many crazy things which came out well. Selling that many wooden paintings in two years would be a miracle, but so is publishing a miracle.

How any human being could have managed that, let alone a septuagenarian, is beyond imagining. Gathie's stunning act of faith brightened my mood for many days.

—

Once the receivers were in charge, camping episodically in our offices, management had been reduced to the role of visitors, there only to advise and endure. I was numb. Mark's personal resources were exhausted. The other shareholders remained astonishingly silent.

The day the news broke, Ron Stern was on the phone again with the thought that he might purchase the company out of receivership. Formal bankruptcy still loomed, but a softer landing might be possible. Ron and I had a long conversation that evening. When I asked, with considerable trepidation, if he might offer, he said he needed to sleep on it. We would talk again the next morning.

Ron was as good as his word and put a verbal offer on the table the next morning. David Bowra suggested that the bank might accept it. Ron and I agreed that, in such circumstances, decisive action is essential, before enthusiasm cools or events intrude.

When Ron's offer arrived in writing, it was lower by an amount equal to the bank's diminished exposure. During the intervening months, our cash flow had improved as HarperCollins was continuing to honour its contract payment terms, although under pressure from head office to break them. For some combination of reasons to which I was never privy, the bank was advised not to accept Ron's offer. Clear action was derailed by the inevitable surrounding murk. I wish I had demonstrated more temper, but I had been utterly ground down by the endless agony of the process. Mark had no solutions.

Wrinkles came and went as the days stretched on. Each day, after reading the morning papers with my stomach in a knot, I drove into the office with debilitating trepidation. Initial conversations were always with lawyers and the receivers, not acrimonious but hardly pleasant.

Ron's offer had come with one important caveat. He wanted assurance that Heritage and Canada Council grants would continue. I was supposed to solve this.

I set up a phone call with three senior staff within Heritage to explain the circumstance, and the urgency of the timing. The conversation was always going to be difficult, but it went off the rails quickly.

We were fighting to protect our authors' royalties, whatever the eventuality, and we had a plan. We proposed that monies owing to D&M under the Canada Book Fund, which based upon our sales the previous fall might amount to several hundred thousand dollars, be put into escrow and deposited with our lawyers. One hundred percent of any monies received would go to pay outstanding author royalties, with full transparency and accountability. This plan had been discussed with the receivers and the lawyers, and while nothing was guaranteed, the idea had been well received.

I was on the phone with three senior Heritage officials, two of whom I had worked directly with in the past. The trio had some decision-making ability, perhaps. I began by outlining that we had an offer to solve the problem from a group of wealthy Vancouver investors. If the receivers and the bank accepted it, land was on the horizon. Critically, there was a possibility of making the authors whole, our essential imperative.

I could hardly get a full sentence out before the chorus interrupted: "We don't fund hypothetical."

"We're not asking you to do that," I replied. "What we are suggesting is that the management of funds due under the terms of the existing program be handled at arm's length by lawyers and the receiver, with the prior blessing of the bank. Nothing would unfold until the deal was consummated, and final legals were in place. All we are seeking is an acknowledgement in principle."

The echo came back, several times, as the discussion continued: "We don't fund hypothetical."

It was a profoundly unsettling conversation. The debate went on for some time, and every suggestion we made ran into a granite wall. There was no sympathy, and no interest in entertaining anything that might help the company and its authors.

Canada was about to lose one of its leading independent book publishers, the largest in the West, and the ministry charged with supporting the industry seemed to be washing its hands of the circumstance. The attitude seemed to stretch up to the minister. Whatever the reasons, and I never discovered them, there seemed to be no interest within Heritage in even attempting to find a solution.

The Heritage response was appalling. The words "we don't fund hypothetical" are seared into my memory. The insulting intransigence of Heritage ultimately proved to be immaterial, but I will never forgive the apparent indifference of the department and some of the people within it. All we were asking for was some assurance that Canadian authors would be protected.

—

Once receivership was formally triggered, the receivers wanted all staff laid off, immediately, without warning and without severance. The next day, we convened an all-staff meeting in our boardroom, with the receivers and out-of-house crisis support in the room. Packages were distributed to each employee, outlining the circumstances as we then understood them to be. Jesse Finkelstein, who was in charge of this ugly file, later confessed that the debilitating headaches she had been living with for some weeks had intensified. She had been an unfailing stalwart in maintaining staff morale during an impossible time. We had no idea what to expect, nor how much agony and fury might erupt.

To everyone's palpable relief, the shocking news was absorbed in silence. The boardroom quickly emptied. Numb employees returned to their offices. The only sound I heard walking back to my own office was loud sobbing behind some doors. Heartbreaking.

We had assumed that staff would simply pack up their offices and vanish. I hoped we might take a few moments to honour all that we together achieved, and the extraordinary loyalty of staff. The receivers suggested that any expression of goodwill following what had just unfolded was wishful thinking. Shock would soon turn to anger, perhaps demonstrable fury.

Stunningly, an eruption of goodwill poured out instead. A group of staff approached me to ask if they could throw a party, in our offices, that very afternoon. It was quickly organized, and appropriate liquids were found. The receivers elected to stay. The event might lance the boil.

As shock wore off, and amber liquid took hold, the mood became nostalgic. There were more tears, emotional speeches, and the gradual emergence of a warm glow. Some of the most deeply felt words poured out of the mouths of normally taciturn people. The receivers were stunned, confessing that they had never seen anything like it. The moment turned into a profoundly heartfelt, cathartic outpouring of proud memories.

—

Nasty stuff remained before us. We had to discover if there remained any way to save the company. The receivers were in charge. The only contribution we could make was helping to generate possible purchase offers for the company's assets. Ron Stern, having been again rebuffed, seemed no longer part of the equation.

Rob Sanders and I had differing views about possible solutions. For obvious reasons, Rob thought that the company should be split into its remaining constituent parts, which would protect Greystone. Always an advocate of sales volume as necessary in an evolving world, I wanted the company to be kept whole. It seemed essential to attract the scale of corporate money now required. If the company was run through a bankruptcy proceeding, however painful, it could begin life anew with its backlists and contracts intact, liberated from historical payables and bank debt. Such restructuring had saved many companies, including many publishing houses, although it was always agonizing to endure.

My personal fight was protecting the authors. Making them whole was my sine qua non. As for my personal future, I had already made it clear that, whatever happened, I wanted no part of it, other than perhaps retaining a minor role on the board or as a consultant, depending upon the outcome.

—

Over the next 60 days, the receivers, Rob, and I approached a dwindling list of likely candidates to acquire the company as a whole. To Rob's credit, he remained actively engaged in the process. My heart wasn't in it. One by one, the options narrowed. The receivers were becoming impatient with what they felt were the dilatory business realities of the industry. D&M, with its three constituent parts, was a complicated animal to swallow.

The larger companies wanted all of D&M — the mother ship, Douglas & McIntyre, along with Greystone and New Society — kept together. Given the environmental idealism that had driven the evolution of New Society, it seemed reasonable that it might re-engage with Renewal Partners, securing a soft landing by returning to its original supportive ownership. I felt it essential that Douglas & McIntyre and Greystone remain together as a single entity leveraging existing editorial strengths and reputation, together maintaining sufficient size and clout.

Time was not on our side. Under pressure from the receivers, and in turn under pressure from the bank, we were working the phones. I recall an animated conversation with Kenneth "Ken" Whyte, then still at Rogers, suggesting that Rogers could acquire a prestigious book publishing unit at a bargain price. Ken was enthusiastic; senior Rogers management quickly dismissed the possibility. We were tainted by the prevailing baggage that book publishing was a terrible business, already undermined by the looming juggernauts of the digital world.

Rob had generated interest from Rodger Touchie at Heritage House for Greystone alone, predicated on the Suzuki Foundation's willingness to make an investment plus transfer its publishing program, which Rob had very effectively grown. But the Suzuki board had said "no" twice, quite reasonably questioning whether book publishing was an appropriate use of its resources.

At that point, the sale of Greystone as a stand-alone was becoming critical and turned on a positive third and final vetting from the Suzuki board. I called Tara Cullis Suzuki, still influential on the Suzuki board, to intervene and to set up an out-of-office meeting. In the end, I abandoned the thought and cancelled the meeting. My fire was out. Even if an intervention from me with the Suzuki board might have proven effective, I no longer saw the purpose. The board ultimately agreed, allowing the Heritage House–Greystone alliance to go ahead.

Douglas & McIntyre had turned into the orphan. It was deemed to be worth nothing. As that painful truth unfolded, I hit bottom in a pit of absolute despair. I just wanted to wash my hands of further agony and get out.

One remaining possibility was the House of Anansi, and Scott Griffin was weighing options. I thought it was a perfect match; Scott's colleagues thought otherwise. His rather terse rejection letter arrived on Christmas Eve, not quite the hoped-for present.

———

Senior D&M colleagues could sense my palpable despair. We had been allowed by the receivers to keep a skeleton staff. What was unfolding daily was painful for them to watch. Toward the end, Trena White, one of the two people I had elevated into senior positions in the company should it survive, ventured into my office, closed the door, and unleashed. How can you give up? she demanded. If for no other reason than your legacy, surely you still have levers to pull.

She had successfully pricked my conscience. The next day, I called Michael Audain to request a meeting. Michael had always been a supporter, and I knew he cared deeply about his home province, its visual artists, and the achievements of Douglas & McIntyre. We met, and he was, as always, gracious. I left his office encouraged, not knowing what to expect next.

Michael swung into action. He phoned a few of his friends. Within 48 hours, he had gathered a small group of wealthy Vancouver investors to commit sufficient money to solve the problem. Ron Stern had returned and would be lead investor, now in partnership with a group of sympathetic colleagues. The financial package was substantial, and this group had the ability to write the necessary cheques.

The combined offer was again made through Ron Stern's people. It seemed reasonable, immediate, and of sufficient scale to avoid the hourglass running out of sand. The receiver felt otherwise. For reasons I was never given a straight explanation of, the offer was not even acknowledged. It was sent a second time. Silence. Finally, I had a stiff conversation with one of the receivers. Still, the offer was rejected, with no satisfactory explanation. I was in no position to demand one.

I had been pushed out of any useful relationship with the bank, and that seemed the end of it. When the offer was rejected for the third time, without even an opening for further discussion, it was withdrawn. The other potential investors who had agreed to help needed assurance that Ron would take the lead in overseeing the business going forward. When Ron withdrew, it was over.

After weeks of uncertainty, resolution was reached. There was not going to be a buyer for all of D&M. The two offers on the table — Heritage House in combination with the Suzuki Foundation for Greystone, and Renewal Partners' repurchase of New Society — were accepted. The existing staff of New Society could return to their passionate mandate, and Rob would take on the running of Greystone, which had always been his baby.

Howard White of Harbour Publishing stepped up to purchase Douglas & McIntyre. Rob had made the decisive call to Howard. After some nervous hesitation, as Howard and his wife, Mary, were risking some of their retirement nest egg, an offer of reasonable size was put forward, and accepted.

By then, two new start-ups led by D&M executives were ready on the sidelines. Chris Labonte and two senior D&M colleagues launched Figure 1, specializing in high-end illustrated books, continuing that central strand of our former program. Jesse Finkelstein and Trena White launched Page Two, which would "help thought leaders, subject matter experts, and organizations publish leading non-fiction books." Ten years on, both are flourishing, as are the "legacy" parts of D&M. Greystone has grown and prospered, particularly in the US and UK. The idealism we instilled in everyone, and the publishing craft we encouraged, remains undiminished. With the luxury of time to reflect, I have come to accept that this was not a bad outcome.

—

The pieces of the puzzle fell into place in early 2013. The three offers in total were sufficient to allow the receiver to recommend acceptance to the bank. The bank agreed, and the final paperwork was completed. Contracts for the few remaining staff who had lingered on, sustained by a mixture of hope, goodwill, and a few more months of income, were terminated. Now, it was over. Offices were bare and the doors were locked.

I took a final, profoundly disconsolate walk through our empty offices. I felt too drained to put all that had unfolded into perspective. Apparently, that was evident on my face: A good friend suggested that I return to swimming laps every morning, something I had pursued over the previous decade to maintain my sanity. Get back to it, she urged: "You look awful!"

L'ENVOI

In February 2014, Corky and I spent an afternoon with Farley and Claire Mowat, for the last time, in their Port Hope home. I was a visiting fellow at Trent University's Traill College. Port Hope was an easy drive down the road, even in winter. Claire made lunch, and Farley and I reminisced over a glass of his good Scotch, which he had poured but barely touched.

A life preserver from the Rotterdam-registered ship *Farley Mowat* occupied a prominent place on the living room wall. That ship had a reputation as the one that shut down the Canadian seal hunt. The life preserver was a gift from Paul Watson, a Canadian-American activist who had founded the Sea Shepherd Conservation Society and had slipped into Canada despite an outstanding Interpol arrest warrant. Farley had provided a safe harbour.

Farley had been living under the dark cloud of a serious aneurysm for many years. He had chosen to defy it, but fate always wins. He died, at 92, a few months following our visit. He had signed our copy of his last book, "To Corky and Scott, with much love, to be shared on an equal basis. All is forgiven. Farley."

I had become Farley's final publisher in 2012, launching a program to reissue 13 new paperback editions of those of his non-fiction books then languishing out of print. I wrote a personal note to introduce the program, concluding with the words: "Feisty icon; passionate Canadian; unrelenting foe of all pretension; energetic provocateur-at-large and, most importantly, superb and dedicated writer. Farley, I salute you."

As Jack McClelland had died many years before, and Anna Porter, his last publisher, could not be tracked down on short notice, I became the voice the media pursued for comment on his death. It was an unexpected opportunity to honour a great writer and a friend. Corky still treasures his kilt pin.

Farley never forgot past episodes. When I retired in 2013, his note was addressed to "The LAST <u>LAST</u> Canadian Publisher!":

> For Cork and Scott. We'll meet again, Don't know when . . . but it will probably be in a chartered aeroplane at midnight on a rainy night, 10,000 feet over the Strait of Georgia, with Scott weeping on my shoulder as he tries to think how to tell Jack McClelland that he had let me hire a plane to get from Sechelt to Van . . . at Jack's expense.
>
> Good cess to ye both!

Farley had been a touchstone throughout the entire arc of my publishing career. His final note was a bittersweet reminder of our long and cherished relationship.

There was one final surprise. Unbeknownst to me, plans were made to give me a retirement party. Led by Karen Love, a curator with whom I had worked closely at the Vancouver Art Gallery, and orchestrated by Chris Labonte, it was held on February 27, 2013, in Andy Sylvester's Equinox Gallery. The event was deeply touching, with almost 100 friends, colleagues, authors, and D&M staff gathered for the celebration. Elegant stacks of D&M books filled one of the galleries. Unexpectedly, our son made the trek north from L.A. In memory of what D&M had done for their, and other, First Nations, the Squamish organized a blanket ceremony, a rare homage, in my honour.

I was drummed in, and "blanketed." Four other blankets were placed in front of me to "catch the intent" of the speakers, "witnesses," each of whom spoke briefly about what my work, and D&M, had meant to them personally. Next, it was my turn to speak. My first words were "My heart is full." I then gifted the four blankets to Corky, Robert Bringhurst, Michael Audain, and Karen Love. Michael had spoken about what D&M art books had meant to him, suggesting that, after decades of helping others to tell their stories, perhaps it was time for Scott McIntyre to write his own.

—

Writing this book has led me back in time, to a journey fuelled by passion, with many highs and lows. Defying the odds for so long became a matter of obstinate pride. From a standing start, we reached a peak amongst Canadian independent publishing houses. It was a deliberate, determined, and successful dare. For almost 50 years, we contributed to Canada's national dialogue, ensuring that voices from beyond the shining mountains were heard.

The friendships, the books, and the impacts they made across Canada and abroad introduced me to a community dedicated to a cause. Becoming part of such a community was a great gift.

As I peruse the books on my shelves at home — the great, the good, and the disappointing — it kindles deep satisfaction at what Douglas & McIntyre, including the dedicated people within it, accomplished. For all the raw edges, it was an extraordinary way to make a life.

ACKNOWLEDGEMENTS

I swore that I would never write a memoir. But over the years, authors, friends, and respected colleagues began to push.

An invitation to deliver a series of John V. Clyne Lectures at the University of British Columbia's Green College was determinant. These three lectures on the postwar publishing world and Canada's place in it, delivered in late fall 2019 and early spring 2020, became the genesis for this book. I gratefully acknowledge the personal encouragement of Mark Vessey, then principal of Green College, for pursuing this idea with the full backing of the University of British Columbia. I want to thank all those colleagues who pushed me to turn those lectures into a full-blown memoir.

I owe a debt of gratitude to those who most effectively provoked me, and generously read the manuscript along the way, usually offering encouraging words. Anna Porter was on my side from the beginning, always provocative, always supportive; and Wade Davis, one of the world's most persuasive voices, as well as a great friend, never let me off the hook.

Close friends we have named the "Gang of Six" were supportive from the beginning: Max Wyman, Susan Mertens, Nini Baird, and Bob Smith (Corky and I were the other two). All are passionate about the arts in Canada, and each in their own way has made significant contributions.

Other colleagues and friends read chapters, commenting on specific issues: Robert Bringhurst; Jack Austin and his daughter, Edie; the late Gordon Gibson; Geoff Plant; Ron Stern; Karen Gilmore; Tony Penikett; and Richard Stursberg. I thank them all for their time and support.

Corky and I are particularly grateful for the friendship and goodwill Nezhat and Hassan Khosrowshahi showed along the way.

As a former publisher, I found it a very pleasant surprise to discover and work with Jack David, a publisher who remembers and honours the old ways. He should join the pantheon. Jack shared many of the agonies that have characterized Canadian publishing over the past two decades, and he has emerged with his company, his idealism, and his wit intact. That is no mean feat.

My indefatigable agent, Michael Levine, took me on despite the skimpy earning power and was always there when needed.

Writers can be offended by editors, the best of whom point out everything that is sloppy, or wrong, in a manuscript. I was blessed. To my astonishment, the first step was a month of careful fact-checking from Adeeba Noor. Lesley Erickson reminded me that good editing, and a shrewd eye on chronological logic, matters. Her skillful nipping, tucking, and cutting of excess, however painful, tightened the narrative. Finally, managing editor Sammy Chin inherited the process of managing both me and all the last steps. As I once said to her along the way, "If we were going into battle, I'd want you on my side." Throughout the entire process, every email was answered within a day, and every concern was carefully resolved. I bow in obeisance to the team at ECW.

Both my personal and the Douglas & McIntyre archives reside in the basement of the SFU Library. While I have a full set of catalogues and every book D&M published on crowded shelves at home, whenever my memories needed bolstering, Melissa Salrin, head of special collections and rare books in the library, and her people made time, sometimes on short notice.

I also want to acknowledge Vasgen Degirmentas. An Armenian born in Istanbul, trained there and in Italy and the UK, he is a magician in both the print and digital worlds, who helped me with scanning and formatting digital files. He was always willing to take the extra step.

I was saved from much sloppy writing, or fading memory, by Corky, a professional reference librarian with skills vastly exceeding mine, including a shrewd judgement of people and situations. She has little patience for pieties or indulgences and made quick work of excising all of mine. She lived the entire journey and remained my conscience along the way.

Memory can be a fickle thing. Any errors of fact, or misrepresentations of either people or events, fall squarely on my shoulders.

INDEX

Abrams Books, 63, 173, 180, 182
Afghanistan, War in, 196–97
Aguirre, Carmen: *Something Fierce*, 262
Aldana, Patsy: background, 87; Canada Book Fund intervention, 85; D&M's educational publishing and, 111; Douglas & McIntyre Publishing Group structure and, 244; fiction program and, 208–9, 213, 215; financial fragility and, 250; FS&G distribution and, 151; Groundwood Books and, 88, 138–39, 240–41, 251–52; M&S's purchase offer and, 247; relationship with author, 87–88; sale of D&M and, 253; transition to UTP distribution and, 94
Alexander, Vikky, 179
Alfred A. Knopf (publishing house), 55, 73–74, 90
Ali, Muhammad, 64
Allan, Richard, 117
Allemeier, Michael, 203
Amiel, Barbara, 28
Anderson-Dargatz, Gail, 209
Andras, Robert "Bob," 70, 85, 86–87
Andrews, Keith, 17–18
Antonson, Rick, 92–93, 103, 142, 253
Appeldoorn, Beth, 62
Arctic, 233–34
Arden, Roy, 179
Arnold, Eddy, 59
Arscott, Glenn, 22, 30
art books, 79–80, 172, 174, 175–76, 180, 185–86

Art Gallery of Ontario (AGO), 184–85
Asgard, Stewart, 47
Asian-Canadian writers, 214–17
Asian Canadian Writers' Workshop Society, 214
Asia-Pacific Economic Cooperation (APEC), 182
Assathiany, Pascal, 209–11
Association for the Export of Canadian Books, 61
Association of Book Publishers of British Columbia, 62, 84, 92
Association of Canadian Publishers (ACP), 61–62, 84, 85, 87, 107, 140
Atheneum Books, 16–17
Athill, Diana, 63
Atkins, Don, 253
Atleo, Shawn, 237
Atwood, Margaret, 14, 58, 208, 218, 219, 224–25
Audain, Michael, 171, 177, 267, 274, 278
Augaitis, Daina, 175

Bach, Richard: *Jonathan Livingston Seagull*, 59
backlist, 239
Bahamas, 11–12
Balkind, Alvin, 7, 173, 187
Bank of Montreal, 93, 101, 116, 123–26, 153, 252
Barbarian Press, 70, 75
Barbeau, Jacques, 178
Barrett, Dave, 161
Bartels, Kathleen, 175, 185–86

283

Bata, Sonja, 181, 182
Bata, Thomas, 181, 182
Bata Shoe Museum, 181, 182
Bawlf, Sam, 84
BC Hydro, 123, 163–64
Beckmann, Jon, 95
Beedie, Ryan, 206
Beketov, Nicholas, 191
Bell, Martin, 194
Bennett, Avie, 145, 247
Bennett, Bill, 136, 158
Bennett, W.A.C., 161, 169
Beny, Roloff, 46–47, 64, 183–84, 230; *People*, 183–84; *Persia*, 46, 183; *A Time of Gods*, 183; *Visual Journeys*, 183–84
Berger, Thomas "Tom," 51, 163, 167–71; *Fragile Freedoms*, 169; *A Long and Terrible Shadow*, 169–70; *Northern Frontier, Northern Homeland*, 168, 169; *One Man's Justice*, 171
Berra, Yogi, 245
Berton, Pierre, 14, 30, 45, 193
Bevington, Stan, 20, 21
Binning, Bert, 7, 8, 173
Binning, Jessie, 173
Birney, Earle, 215
Bishop, John, 91, 201–3
Blackman, Margaret B.: *During My Time*, 129–30
Blades, Ann: *A Salmon for Simon* (with Waterton), 88–89
Blondin, Claire (Sister Claire Marie), 86
Bloomsbury Publishing, 226
Bohne, Harald, 93–94
book fairs, 105. *See also* Frankfurt Book Fair; London Book Fair; Montreal International Book Fair
BookRiff Media, 255, 257, 264
bookselling: author's employment in, 39–40, 41–43; BC's independent scene, 40–41, 49–50; book tours, 45–47, 48; "Canadian Day" event, 44; Chapters, 144–46, 149; Indigo Books and Music, 50, 83, 146, 185, 251; Julian Books initiative, 64–65; McIntyre & Stanton sales agency, 43–45, 52, 65, 69, 70–71; M&S's overstock inventory sale, 29–31; radio and, 48–49, 50; superstores approach, 144–46, 149. *See also* distribution; publishing industry
book tours, 45–47, 48
border issues, 82
Bosnian War, 193–94, 195
Bowra, David, 267, 269
Bowra Group, 267
Boyd, Denny, 156

Bradley, Jessica, 184
Brett, Brian, 241
Brewster, Hugh, 63–64
Bringhurst, Robert, 77–79, 85, 91, 131, 134, 278; *Classical Haida Mythtellers and Their World* trilogy, 236; *The Elements of Typographic Style*, 78; *A Story as Sharp as a Knife*, 217–19
British Columbia: bookselling scene, 40–41, 49–50; changing economic base, 122; educational publishing, 84, 107, 108–9, 115–16; encyclopedias of, 56, 163–64; labour relations, 158; media, 156; publishing community, 60–62; support from, 94; W.A.C. Bennett government, 161; wilderness protection, 133
Broadfoot, Barry: *The City of Vancouver*, 66–67, 178
Broadhead, John, 133
Brody, Hugh, 128–29; *Maps and Dreams*, 129; *The Other Side of Eden*, 164–65
Brown, Sharon, 85
Bruno, Ulli, 101–2
Bukowski, Denise, 216
Burghead Bull, 74–75
Burnford, Sheila, 14
Busby, Adam, 203
Byers, Michael: *Who Owns the Arctic?*, 233
Byng, James "Jamie," 219

Cahill, Leo: *Goodbye Argos*, 45
Campbell, Gordon, 67
Campbell, Gray: *Wildflowers of British Columbia*, 67
Campbell, Maria, 50–51; *Halfbreed*, 50; *Riel's People*, 88
Canada: in Afghanistan, 196; "cultural diversity" protections, 242–44, 249–50; culture and free-trade negotiations, 141–42, 241–42; at Frankfurt Book Fair, 37–38, 62–63, 103; nationalism, 93, 107–8, 176, 265; publishing industry, 13–14, 37–38, 60–62, 85–87, 107–8, 140, 146, 210, 241, 247, 265–66; Quebec nationalism and, 24–25. *See also* British Columbia; Quebec
Canada Book Fund, 85–87, 245, 269
Canada Council for the Arts, 61, 211, 266, 269
Canadian Book Publishers Council, 37–38
Canadian Encyclopedia, 163
Canadian Heritage, Department of, 87, 245, 266–67, 269–70
Canadian Museum of Civilization, 186
Canadian Review of Materials (journal), 119
Canadian Textbook Publishers Institute, 108–9

Canadian War Museum, 197, 198
Canadian Women's Press, 87
Canda Reads (CBC), 221, 262
Candlewick Books, 146
Canfield, Cass, Jr., 63, 102
Canongate Books, 219
Carney, Patricia "Pat," 161
Carr, Emily, 3; *The Art of Emily Carr* (Shadbolt), 80–83, 84, 175
Carter, R.J. "Jim," 115, 116
Cater, David, 153
CBC (Canadian Broadcasting Company): Canda Reads, 221, 262; *As It Happens*, 129; LaMarsh book launch and, 27; *Reach for the Top*, 6–7
C&C Offset Printing, 176
Cemp, 19, 20
Cerf, Bennett, 14
Chamberlin, J. Edward, 237
Chapters, 144–46, 149
Cheetham, Anthony, 146–47
Chenelière, Michel de la, 252
children's books, 87, 88–89, 138–39, 239–41
Chong, Denise, 214
Chow, Carol, 203
Choy, Wayson, 90, 214, 215–17; *The Jade Peony*, 215–16, 217
Chrétien, Jean, 168, 186, 230
Chrétien, Raymond, 248
Christie, Heather, 39, 44, 57
cinema, 7–8
City of Vancouver Book Award, 76
Clare, Bill, 108–9, 110, 114, 118
Clark, Penney, 121
Clarke, Irwin & Company, 14, 76, 80, 83, 88, 93, 138
Clarke, William "Bill," 76, 81, 82
Clarkson, Adrienne, 28, 187, 198, 203
Classics (bookstore chain), 21, 65
Clavell, James, 51–52
Coach House Press, 20–21
Coalition for Cultural Diversity/La coalition pour la diversité culturelle (CCD), 243, 248
Cobham, Alan "Al," 140
Cohen, Leonard, 14, 30–31
Cohen, Matt, 14, 213, 244
Colbert, Nancy and Stanley "Stan," 194
Coles (bookstore chain), 65, 82, 144–45
Collins, William "Billy," 56–57
Committee for an Independent Canada, 107
company histories, 122–23
cookbooks. *See* Bishop, John; Feenie, Rob; Menghi, Umberto; Posteraro, Pino; Vij, Vikram

Copps, Sheila, 198, 242, 245, 248, 249
Coupland, Douglas "Doug," 60, 90–91, 179, 227–30; *City of Glass*, 227–28; *Generation X*, 227; *Shampoo Planet*, 227; *Souvenir of Canada* compilations, 227, 229; *Terry*, 227, 229–30
Courtemanche, Gil, 211
Crey, Ernie, 165–66; *Stolen from Our Embrace* (with Fournier), 166
Crichton, Sarah, 151
culture: "cultural diversity" protections, 242–44, 249–50; free-trade negotiations and, 141–42, 241–42
Cummings, Al, 63–64
Curzi, Pierre, 243, 249
customs issues, 82

Davidson, Florence, 68, 129–30, 236
Davidson, Robert, 69, 78
Davies, Robertson, 208
Davis, Chuck: *The Vancouver Book*, 67–68
Davis, Wade, 90, 225–27, 237; *The Clouded Leopard*, 226; *Light at the Edge of the World*, 223, 226–27
Dawson, Blair, 88, 239
de Gaulle, Charles, 28
de Grandmaison, Nicholas: *History in Their Blood* (Dempsey), 102, 123, 124–26
Delgado, James "Jim": *Across the Top of the World*, 102
Dempsey, Hugh A.: *History in Their Blood*, 102, 123, 124–26
DePoe, Norman, 27
Derreth, Reinhard, 81
Deutsch, André, 63
Dhalwala, Meeru: *Vij's* (with Vij), 203–4; *Vij's at Home* (with Vij), 203–4
Diefenbaker, John, 43–44, 186
distribution: advantages and disadvantages, 148–49; challenges and changes, 76, 93–94, 149–50, 245–46; by HarperCollins Canada, 265; international partnerships, 101–2, 146, 147–48, 150–51. *See also* bookselling
Dobbs, Kildare, 25
Döblin, Alfred, 89
Dodd, Mead & Co., 16–17
Dopping-Hepenstal, Maxwell Edward, 190–91
Douglas, James: "Douglas Treaties," 170
Douglas, Jim: *The Art of Emily Carr* (Shadbolt) and, 80, 81; Association of Canadian Publishers and, 61–62; background and reputation, 10, 38–39; "Canadian Day" bookselling event, 44; and Clarke, Irwin & Company, 80; *The Distemper of Our Times*

(Newman) and, 22; D&M and, 74–75, 76, 84, 253; educational publishing and, 109–10, 114, 116, 120–21; fiction program and, 208; Julian Books initiative and, 64–65; on M&S fall 1969 catalogue, 35; partnership with author, 31–32, 33, 38, 43; Paul St. Pierre and, 212; publishing strategy under, 55; SFU's publishing studies and, 253. *See also* Douglas & McIntyre; J.J. Douglas Ltd.
Douglas, Stan, 179
Douglas Agencies, 43
Douglas & McIntyre. *See also* J.J. Douglas Ltd.
Douglas & McIntyre (D&M): 25th anniversary, 152; about, 171, 278; art books, 79–80, 172, 174, 175–76, 180, 185–86; author's roles, 84, 142–43, 255–56; backlist, 239; BookRiff Media and, 255, 257, 264; Burghead Bull graphic device, 74–75, 76; company histories, 122–23; creditor protection, 267–75; development, 89–90; distribution, 76, 93–94, 101–2, 149–50, 245–46; Douglas & McIntyre Publishing Group structure, 244; education division, 121, 138, 139–41; fiction program, 208–9; financial fragility, 101, 152–53, 246–48, 250–51, 252–53, 257–58, 262, 263–65; at Frankfurt Book Fair, 62–64, 101–3; Greystone Books and, 143–44, 155, 241, 250, 256, 264, 272, 273, 274–75; Groundwood Books and, 88, 138–39, 146, 155, 214, 239–41, 250, 251–52; growth, 76, 84, 93, 138–39, 152–53, 155; HarperCollins negotiations, 265–67; Indigenous titles, 9, 77, 78, 79, 88–89, 102, 129–30, 131–33, 134, 165–67, 169–70, 186, 217–22, 237–38; international distribution partnerships, 101–2, 146, 147–48, 150–51; Key Porter and, 230–31; legacy, 275; limited editions, 174, 175, 219; marketing and sales, 91–93; Mark Scott ownership, 253–56, 257–58; Mount Pleasant office, 154–55; M&S and, 138, 187, 247; New Society Publishers and, 256–57, 262, 272, 274–75; personnel, 90–91, 92–93, 142–44, 153–54, 264; purchase offers from Stern, 231, 262–63, 268–69, 272, 274; sale to Howard and Mary White, 275; staff layoffs, 270–71; transition from J.J. Douglas, 73. *See also* J.J. Douglas Ltd.; *specific authors*
Douglas & McIntyre (Educational) Ltd.: BC textbook opportunity and contract, 107, 108–9, 115–16; challenges, 111–12, 114–15, 118–19; decision to pursue, 109–10; establishment and structure, 110–11; finances, 119–21; merger with D&M, 121, 138; printing by Evergreen Press, 112, 116–17; sale to Nelson, 139–41; textbook development, 112–14, 116, 117–18

Doyle, Brian, 88, 239
Dubrovnik, 13, 15, 195
Duff, Wilson, 9, 65
Dunfield, Gary, 259
Dunne, Thomas "Tom," 63
Durbach, Audrey, 203
Duthie, Bill, 40–41
Duthie Books, 8, 65, 75

Eaton's, 27, 41, 46
Eberle, Corinna, 129
Ecotrust Canada, 235
ECW Press, 245
Edenshaw, Charles, 130, 131
Edenshaw, Gary (Gidansda Guujaaw), 235–38
educational publishing, 84, 107–9, 121. *See also* Douglas & McIntyre (Educational) Ltd.
Eggleton, Art, 242
Eisenstein, Sergei, 8
Ellegood, Donald "Don" R., 56, 131
Ellis, Bill, 77
Ellis, Sarah, 239
Elsted, Crispin, 70–71, 75, 85
Elsted, Jan, 70, 85
Endicott, Marina, 209
Entrekin, Morgan, 219
Erdrich, Louise, 221
Erickson, Arthur, ix–x, 60, 67, 134, 173, 186–89; *The Architecture of Arthur Erickson*, 102, 187–88
Esquire (magazine), 6
Esso Canada, 25
Evergreen Press, 68, 112, 116–17

Faber, Geoffrey, 261
Faber & Faber, 128, 165
Fafard, Joe, 186
Falk, Gathie, 268
Farrar, Straus and Giroux (FS&G), 148, 150–51, 165, 257, 263–64
Feenie, Rob, 91, 203, 204–5; *Feenie's*, 205; *Lumière Light*, 205; *Rob Feenie Cooks at Lumière*, 205
Feilding, Geoff, 11, 15
Ferguson, Ian: *How to Be a Canadian* (with Ferguson), 223, 225
Ferguson, Will, 223–25; 419, 225; *Bastards and Boneheads*, 224; *How to Be a Canadian* (with Ferguson), 223, 225; *I Was a Teenage Katima-Victim*, 224; *Why I Hate Canadians*, 223, 224
F.H. Hayhurst (advertising agency), 10
fiction, 208–9
Figure 1 Publishing, 275

Finkelstein, Jesse, 264, 271, 275
First Nations. *See* Indigenous peoples
Fisher, Douglas, 57–58
Fitzhenry & Whiteside, 109
Fladell, Ernie, 67, 75
Flick, Jane, 10
Flick, Robert "Bob," ix–x, 8, 9–10
Flight, Nancy, 91
Folio Society, 219
Foon, Dennis, 221
Fotheringham, Allan, 58, 156, 159, 162, 230; *The World According to Roy Peterson* (with Peterson), 79
Fournier, Suzanne: *Stolen from Our Embrace* (with Crey), 166
Fox, Francis, 86
Fox, Michael J., 137
Fox, Terry, 135, 227, 229–30
France, 243, 244
Francis, Daniel, 163
Frankfurt Book Fair: about, 36–37, 63–64, 95, 97; author's first visit to, 37; Canadian representation, 37–38, 62–63, 103; D&M (J.J. Douglas) at, 62–64, 101–3; Frankfurt Fever, 101; geopolitics and, 100; hotels and parties, 98–99; Paris gatherings and drive to Frankfurt, 95–97; returning home from, 103; Richler encounter, 105–6; security, 99–100; weather, 98
Franklin, Elsa, 30
Frederking & Thaler, 182
free-trade negotiations, 141–42, 241–42
Friesen, David, 259
Friesens (printer), 164, 176, 184, 185, 259
Frum, David, 233
Fry, Pamela, 15, 34
Furlong, John, 136–37; *Patriot Hearts* (with Mason), 261–62

Gage (publisher), 107
Gagné, Jean-Pierre, 98
Galassi, Jonathan, 151
Gaspereau Press, 258, 259
Gay, Marie-Louise, 239
General Distribution Services (GDS), 150, 154, 245
General Publishing, 231, 247
Germany, 100. *See also* Frankfurt Book Fair
Ghandl (Haida poet), 217, 218
Gibson, Douglas, 247
Gibson, George, 95
Gibson, Gordon, Sr.: *Bull of the Woods* (with Renison), 126
Gill, Charlotte, 241; *Eating Dirt*, 262

Gill, Ian, 234–35; *All That We Say Is Ours*, 233, 234, 237–38
Giller Prize, 258
Gilmore, Karen, 153–54
Gingrich, Arnold, 6
Glavin, Terry, 197
Glenbow Museum, 123, 124
Gochmann, Claudia, 179
Godbout, Jacques: *Knife on the Table*, 24
Godine, David, 95, 251
Gorbachev, Mikhail, 97
Gordon, Walter, 5
Gosewich, Arnold, 194
Gosnell, Joseph, 237
Gotlieb, Allan, 142
Gottlieb, Paul, 63, 180, 182
Graham, Rodney, 179
Granatstein, Jack, 198
Grant, Jon, 233, 234
Grant, Peter, 242
Grant, Shelagh: *Polar Imperative*, 233–34
Gray, John, 10, 34
Greenpeace, 57
Greystone Books: D&M creditor protection and sale of, 272, 273, 274–75; *Eating Dirt* (Gill) and, 262; financial fragility and, 250; growth, 155, 241; launch and place within D&M, 143–44, 257; oversight of, 256, 264
Griffin, Scott, 251–52, 258, 273
Groundwood Books, 88, 138–39, 146, 155, 214, 239–41, 250, 251–52
Grove Press, 219
Guujaaw, Gidansda (Gary Edenshaw), 235–38
Gwaii Haanas National Park and Haida Heritage Site, 133
Gwyn, Richard, 23–24; *The Northern Magus*, 24; *Smallwood*, 23

Habitat I (UN conference), 66–67
Hachette, 105, 147, 150
Hahn, Charlie, 99
Haida, 68, 78, 118–19, 129–31, 133–34, 217–19, 237–38
Haida Gwaii, 235–37, 238
Haida Gwaii Museum, 236–37
Halton, Matthew, 192
Hansen, Andrew, 176
Hansen, Rick, 134–37
Harbour Publishing, 163
Harcourt, Mike, 75–76
Harcourt Brace Jovanovich, 99
Hardin, Herschel: *A Nation Unaware*, 57–58
Harlow, Robert "Bob," 209
Harper, Russell, 124

HarperCollins, 96, 97, 194, 265–67, 269
Harper & Row, 63, 101, 102, 187
Harris, Lawren and Bess, 173
Hart, Jim, 237
Hassell, Robert "Bob," 228
Hawthorn, Audrey, 9, 65; *Kwakiutl Art*, 79
H.B. Fenn and Company, 231
Heath, Chuck, 109, 110, 111, 112
Heath, Terrence, 186
Helm, Michael, 209
Hemlock Printers, 78, 132–33, 173, 174, 176, 178
Henley, Thom, 133
Heritage. *See* Canadian Heritage, Department of
Heritage House Publishing, 273, 274
Herzog, Fred, 67, 175, 178–80; *Fred Herzog Photographs*, 179
Hill, Charles, 185
Hill, Frederick "Fred," 96
Hodgeman, Marge, 15
Hogg, Helen, 41
Holgate, Edwin, 3
Holmes, Willard, 175
Holt, Simma, 156
Hoppener, Henk, 37
House of Anansi Press, 44, 251–52, 258, 273
Hudson Hills (publisher), 125
Hughes, E.J., 175, 177–78
Hughes, Shirley, 239
Hunter, Robert, 156
Hunter-Rose (printer), 56, 67
Hurley, Maisie, 169
Hurtig, Mel (Hurtig Publishers), 10, 44, 49, 57, 65, 107, 163
Hutchison, Bruce, 126–28; *Canada: Tomorrow's Giant*, 229; *To Canada with Love and Some Misgivings*, 128; *Uncle Percy's Wonderful Town*, 126
Hyatt, Glenn, 112, 116–17

ICBC, 163
Independent Publishers Association, 61. *See also* Association of Canadian Publishers
Indigenous peoples: D&M (J.J. Douglas) titles on, 9, 66, 68, 69, 77, 78, 79, 88–89, 102, 129–30, 131–33, 134, 165–67, 169–70, 186, 217–22, 237–38; *Halfbreed* (Campbell), 50; Hugh Brody and, 128–29; resurgence, 65–66; Sparrow case, Nisga'a Treaty, and Aboriginal title, 170–71; Tom Berger and, 169. *See also* Haida; Inuit; Nisga'a Tribal Council; Squamish Nation; Stó:lō Nation
Indigo Books and Music, 50, 83, 146, 185, 251
Inuit, 49, 118, 130, 180–82
Investment Canada Act, 265–66

Isenberg, Joy, 263–64
Islands Protection Society: *Islands at the Edge*, 133

Jacob, Michel, 204, 205
Jacobs, Ben, 102
Jam, Teddy, 239
James Lorimer & Company, 44
Jarislowsky, Stephen, 178
J.J. Douglas Ltd.: author's involvement, 43, 52; as distributor, 10, 44; editorial program and launch, 55, 56–58; growth, 64, 65, 68; Indigenous titles, 66, 68, 69; *Johann's Gift to Christmas* (Richards), 58–59; transition to Douglas & McIntyre, 73; Vancouver titles, 66–68. *See also* Douglas & McIntyre
John Murray (publisher), 63, 104–5
Jovanovich, William, 99
Julian Books, 65

Kane, Hugh, 11, 13, 15, 18, 19, 33–34, 37, 43–44, 126
Karl, Jean E., 138
Kasztner, Rezso, 232
Katimavik (volunteer youth corps), 224
Katz, Welwyn Wilton, 239
Keneally, Thomas, 232
Kent, David, 265, 266, 267
Kerr, Catherine, 79
Key Porter Books, 183, 224, 230–31, 245. *See also* Porter, Anna
Keziere, Robert, 66, 67, 182
Kilian, Crawford, 113–14; *Icequake*, 77
King, Thomas, 239
Kipp, Charles D.: *Because We Are Canadians*, 193
Klein, Judy, 148
Knopf (publishing house), 55, 73–74, 90
Knopf, Alfred, 14, 73
Knopf, Alfred "Pat," Jr., 17
Knopf, Blanche, 73, 74
Koch, Eric: *The French Kiss*, 28
Kolber, Leo, 20–21
Kolber, Sandra: *Bitter Sweet Lemons and Love*, 20–21
Kouwenhoven, Dick, 178
Kovach, Rudy, 67

Laberge, Georges, 85
Laberge, Marc, 184
Labonte, Chris, 209, 221, 259, 275, 277
Laferrière, Dany, 211
LaMarsh, Judy, 26–27, 162; *Memoirs of a Bird in a Gilded Cage*, 26–27

Lambert, Phyllis, 188–89
Langford, Carol, 109, 110, 111, 112, 114, 117, 120, 139–40
Lau, Evelyn, 214
Laughlin, James, 55
Laurence, Margaret, 14, 208
Layton, Irving, 14
Lee, Bennett: *Many-Mouthed Birds* (with Wong-Chu), 214
Lee, Carol, 207
Lee, SKY: *Disappearing Moon Cafe*, 214, 215
Les Éditions de la Chenelière, 252
Les Éditions du Boréal, 209–11
Leventhal, Lionel, 104
Levin, Martha, 96
Lévi-Strauss, Claude, 132, 171
limited editions, 174, 175, 219
Linton, Diane, 15
Lippincott (publisher), 17
LiterASIAN (festival), 215
Little, Brown and Company, Canada, 17
Lo, Charlie (Lo Chi-Hong), 176
London Book Fair, 103–4
Lord Byng Secondary School (Vancouver), 5–6
Love, Karen, 277, 278
Lowry, Malcolm, 209
Lum, Ken, 179
Lunn, Janet, 239
Lyons, Kim, 154

Macdonald, Donald, 86
MacDonald, Flora, 142
MacDougall, Allan, 17, 69–70, 253
MacDougall, Angie, 69–70
MacKenzie, Lewis "Lew": *Peacekeeper*, 193–95
Mackenzie Valley Pipeline Inquiry, 168
Macmillan, 10–11, 14, 33–34, 39, 43–44, 55, 64, 73, 208, 264
Macpherson, Duncan, 26
Madison Press, 63–64
Manguel, Polly, 231
Marks, Binky, 8, 41
Mason, Gary: *Patriot Hearts* (with Furlong), 261–62
Masse, Marcel, 140
Massey, Geoffrey, ix–x
Mather, Barry, 156
Mayer, Peter, 94
Mays, John Bentley, 83
McClelland, Jack: author and, ix–x, 32–33, 35, 40, 53–54, 71–72; Beny inventory problem and, 183–84; on book superstores, 145; on book tours, 45; Committee for an Independent Canada and, 107; death, 277; fall 1969 catalogue and, 35; at Frankfurt Book Fair, 63, 64; at M&S, ix, 14, 15, 18, 19, 21–22; *A Nation Unaware* (Hardin) and, 57; overstock inventory sale and, 31; Paul St. Pierre and, 212; on publishing, 55, 89–90, 247
McClelland & Stewart (M&S): about, 14; Anna Porter and, 28–29; art books, 80; author's employment and departure, 10–11, 12, 13, 14–16, 19–20, 29, 31–34, 35, 53–54; distribution partnerships, 150–51; D&M (J.J. Douglas) and, 55, 138, 187, 247; Douglas at, 39; fall 1969 catalogue cover, 35; fiction program, 208; financial fragility, 18–19, 29, 61; Gwyn's *Smallwood* launch, 23; Hollinger House offices, 13; under Jack McClelland, ix, 14, 15, 18, 19, 21–22; Koch's *The French Kiss*, 28; Kolber's *Bitter Sweet Lemons and Love*, 20–21; LaMarsh's *Memoirs of a Bird in a Gilded Cage*, 26–27; McIntyre & Stanton and, 44; Newman's *The Distemper of Our Times*, 21–23; overstock inventory sale, 29–31; parties, 47–48; Richler's *Hunting Tigers Under Glass*, 25; Roloff Beny and, 46–47, 183; sales conferences, 16–17, 22
McCormack, Thomas "Tom," 63
McElderry, Margaret K., 138
McGeer, Pat, 108
McGill, Dave, 15
McGill-Queen's University Press, 10, 44, 92
McIntosh, Susan, 92
McIntyre, Corky: author's retirement party and, 278; departure from Toronto and return to Vancouver, 31, 32, 33, 38; D&M and, 116, 154, 250, 254; Farley Mowat and, 47–48, 276, 277; gift from Gathie Falk, 268; Haida Gwaii trip, 235–37; honeymoon, 13, 15, 195; Keith Andrews and, 18; Leonard Cohen and, 30–31; Robert Bringhurst and, 79; son's birth, 58; support from, 54; at UBC, 8–9; wine incident, 165
McIntyre, David (son), 58, 81, 85, 127, 159, 277–78
McIntyre, Harry Beecher, 2
McIntyre, Scott: Bahamas holiday, 11–12; bookselling in BC, 39–40, 41–43; childhood and education, 1, 3–4, 5–9; decision to focus on publishing, 69, 70–72; departure from Toronto and return to Vancouver, 31–34, 38; family background, 1–3, 190; father's death, 18; financial fragility, 246, 250; first job, 9–10; honeymoon, 13, 15, 195; McClelland and, ix–x, 32–33, 35, 40, 53–54, 71–72; military history and, 190–92; M&S

and, 10–11, 12, 13, 14–16, 19–20, 29, 31–34, 35, 53–54; North Vancouver home, 59–60; partnership with Douglas, 31–32, 33, 38, 43; retirement party, 277–78; Richler and, 25–26, 105–6; son's birth, 58. *See also* Douglas & McIntyre; Frankfurt Book Fair; J.J. Douglas Ltd.
McIntyre & Stanton (sales agency), 43–45, 52, 65, 69, 70–71
McKnight, Linda, 193, 194
McMaster, Gerald: *Indigena*, 186
McNeil, Fred, 123
McNeil, Jo, 20
McRae, Julia, 138
McTaggart, David: *Outrage!*, 57
Melzack, Louis, 21
Menghi, Umberto, 200–201, 202, 206; *Toscana Mia*, 199, 201; *Umberto's Kitchen*, 201
military history, 190–92. *See also* Canadian War Museum; Kipp, Charles D.; MacKenzie, Lewis "Lew"; Wiss, Ray; Zuehlke, Mark
Miller, Peggy, 148
Milroy, Sarah, 179, 180
Milsom, Lois, 60
Mitchell, Howard (Mitchell Press), 9
Moldow, Susan, 96, 97
Monk, Lorraine, 183
Montreal International Book Fair, 61
Moriyama, Raymond, 182, 197–98; *In Search of a Soul*, 198
Mowat, Claire, 276
Mowat, Farley, 14, 39, 45, 47–48, 58, 182, 190, 276–77; *And No Birds Sang*, 192
Mulgrew, Ian: *Webster!* (with Webster), 160
Mulholland, William, 124–26
Mulroney, Brian, 141, 161
Munk, Peter, 232
Munro, Jack, 157–59, 162; *Union Jack*, 158
Munro, Jim, 41, 163
Munro's Books, 41
Murray, Jock, 63, 104–5
Museum of Anthropology (UBC), 67, 187

Nasgaard, Roald: *Abstract Painting in Canada*, 91, 186
National Gallery, 185, 186
National Geographic, 226
nationalism, 93, 107–8, 176, 265
natural history, illustrated, 143, 144, 241
Neale, Gladys, 116
Nelson Canada, 140
Neurath, Eva, 63, 180
Neurath, Thomas, 63, 180
New Directions Publishing, 17, 55

Newfeld, Frank, 15–16, 35, 126
Newman, Peter C., 14, 21–23, 107, 163, 232; *The Distemper of Our Times*, 21–23
New Press, 42, 44
New Society Publishers, 256–57, 262, 272, 274–75
Nichols, Marjorie, 156, 157, 160–62; *Mark My Words*, 162
Nikiforuk, Andrew, 241
Nisga'a Treaty, 170–71
Nisga'a Tribal Council: *Nisga'a*, 166
Norris, Len, 58–59
North American Free Trade Agreement (NAFTA), 241–42. *See also* free-trade negotiations
North Vancouver, 60
Nowell, Iris: *Painters Eleven*, 186
Nurnberg, Andrew, 96, 97

Oakes, Jill: *Our Boots* (with Riewe), 180–82
Oberlander, Cornelia, 67, 173, 187
Oberlander, Peter, 67, 173
Off, Carol: *The Lion, the Fox and the Eagle*, 195
O'Hara, Jane, 157, 158, 162
Olympics, Vancouver Winter (2010), 136–37, 261–62
Ontario Arts Council, 61
Ontario Development Corporation (ODC), 93
Ontario Royal Commission on Book Publishing, 61, 93, 108
Order of St. Clare's Monastery (Mission, BC), 86
Orion Publishing Group, 146, 147, 150, 252
Ortona, Battle of, 192
Oxford University Press, 14

Page Two, 275
Palmer, Vaughn, 128
Pantheon Books, 129
Parry, Mac, 227
Pathfinder Capital, 144–45
Peacock, Don, 123
Pearson, Lester, 28
Perrin, Nick, 104–5
Peter Martin Associates, 44
Peterson, David, 145
Peterson, Roy: *The World According to Roy Peterson* (with Fotheringham), 79
Pettigrew, Pierre, 242
Philip, Prince, 158
Pinder, Leslie Hall, 129
Plant, Judith and Christopher, 256–57
Poliquin, Daniel, 211; *In the Name of the Father*, 211

Porter, Anna, 17, 28–29, 159, 183, 230–33, 247, 277; *The Ghosts of Europe*, 232–33; *Kasztner's Train*, 227, 232. *See also* Key Porter Books
Posteraro, Pino, 199, 206
Prentice Hall, 116, 117–18, 119
Prestel Publishing, 176
Proulx, Annie, 212
Proulx, Monique, 211
Pryde, Duncan: *Nunaga*, 49
publishing industry: art books, 79–80, 172, 174, 175–76, 180, 185–86; backlist, 239; in BC, 60–62; book fairs, 105; business models and program development, 54–55, 89–90; in Canada, 13–14, 37–38, 60–62, 85–87, 107–8, 140, 146, 210, 241, 247, 265–66; company histories, 122–23; educational publishing, 84, 107–9, 121; fiction, 208–9; illustrated natural history, 143, 144, 241; limited editions, 174, 175, 219; McClelland on, 55, 89–90, 247; quarterly fiscal results, 261; in Quebec, 210; returns, 82–83, 149, 210; social side, 83. *See also* bookselling; distribution; Douglas & McIntyre; Frankfurt Book Fair; J.J. Douglas Ltd.; McClelland & Stewart; *other specific publishers*

Quarrington, Paul, 241
Quebec, 24–25, 28, 141, 209–11, 243
Quebecor, 252

Rabinovitch, Jack, 258, 259–60
radio, 48–49, 50, 160
Raincoast Books, 17, 264
Random House, 63, 252
Rasky, Frank: *The Taming of the Canadian West*, 16
Rawling, Percy, 127
Reid, Amanda, 135
Reid, Bill, 118–19, 130–33, 219, 236; *The Black Canoe*, 134; *The Raven Steals the Light*, 131–32; *The Spirit of Haida Gwaii* (canoe), 134
Reid, Dennis, 185; *Krieghoff*, 184–85
Reisman, Heather, 146
Reisman, Simon, 141, 142
Reksten, Terry: *The Illustrated History of British Columbia*, 163–64
Renewal Partners, 256, 272, 274
Renison, Carol: *Bull of the Woods* (with Gibson), 126
returns, book, 82–83, 149, 210
Reynolds, Margaret, 92
Rice, Condoleezza, 249
Ricepaper (journal), 214–15
Richards, Jack: *Johann's Gift to Christmas*, 58–59

Richardson, Bill, 90
Richardson, Miles, 237
Richardson, Sally, 63
Richler, Mordecai, 25–26, 101, 105–6, 208; *Hunting Tigers Under Glass*, 25
Riede, Jack, 99–100
Riewe, Rick: *Our Boots* (with Oakes), 180–82
Riger, Robert, 96
Riis, Sharon, 209
Ritchie, Larry, 53
Roberts, Edward "Ed," 23
Roberts, John, 86
Roche, Peter, 147
Rogatnick, Abraham "Abe," 7, 173
Rogers, 273
Rohmer, Richard, 61
Rombout, Luke, 175
Rose, Clyde, 108
Rotstein, Abraham, 58
Rowntree, David, 253
Roy, Gabrielle, 14
Royal Commission on Book Publishing (Ontario), 61, 93, 108
Rushdie, Salman: *The Satanic Verses*, 100
Ryerson Press, 13, 107

Sackheim, Paula, 15
Sackheim, Sherman, 15
Sacks, Don, 110–11, 114
Sacks, Marilyn, 110–11, 114, 226
sales conferences, 16–17, 22
Salmon, Patricia, 177–78
Sanders, Rob, 103, 142–44, 154, 159, 241, 250, 256, 272, 273, 275
Sarajevo, 193–94, 195
Savage, Candace: *Wolves*, 143
Schloss Bühlerhöhe (Black Forest), 96–97
Schroeder, Andreas "Andy," 85
Schulte, Anthony "Tony," 63, 255
Schwartz, Gerald "Gerry," 146
Scott, Jack, 156
Scott, Mark, 253, 255, 257–58, 262, 263, 264, 265, 268, 269
Second International Meeting of Cultural Professional Organizations, 248–49
Senft, Rod, 253
Seton, Ernest Thompson, 1, 2
Seymour Books, 41
Shadbolt, Doris, 80–83, 131, 163, 172–73, 175, 178; *The Art of Emily Carr*, 79, 80–83, 175; *Bill Reid*, 132–33
Shadbolt, Jack, 81, 83, 172–74, 202
Shadbolt, Maurice, 57
Sharon, Lois & Bram (music group), 239

Sherlock, John, 201
Shinker, William "Bill," 96
shipping, cross-border, 82
Sierra Club Books, 95, 144, 146, 241
Sifton, Elisabeth, 151
Simon, Mary, 164–65
Simon Fraser University (SFU), ix–x, 9–10, 187, 252–53
Sino United Publishing, 176
Skaay (Haida poet), 217, 218
Skibsrud, Johanna: *The Sentimentalists*, 258, 259–60
Smallwood, Joseph "Joey," 23
Smith, Brian, 107, 115–16, 163–64
Smith, Gordon, 173, 175, 176–77, 187, 202
Smith, Joan Ashton, 46
Smith, Julian "Buddy," 64–65
Smith, Marion, 173
SmithBooks (WH Smith), 65, 144–45
Sparrow case, 170
Spieler, Joe, 96
Squamish Nation, 278
Staehling, Rick, 113
Stanton, Mark, 42, 43–45, 52, 69, 70, 253
Steeves, Andrew, 259
Steltzer, Ulli, 68–69, 88, 134; *Coast of Many Faces*, 79; *Indian Artists at Work*, 68, 69, 176; *Inuit*, 130
Stenson, Fred, 209, 213; *Lightning*, 213; *The Trade*, 213
Stern, Ron, 231, 262–63, 268–69, 272, 274
Stevenson, Lawrence "Larry," 144–45
Stevenson, Michael, 253
Stewart, Hilary, 77, 130; *Cedar*, 130; *Indian Fishing*, 77; *Looking at Indian Art of the Northwest Coast*, 77, 78; *Robert Davidson*, 78, 79
St. Martin's Press, 63, 227
Stoddart, Jack, 150, 231
Stó:lō Nation: *A Stó:lō–Coast Salish Historical Atlas*, 166–67
Stouck, David: *Arthur Erickson*, 188–89
St. Pierre, Paul, 156, 209, 211–13; *Breaking Smith's Quarter Horse*, 212; *Chicotin Holiday*, 212; *In the Navel of the Moon*, 212
Strauss, Roger, 64, 148, 151
Stravinsky, Igor, 173
Stuart-Stubbs, Basil, 61
Suzuki, David, 28, 144, 237–38, 241
Suzuki, Tara Cullis, 144, 273
Suzuki Foundation, 144, 241, 273, 274
Sylvester, Andy, 178, 277

Tappage, Mary Augusta: *The Days of Augusta*, 66

Taylor, Jim, 135, 136
Taylor, Timothy, 254–55
Teitelbaum, Matthew, 184
Telus, 164
Ten Speed Press, 205
Thames & Hudson (T&H), 63, 98, 102, 146, 174, 180, 182, 183, 187
Theroux, Paul, 129
Theytus Books, 79
Thom, Ian: *E.J. Hughes*, 177–78; *Gordon Smith*, 176–77
Thom, Ron, 228
Thomas Allen & Son, 10
Thompson, Ernest Cameron "Gramps," 4–5
Thompson, Peggy, 91
Thomson, Tom, 185
Thornhill, Arthur, Jr., 17
Timmings, Mark, 185
Totem (UBC yearbook), 8–9
Touchie, Rodger, 273
Treasury Board, 85, 86, 116, 245
Trécarré (publisher), 184
Trudeau, Pierre, 24, 160, 161, 169, 224
Truss, Jan, 239
Turley, Rae, 124, 125
Turnbull, Linda, 141
Turner, John, 161
Tutu, Desmond, 197

UNESCO, 243–44, 248–49
UNESCO Convention on the Protection and Promotion of the Diversity of Cultural Expressions, 249
United States of America, 82, 141–42, 241–42, 249
University of British Columbia (UBC), 7–9
University of Chicago Press, 130
University of Nebraska Press, 219
University of Toronto Press (UTP), 10, 14, 44, 80, 93–94, 138, 149–50
University of Washington Press (UWP), 56, 78, 82, 131, 167
Usukawa, Saeko, 90–91, 164, 208, 215, 223

Vaillant, John, 237
Valgardson, W.D., 209, 239
Van Camp, Richard, 219–20; *Lesser Blessed*, 219–20
Vancouver: books about, 66–68, 75–76, 227–28; booksellers, 41; cultural life, 173; food scene, 200, 207; Winter Olympics (2010), 136–37, 261–62
Vancouver Art Gallery, 174, 175, 178, 229
Vancouver Public Library, 56, 216

Vancouver's First Century (book), 75–76
Vancouver Sun (newspaper), 56, 59, 156–57, 162
Vanguard Books, 95
Van Nostrand Reinhold (publisher), 42, 43
Van Oudenallen, Captain, 191
Vaugeois, Denis, 209
Vigneault, Guillaume, 211
Vij, Vikram, 203–4; *Vij's* (with Dhalwala), 203–4; *Vij's at Home* (with Dhalwala), 204
Vogel, Richard, 94

Wagamese, Richard, 220–22; *Indian Horse*, 221–22, 262; *One Native Life*, 221; *Richard Wagamese Selected*, 222; *Starlight*, 222
Wagner, Erica, 219
Wah, Fred, 214
Walbran, John T.: *British Columbia Coast Names*, 56
Walker Books, 139, 146
Wall, Jeff, 179
Wallace, Ian, 179, 239
Walt, James, 203
Walter and Duncan Gordon Foundation, 5
Wasserman, Jack, 156
Waterton, Betty: *A Salmon for Simon* (with Blades), 88–89
Watson, Paul, 276
Watson, Scott: *Jack Shadbolt*, 173–74
Webster, Jack, 49, 50, 157, 158, 159–60, 162, 230; *Webster!* (with Mulgrew), 160
Webster Awards, 160
Weidenfeld, George, 103, 147
Weidenfeld & Nicolson, 147
Weinberg, Susan, 96
Weir, Ian, 209
Wells, Andy, 230
Werschler, Terri, 154
West Coast modernism, 60, 228

Western Producer Prairie Books, 142, 144
Wheeler, Anne, 66
White, Howard "Howie," 163, 275
White, Mary, 275
White, Trena, 264, 274, 275
WH Smith (SmithBooks), 65, 144–45
Whyte, Kenneth "Ken," 273
Wilkie, Bob, 15, 20
Williams, Lorna, 118
Williams, Robert "Bob," 163
Wilmot, Norah Mannion: *Cooking for One*, 56–57
Wilson, Catherine, 19, 22, 35
Wilson, Michael, 241–42
Wiss, Ray: *FOB DOC*, 196–97; *A Line in the Sand*, 197
Woll, Tom, 95
Wong-Chu, Jim, 214–15; *Many-Mouthed Birds* (with Lee), 214
Wood, Alan, 202
Woodcock, George and Inge, 173
Woodward's, 41
Woolliams, Nina G.: *Cattle Ranch*, 79
World Trade Organization (WTO), 242
World War II, 192–93, 197, 232
Wright, Andy, 41
Wright, Frank Lloyd, 187
Writers' Union of Canada, the, 61
Wyman, Max, 243–44
Wynne-Jones, Tim, 239

Yee, Paul, 214, 239; *Saltwater City*, 214
Yeo, E.L., 6
Young, Walter D., 115–16
Young Canada Health program, 120, 139, 140

Zuehlke, Mark, 192; *Ortona*, 192

Entertainment. Writing. Culture. ─────────────

ECW is a proudly independent, Canadian-owned book publisher. We know great writing can improve people's lives, and we're passionate about sharing original, exciting, and insightful writing across genres.

───────────────── **Thanks for reading along!**

We want our books not just to sustain our imaginations, but to help construct a healthier, more just world, and so we've become a certified B Corporation, meaning we meet a high standard of social and environmental responsibility — and we're going to keep aiming higher. We believe books can drive change, but the way we make them can too.

Being a B Corp means that the act of publishing this book should be a force for good — for the planet, for our communities, and for the people that worked to make this book. For example, everyone who worked on this book was paid at least a living wage. You can learn more at the Ontario Living Wage Network.

This book is also available as a Global Certified Accessible™ (GCA) ebook. ECW Press's ebooks are screen reader friendly and are built to meet the needs of those who are unable to read standard print due to blindness, low vision, dyslexia, or a physical disability.

The interior of this book is printed on Sustana EnviroBook™, which is made from 100% recycled fibres and processed chlorine-free.

ECW's office is situated on land that was the traditional territory of many nations, including the Wendat, the Anishinaabeg, Haudenosaunee, Chippewa, Métis, and current treaty holders the Mississaugas of the Credit. In the 1880s, the land was developed as part of a growing community around St. Matthew's Anglican and other churches. Starting in the 1950s, our neighbourhood was transformed by immigrants fleeing the Vietnam War and Chinese Canadians dispossessed by the building of Nathan Phillips Square and the subsequent rise in real estate value in other Chinatowns. We are grateful to those who cared for the land before us and are proud to be working amidst this mix of cultures.

ecwpress.com